MEMOIR

OF

ELIZABETH GEORGE.

BY THE

REV. HENRY J. PIGGOTT, B.A.

"Pure religion and undefiled before God and the Father is this,
To visit the fatherless and widows in their affliction, and to keep
himself unspotted from the world." (James i. 27.)

LONDON:

PUBLISHED BY JOHN MASON, 14, CITY-ROAD;

SOLD AT 66, PATERNOSTER-ROW.

—

1858.

PREFACE.

THE appearance of a new biography, and especially of a new religious biography, inevitably provokes the question, Why this addition to the almost numberless books of the same class already in existence? What was there sufficiently extraordinary about *this* life, to justify the publication of its history?

Should such an inquiry suggest itself to any one on opening these pages, it is hoped that a candid perusal of them will furnish a not unsatisfactory reply. It has not been merely for the sake of the eminent piety they exhibit, that these records of a brief but well-spent life have been preserved; but rather for the sake of the peculiar manifestations of that piety,—the zeal for truth, the tenderness and catholicity of affection, and the self-denying activities, in which it displayed itself. It is thought that, especially to those of the same sex and age, such an example may not be without its use.

What there is of *ordinariness* about this example will, perhaps, serve to render it the more imitable. Many biographies lose much of their force as incentives, on account of the distance to which, in position and mode of life, their subjects are removed from their readers. The life of one who, in point of rank, endowment, and culture, stood at no elevation above the majority of those by whom her memoir will be read,—who only distanced them on a field in which competition is open to all,—may, perhaps, possess recommendations peculiarly its own.

It may possibly occur to some, that there is too much of detail in these pages; that to furnish an almost daily account of the progress and development of the spiritual life of any one, is to fall into a faulty and excessive minuteness. To this the Biographer can only reply,—first, that his subject left him no choice; that a story extending over little more than three years must, of necessity, if written at all, go much into detail;—and, secondly, that since it is day by day that the Christian warfare has to be fought, and Christian duty to be discharged, this very detail may add to the use and *practicalness* of the example.

It is for the young that this book has been written, and especially for *young females*. The writer will be abundantly repaid, if, by the perusal of its pages, any of this class be led to see that there is within their reach a standard of Christian attainment and happiness higher than they have yet aspired to gain; and that there are around them opportunities of Christian service, wider and more glorious than they have yet embraced.

HASTINGS, *September*, 1858.

CONTENTS.

MEMOIR

OF

ELIZABETH GEORGE.

CHAPTER I.

CHILDHOOD.

"The unfeigned faith—which dwelt first in thy grandmother
Lois, and thy mother Eunice; and I am persuaded that in thee also."
(2 Tim. i. 5.)

PIETY is not hereditary. It is not transmitted along
the line of family descent by any natural law, as bodily
or mental endowments sometimes are. Yet it would be
contravening Scripture and common observation to deny
that ancestral piety does often reappear in successive
generations. The children are blessed for the father's
sake. The house of Jonadab does not want a man to
stand before the Lord. The prayers and faithful service
of His people come up before God " for a remembrance,"
which is not " cut off" when they have departed from
the earth.

In the case of the young Christian the story of whose
life is told in these pages, a striking illustration is
afforded of the truth of these remarks. She drew her
descent on the mother's side from a family of which
honourable mention is made in the earliest annals of
Methodism. The EDENS were amongst the first sup-

porters of this great work of God in the town and
neighbourhood of Evesham. They were familiarly
known to the Wesleys themselves, and furnished a
home to their "Assistants." From that period, during
more than a hundred years, there have never been
wanting some members of the family to continue the
honourable succession, and maintain the primitive piety
and hospitality.

The mother of ELIZABETH GEORGE was a worthy scion
of this godly and generous stock. Her conversion was
late, and her subsequent lot one of suffering and trial;
but by meekness and patience, and a tender and diffusive
charity, she magnified the grace of God. Elizabeth was
the sixth child of this excellent lady, and was born at
the village of Pebworth, in Gloucestershire, on the 27th
of April, 1831.

At the time of her birth, both her parents attended
the services of the Established Church, but, though
observant of the forms of religion, were destitute of its
reality. The souls of their children were not, however,
uncared for during those critical years when the unfolding character is most easily influenced for good. A
pious invalid aunt, a true representative of the old Eden
lineage, came to reside in the family. She was one of
those to whom the discipline of suffering has taught the
lesson that affliction does not absolve from service, and
that within the narrow limits of a sick room there is
scope enough for many a work of faith and love. She
studiously turned the leisure of her long imprisonment
to the benefit of the younger members of the household.
They were had daily to her bed-side, and taught with
many prayers and gentle earnestness the truths of religion. The good aunt possessed peculiar aptitude for
such a task. She knew how to clothe her instructions

with the familiar illustrations and simple homely words which children understand and love. Told in her vivid way, the Bible-story became to her little sympathizing audience a scene their own eyes had witnessed; and, conveyed through the happy vehicle of anecdote or parable, truth gained at once in clearness and attraction.

On the mind of Elizabeth, the youngest of the group, this mode of teaching produced singular effects. To her childish simplicity every statement was literally true, and to her lively fancy every scene was actually present. On one occasion, Elijah's translation had been the theme, and with eager wondering ears she had listened to the narrative. Shortly afterwards, she happened to be reclining with her face opposite to the window of the room. She could see, as she lay, the heavens glowing in the hues of sunrise. Soon the whole scene seemed to be transfigured. Yonder ruddy group of clouds became a chariot of fire, like that in which the Prophet had been caught up; and in great excitement the child began to pray aloud that it might descend for her also. Nor was the illusion broken, until she had been summoned a second time to her aunt's room to be soothed by suitable explanations.

On another occasion, the text for the lesson had been furnished by some of those strong words of Christ which speak of the power of faith. No sooner was it over, than Elizabeth was in the garden, intent upon putting the truth of what she had heard to practical proof. She bade the garden-pond be dried up, and the shrubbery-trees be transplanted; and, because no change followed, flew back to her aunt, in not a little perplexity and trouble, to ask why she had been unsuccessful.

Nor was it only in such isolated and somewhat grotesque cases that she exhibited the effect of her aunt's teaching. Her convictions of the efficacy of prayer became so strong, that all her childish griefs and wants were habitually carried to the ear of God, and that not as a prescribed duty, but of her own accord, in her own simple child's talk, and with the fullest persuasion that she was heard and answered.

Elizabeth grew up, an active, sprightly, intelligent girl. She displayed an intense love of knowledge, and much aptitude in acquiring it. Her vivacity was extraordinary, even for a child. Those who knew her at this early age, still speak with pleasure of her bright laughing countenance and agile movements. With the Wesleyan Ministers, who after her mother's conversion became again welcome and honoured guests of the family, she was an especial favourite; while to Elizabeth, on the other hand, the days on which their periodic visits occurred were the happiest of the year. The most coveted post for the time being was at the chair-back, or by the side, or on the knee, of the servant of God. When the hour of departure came, if the hat or stick were missing from the hall, be sure that Elizabeth had spirited them away. If permitted, as was not unfrequently the case, to escort them to a little distance from the village, her childish glee knew no bounds. To see her, as from very exuberance of spirits she gambolled to and fro, or strutted proudly under the self-imposed burden of the carpet-bag, was enough to provoke laughter from a cynic.

But underneath this sparkling exterior grave thoughts soon began to work. While Elizabeth was yet a child, her mother was converted to God, and began with her whole family to attend the Methodist ministry. A year or two afterwards a new chapel was erected in the village, and a Sabbath-school commenced. Elizabeth became a scholar in the class of an elder sister. And now the religious impressions, first received in her aunt's sick room, revived. Divine truth became very real to this young child. She felt that she had to do with a God who hated sin, and whose eyes were in every place. Her conscience became very sensitive, and filled her often with sorrow and alarm. When guilty, as she sometimes was, of passion, or deceit, or some other of the sins of childhood, her compunction was keen and instant. For some years, at intervals, she continued in this state. An uneasy strife was waging in her heart: "the flesh lusted against the spirit, and the spirit against the flesh." It was the same strife, in all its essential elements, through which, in a subsequent period of her religious history, she had to struggle for several miserable years; only that *then* the discord was the more active and bitter, in proportion as on the one hand the voice of conscience had become more loud and clear, and on the other the tendencies of a corrupt nature had also grown in strength.

Unfortunately, her condition was not understood by those who had chiefly to do with her training. Sufficient credit was not given her for the depth and sincerity of her convictions. She failed, therefore, in obtaining that thorough sympathy and encouragement which were perhaps all that she needed to lead her, even at this early age, to Him to whom the little ones are welcome. This, though to be regretted, was hardly to be helped; for Elizabeth had an almost morbid habit of concealing her gravest thoughts and feelings. She would brood over her griefs in private, but in the presence of others she was only a merry, careless, impulsive child. It required, therefore, an eye of more than ordinary penetration to detect what was passing in her

secret soul. Still it was unfortunate that she was not
better understood; for her religious desires, chilled thus
in their first unfolding, gradually shrunk and faded
away.

In subsequent years, when Miss George had herself
much to do with the training of the young, she gathered
wisdom from her own childish reminiscences. They
taught her to have great faith in the religious suscep-
tibility of very young children. She believed that with
the very first awakening of the intellect and the heart
the Spirit's influences may be blended; that, as soon as
the child may be taught anything, it may be taught the
simple primary truths of religion; and, as soon as it can
feel anything, it can feel the essential saving emotions
of religion. On this belief she acted, and, as some after-
parts of this Memoir will show, with the happiest
results.

In May, 1844, Mr. George died; and shortly afterwards the bereaved family removed to the neighbouring
village of Welford-on-Avon, where Mrs. George and her
two oldest daughters opened a boarding-school. Elizabeth, meanwhile, had been sent to a school at Birmingham. She continued there about twelve months, and then
returned to pursue her studies under the tuition of her
sisters. She was thus employed until her seventeenth
year, when she began herself to assist in the management of the school.

During the greater part of this period, her spiritual
history is a blank, or worse. She returned from her
residence at Birmingham greatly changed, her religious
impressions almost obliterated, even her thirst for knowledge much abated from its former ardour. She had
formerly taken great delight in the study of the natural
sciences, more especially in astronomy, poetry, and

general literature; but all graver pursuits now for a while yielded precedence to frivolities more dearly loved. For all this her character developed into much that was amiable: she was kind and generous, if gay and thoughtless; was, in fact, just one of the buoyant-hearted, vivacious girls we so often meet with and sorrow for, who live only for present enjoyment, and throw recklessly off every serious concern. This state of things lasted for a year or two. It was a critical time; for if there is one period more than another in which the character gets definitely and durably shaped, it is that on which Miss George was now entering.

Happily, however, this important crisis of transition from girlhood to womanhood was not all trifled away. In her sixteenth year she began again to manifest religious concern. Probably all along, in her secret conscience, she had heard an undertone of reproach, which had made her more ill at ease than she cared to confess. It was the perusal of Bunyan's immortal allegory which now fairly roused her to emulate the "Pilgrim's Progress to the Celestial City." She joined herself to the Methodist Society at Welford. She began to teach in the Sabbath-school, and threw into the work her characteristic energy. Yet for a long time her religious desires were weak and fitful. The promptitude and resolution which entered largely into her character were not yet applied to the working out of her salvation. In fact, her mind was only half made up. She halted between the claims of piety on the one hand, and the attractions of the world on the other. The inward strife of earlier years revived. Still her state was an advance upon what it had been. This quarrel of the heart with its own evil, these movements of desire towards God, though indecisive and fluctuating, were

much to be preferred to utter unconcern. Nor did she
ever again wholly relapse into her former apathy; but
this internal discord—sometimes languishing, sometimes breaking forth into bitter paroxysms—continued,
until at length, consenting to be saved on God's own
terms, she received the sentence of death in her old
nature of sin, and rose again into a new and holy life
in Christ Jesus.

CHAPTER II.

THE TRANSITION.

"O wretched man that I am! who shall deliver me from the body of this death? I thank God through Jesus Christ our Lord.

"There is therefore now no condemnation to them which are in Christ Jesus." (Rom. vii. 24, 25; viii. 1.)

A STAGE of conflict and sorrow immediately precedes the peace and freedom which the Gospel promises, and faith in Christ secures. We live with Christ only on condition of being first crucified with Him. We have to learn, and learn bitterly, our guilt and thraldom, and impotence, before we can consent to seek in Him our strength and righteousness.

Sometimes, it is true, this stage is a brief one. The shaft of conviction pierces so truly that self is slain outright. Despairing of all other help, the soul at once stretches out its hands to Christ, and cries, "Save, Lord, or I perish!" No time is lost in applying for perilous shelter to refuges of lies. The pilgrim neither loses his footing in the Slough of Despond, nor is trepanned into the by-path to the town of Legality. He apprehends justly and at once the terms of salvation; such clear light shines upon the way to the cross, that he hies thither forthwith, and drops his burden.

But more generally this transition-period is more or less protracted. With hesitating steps, and after devious wanderings, the sinner finds his Saviour. One of the most frequent causes of this is *a want of decision*. With true penitent feeling and Godward desire there is often blended a pernicious leaven of insincerity. The stricken soul would fain find ease and healing, but is hardly prepared to pay the cost. There is some forbidden thing it would still cling to, or some doubtful path it would still walk in. It casts back longing, lingering looks upon the world it has to abandon. The desire of salvation has not become so vehement and absorbing as to swallow up all old interests and attachments. As with one who came to Jesus in the days of His flesh, the fervid, "Lord, I will follow Thee," is half retracted by the "*but first*" which succeeds it. Such indecision is fatal. So long as it lasts, the soul can never come to Christ. He requires to be sought with the whole heart. "Strait is the gate, and narrow is the way, which leadeth unto life," and we must *agonize* to enter therein.

Another hindrance, that often obstructs the path of the penitent, is *a mistaken view of the terms of salvation*. That God justifies the ungodly wholly for the sake of Christ, and simply on the condition of faith, experience shows to be a truth difficult to receive. Acute and sincere men, with their Bibles open before them, have blundered about it. Nay, many who in theory have held this very sentiment, have, strange to say, wandered into sad error when they should have acted upon it. They have inverted the Divine order of things, making holiness the condition and not the result of receiving the atonement; or, at least, have sought to effect a kind of composition with God, in which the merits of Christ are simply to supplement their own imperfect doings. Such mistaken notions, whether consciously or unconsciously held, will always darken and hinder the way to the cross.

Miss George belonged to this class of long and weary seekers after spiritual comfort. Five years in all elapsed between the time when she was re-awakened to religious concern through reading the "Pilgrim's Progress," and the happy crisis when she found "joy and peace in believing." These were in the main sorrowful years. True, there was an outer life of much vivacity and cheerfulness, and her acquaintance saw little more than that; but beneath this bright exterior there was an inner life of conflict, and trouble, and self-reproach. Conscience was sufficiently aroused and active to embitter the pleasures she sought to derive from the world: like all "halters between two opinions," she had neither the satisfactions of religion, nor such sorry compensations as those who possess no religious aspirations may find elsewhere; often the ache at the heart belied the laugh on the lips, and the remorseful retrospect of the night rebuked the unreflecting gaiety of the day. She was "never at one stay:" now in a paroxysm of compunction and self-upbraiding, and now relapsed into comparative insensibility; now for a while struggling hard to reach a more satisfactory state, and now carelessly succumbing to natural temperament and outward seduction; at one time close upon the goodly land, within sight of its pleasant landscapes, and fore-tasting its delicious fruits, and at another far back again in the desert of drought and barrenness. Yet she never turned her back upon the goal. She knew full well that in Jesus alone was the rest she wanted, and she never ceased altogether to hope and struggle for it.

But a few extracts from her own diary will give the most vivid picture of her state during these years. That diary she began to keep about a year and a half before her conversion: had it, however, extended over the whole of this troubled period, its entries would have been of the same character. It is just what a diary should

be, to be of any worth,—free, spontaneous, artless.
These extracts are made simply because they give, much
better than mere description could do, the features of
this very interesting crisis in her religious life. They
are photographs, taken at the time, of her compunc-
tions and resolves, her struggles and relapses. Probably many readers may find them a mirror, in which a
sorrowful passage of their past or present history is
reflected with some truth and vividness.

The opening entry contains a brief retrospect. "Feb.
25th, 1851.—About three weeks since, simply from a
sense of duty, I once more openly professed myself a
follower of Jesus; that is, I met in class, after neglecting
to do so for six months, during which time I had lived
in a careless state. I felt that my heart was growing
harder and harder; and that the longer I shunned the
cross, the more difficult it would be to take up.

"On Sunday last, how wandering were my thoughts,
how weak my faith, how cold my love! In the evening
I commemorated the dying love of my Redeemer; but,
alas! my heart was hard. I could not realize that the
Saviour died for *me*,—that

> ' *My* sins gave sharpness to the nail,
> And pointed every thorn!'

How long have I been halting between two opinions!
O, may I now be in right earnest to get possession of
true religion!

"Sunday, March 9th.—The last week I have allowed
to pass unimproved. How sinful has been my conduct!
I have neglected prayer, given way to sinful, wandering thoughts, been careless and trifling in my conversation, and grieved the Holy Spirit. All the week I have
been very uncomfortable. Commenced this holy day

without prayer. How could I look for success at school, or anywhere else? For the sake of my Redeemer, Lord, do thou enable me to feel my sinfulness.

"13th.—Since Sunday I have omitted recording my feelings, for shame. God knows how I have spent the time; how sinful have been my thoughts, words, and actions. How can I be so *stupid,* so *mad?*—as if I expected to live for ever on this earth, forgetting I have an immortal soul, the breath of God, which must exist when all worlds are crumbled into dust! On Monday night, after hearing a sermon on 'Watch and pray,' I felt determined to be more diligent in these duties. I left the chapel, and my determination left me. This day I again resolved (by God's assistance, for I have time after time experienced that of myself I am worse than frailty itself) to be more earnest. But how dare I make any resolve? I am so weak, so changeable! But the Infinite God has said, 'My grace is sufficient for thee.' May much of that grace be granted to me, a poor miserable sinner. Help me to come to Thee at once,

' Just as I am, without one plea,
But that Thy blood was shed for me.'

"20th.—On Sunday I enjoyed more than usual; but neglected going to my closet after school, and therefore did not continue in so good a state. How prone I am to forget God! Lord, change this vile hard heart, and help me to love Thee! Why not me? Lord, I know Thou art willing, waiting to forgive: why can I not believe? Help me to come, just as I am, to cast all my sins upon Thee—upon my Jesus, who died on Calvary to atone for them—and find mercy.

"24th.—On Thursday night, while sitting up with a sick friend, I examined myself in God's presence, to

c

see if I really repented of all my sins. I feared I was scarcely willing to give up one sin, my besetting sin— day-dreaming. Even that I resolved to give up, and everything I knew to be sin. On Saturday morning I prayed, and read, and cast my whole soul upon Jesus, and was *determined* to believe. I felt that Jesus died for *me;* that I could not disbelieve; that if I died then I could not be lost, because I was determined to trust my whole soul to Jesus, at all risks to cling to Him. I felt a degree of peace. Frequently through the day I looked to God. I lived by faith, and determined still to believe, and to pray for increased faith, that I might grasp the promises, and cling to Christ more firmly. On Sunday I do not know how I felt. I was fearful that I was not believing rightly: believing ought to bring joy, and none was mine. This morning I determined by God's help to pray and believe, till I can say with confidence, 'My God is reconciled.'

" 28th.—At intervals during the last few days I have felt a peace of mind; no joy, but at times a persuasion that God has forgiven me. God forbid that I should deceive myself!

" April 4th.—Last night at class it was with diffi- culty that I could explain my feelings. I cannot *rejoice* in a sin-pardoning God, although I cannot but think that my sins are pardoned. I want stronger faith, that I may rest more fully on Christ. I frequently pray earnestly for saving faith, and do give my whole heart to Christ, and believe to the best of my ability, God is my witness. I humbly pray that He will teach me what I need to know, and not let me deceive myself."

One word of comment here. It is not easy to speak decisively as to the singular phase which Miss George's religious state just now presented. It may be that she was struggling to trust in Christ for salvation, *before* having with her whole heart forsaken sin,—that she was striving to appropriate the promise of pardon and find comfort in it, while yet secretly clinging to her old idolatries. Not consciously so, perhaps; but her deceitful heart was betraying her unwittingly to this not unfrequent hypocrisy. If it were so, her suspicions were well-founded; her faith *was* spurious; she had yet lower depths of self-renunciation to tread, yet more humiliating discoveries of inward sinfulness to make; and this it was that prevented her from realizing "joy and peace in believing." A corrupt faith, which is in fact no faith at all, can bear no such good fruits. Or it may be that when she wrote, "I cast my whole soul on Jesus, and was determined to believe; I felt that Jesus died for me—that I could not disbelieve—that if I died then I could not be lost, because I was determined at all risks to cling to Jesus;" her faith was genuine, but feeble. The germ of a true faith may then have sprung up in her heart. For it is a great mistake to suppose that always *at once* is the soul so enabled to apprehend and rely on the atoning work of the Saviour, as to start up from its fear and sorrow in the full joyous assurance of cancelled sin and Divine acceptance. In the vast diversity of the Spirit's operations, there may be a gradual growth of faith and a gradual flowing in of comfort upon the soul in the crisis of conversion, as well as a gradual maturing of the renovated affections afterwards. Penitent sinners are too apt to forget this, and to look for one certain definite style of conversion. In the religious biographies they are most familiar with, and in the narrated experience of their Christian friends, they find that the great change has been abrupt, sudden, and strongly marked.

There has been one energetic act of faith, and then a
dazzling rapturous emergence from darkness to light,
from misery to ecstasy, from despair to assurance, from
death to life. And thus they wish that it may be, and
expect that it shall be, in their own cases; thereby
limiting the Holy One, whose infinite wisdom loves to
work in an infinite diversity of modes. The result is
often pernicious. Having prescribed for the Spirit this
one abrupt and rapid method of procedure, the penitent
is not careful to cherish those beginnings of faith and
dawnings of comfort which are truly the work of the
same Spirit, and would, if cherished, lead sooner or later
to the happy issue he so ardently longs for. He relaxes the hold which he has fixed on the provided Refuge,
because it is not so firm and confident a hold as it might
be. Unable to get so near the Saviour as he could
wish, to "touch the hem of His garment" is not enough
for him. He flings away the peace he does feel, because
it is not the lively joy he had hoped to feel. Thus are
many hindered and kept back in a path of darkness and
stumbling, who might long before have been walking
with sure and steadfast feet beneath the clear shining
of God's uplifted countenance.

Thus it may have been with Miss George. If she
had persevered in her determination "to cling to Christ
at all risks," and had not begun timorously to conclude
that her faith was not genuine, because "believing
ought to bring joy, and none was mine," it may be
that she would at this time have attained to that filial
confidence towards God, which, as it was, she did not
reach until many weary months had elapsed, and then
only through the stern discipline of sorrow.

But, to return to the diary, which resumes now its
old tone of compunction and self-reproach :—

"25th.—O that I could feel more happy; feel myself to be a child of God! How long am I to grope in the dark?

"May 30th.—The last two days I think I have felt more in earnest. Yet I am so weak, so changeable! I have been thinking how happy it would be, were I a Christian indeed, a holy person, enjoying constant communion with my Maker. And this is my privilege, God's will concerning me;—nay, my duty. O, why am I thus? Lord, for Jesus's sake, have mercy, quicken me, help me to look by faith on my precious Redeemer.

"July 30th.—I have long neglected writing here. On examining my state, I feel that I am not progressing in spiritual things. For several days after I last wrote I was more in earnest. I did seem to rest my soul on Christ. Afterwards I neglected prayer and reading the Scriptures, as I so often do. When shall I prosper? *Never*, so long as I am so unstable in religious exercises. I know God is ready to bless, and able: the fault is with myself. I am very much troubled with wandering thoughts—sinful, trifling thoughts. Lord, empty my heart of such things, and fill it with Thyself! Make me Thy own adopted child.

"August 13th.—I see and feel the vanity of earthly things: I see that religion is more necessary than anything else. I desire to get in possession of it; but my weakness almost drives me to despair. How many, many times have I been not far from the kingdom of God, yet have not entered!

"September 13th, Sunday.—Five years this day since I received my first ticket of membership. I look back with the greatest shame and confusion of face, feeling that I have dishonoured God and His cause. I

am not one whit nearer heaven now than I was then.
Then I was not far from the kingdom of God; and many,
many times since then I have been very far. My heart
is much, very much harder than it was then. O, if I
had known then that I should be in this state in
five years' time, I should have despaired of ever being
saved at all! Hope has borne me up. I am continually
hoping that soon, very soon, the day of my deliverance
draweth nigh. Then time passes on, and I am still the
same.

"24th.—I have been reading Romans vii., and find
that my experience precisely agrees with what St. Paul
describes. I have indeed a war going on within.

'End, O end this war within;
Set me free, O Lord, from sin!'

"November 27th.—I feel that I am still clinging to
earthly things, though not willingly. I so frequently
do that which I would not, and omit doing that I
would. When shall I be delivered from this bondage
of sin?

"December 18th.—I am seldom long together in the
same mind. Several times of late I have been very
earnest and determined to persevere: then, as I do not
gain my end at once, I tire and grow careless. On
Monday I heard a sermon from, 'Now then we are am-
bassadors for Christ.' It seemed easy, the simplicity
of the way was even startling; but, Lord, to me the
way seems hard!

"February 3d, 1852.—On Wednesday I heard Mr. V.
preach from, 'We have left all, and followed Thee.'
God blessed my soul, and enabled me to resolve to give
up every idol, or whatever I knew would be a hin-

drance to me. I felt able to do so for some time; but, since, I have been much tempted, and through lack of prayer have not so guarded my thoughts as I promised then."

There may be a monotony of unhappiness running through the above extracts, yet what could so well tell the story of such a period as these broken utterances? They are the irrepressible outcries of the heart under the burden of its sorrow. And is there not many a heart which, inaudibly to any but the Omniscient, is pouring out in similar complaints its secret bitterness?

Plainly, as has already been intimated, the great defect which held Miss George so long in this unsatisfactory state, was her want of decision. Deep and poignant as her religious convictions were at times, they had not an abiding predominance. Her heart was divided against itself. She wished to follow Christ, but she would fain also have lingered for a while in the flowery paths of worldly pleasure. Possessed as she was of great buoyancy of spirit, and a keen relish for the enjoyments which the world offers to youth and health, it was a hard thing for her to say to them all, "Farewell! Henceforth my heart is not in you; ye are not my good." She struggled to say this; but the words faltered on her tongue, and the deep, earnest *Yea* was wanting in her heart. It was this halting short of a full and fixed intention, which was at the root of her broken vows, her inconstant efforts, her frequent relapses.

A break of six months now occurs in the diary; and during that interval great changes took place in the family at Welford. Elizabeth's sister, the only one that had remained with her at home, married, and removed to a distance. This separation was painful, but it was not the worst. Three of her brothers, attracted by the

promises which Australia was holding out to youthful
energy and enterprise, determined on emigrating thither.
No dissuasion could move them from their purpose, and
accordingly in the summer of this year they set sail.
To one of them, the nearest to her own age, Elizabeth
was strongly attached, and to part with him was like
rending her own heart asunder.   Thus in a few months
the home was almost broken up. Elizabeth was left
alone with her widowed mother and the one remaining
brother. The conduct and responsibility of the school
devolved wholly upon her. It was a sorrowful time,
but salutary. That clinging to earthly pleasure and
affection, which had so much interfered with her religious earnestness, was now overborne. Her vacillating
purpose was fixed. Her heart, wounded where it was
tenderest, fled to the true Comforter for healing. And,
as soon as she was thus prepared to meet Christ on His
own terms, she found Him faithful to His promise.
But the story of the blessed transition shall be given in
her own words. The following extract is taken from
the entry with which she resumes her diary, and in
which she looks back over the way by which God had
led her :—

"Another sore trial came on about this time—May
and June. My three brothers, Joseph, William, and
Alfred, determined to go out to Australia : no persuasion
could alter their minds. For a length of time, several
weeks, while the matter was deciding, I could do nothing but weep and pray. I prayed that, if the step
would be for their good and God's glory, I might feel
resigned; and that, if otherwise, it might be prevented.
Well, as nothing arose to prevent it in any way, indeed
everything happened to favour it, I was obliged to give
up ; or I thought I never could part with William. A

fortnight before their departure I had resigned them entirely into the hands of God, and felt they were safe. I had no anxiety about them, but trusted them fully to the goodness of Him who has promised to be a Father to the fatherless. They sailed from London about the 24th of July. It has been a great trial; but I now rejoice in it all, for my Father thus led me to look more fully to Him.

"About the 20th of July, I commenced again early rising and reading, which I had sadly neglected the last few months. The first book I read was 'The Memorials of Henley,' a devoted Wesleyan Minister. I praise God that it ever fell into my hands. I much enjoyed it, and was led to see more plainly the way of pardon—the simple way.

"On Thursday, the 22d, while standing in the shrubbery, I read with tearful eyes, and heavy but hopeful heart, one of his letters to a young man, exhorting him at once, while reading, to venture his all, body and soul, on Christ's perfect atonement. The words ran thus:—'Dare to venture yourself on Christ now. Believe that God is now waiting to receive you. Say, Lord, I am Thine: Abba, Father, my Lord and my God!' I did so, and felt that I dared not doubt of God's willingness to receive me just then. I was determined to rely on the atonement. I felt peace, no guilt, no condemnation; yet feared I might not retain the blessing which I thought I had obtained. I had a severe cold; so retired early at night. In the morning I woke early, fell on my knees, and committed myself to God for the day. I had no joy, but a kind of peace, arising from the removal of all fear. I prayed much, and saw clearly how God accepted sinners through His Son. In a few days my strength and faith increased, and I took a firm hold on Christ. I felt that I could say, 'My Father!' Daily I exhorted poor sinners to believe in Jesus; and doing so increased my own faith. Sunday was a good day: God's goodness overflowed my soul."

Thus it was that this young pilgrim, after bearing long and painfully the burden of sin, lost it at the cross. It was, indeed, her own fault that she carried it so long. Had she been willing to comply with Christ's requisitions, He would have spoken the word of release years before. *As soon as she was willing, the deliverance came.* Not, however, until her heart had been sorely wounded in its tenderest affections, did it turn to Jesus, void and bleeding, for the solace and satisfaction of His love. Happier they who need no such stern discipline to lead them to that entireness of self-surrender which the Saviour requires!

It is noteworthy, too, that, when at length the brighter day did break, it was not the sudden influx of light and gladness she had hoped for. She had to live for a time without much lively emotion, simply looking to Jesus, and clinging to God's faithful word. Hers was a faith which, timorous at first, only gradually deepened to a full assurance. The Spirit's "Abba, Father," whispered at first in tones scarcely perceptible, gradually grew in volume and distinctness. Thus God's dealings, even in the first bestowment of His favour, as in so much of the after-history, are often not "according to our mind."

CHAPTER III.

HOLINESS.

"Who gave Himself for us, that He might redeem us from all iniquity, and purify unto Himself a peculiar people, zealous of good works." (Titus ii. 14.)

It is one of the tenets of the religious body to which Miss George was united, that there is a state attainable by Christians on earth, when all inward depravation is removed; when thought, motive, and desire are made pure, and the sanctified inner nature finds appropriate expression in an outer life of perfect obedience. They discover many passages of Scripture, which they believe can only be fairly interpreted on such a supposition. In the practical parts of the writings of the Apostles, for instance, they find regenerate persons continually exhorted to seek a higher state, of which the great characteristic is "walking before God unto all pleasing." Such prayers as, "And the very God of peace sanctify you wholly, and I pray God your whole spirit and soul and body be preserved blameless unto the coming of our Lord Jesus Christ;" such exhortations as, "Having therefore these promises, dearly beloved, let us cleanse ourselves from all filthiness of the flesh and spirit, perfecting holiness in the fear of God;" such statements of Christ's relations to the church, as that in which it is said, He "gave Himself for it, that He might sanctify and cleanse it with the washing of water by the word, that He might present it to Himself a glorious church, not having spot, or wrinkle, or any such thing,

but that it should be holy and without blemish;" are,
they think, unwarrantably stripped of force and meaning on any other belief than the attainableness in this
life of a state of "entire sanctification." This doctrine
Miss George cordially held, and towards this elevated
goal she steadfastly set her face.

Even by those, however, who acquiesce in this belief,
it is usually supposed that a long interval must elapse
between the attainment of the regenerate and of the
sanctified state. They look upon the latter as the maturity of the Christian character, and the result, therefore, of the gradual growth of the graces and affections of
the renewed nature through a course of varied experience.
It is a far-off Beulah land, lying close on the verge of
the river, and visited often by wafts of melody and
gleams of splendour from the city on the other side.
They who have reached it are the veterans of the pilgrimage. At least this state of sanctification is not
generally recognised as the *normal* condition of the
Christian life; as the realization of Christ's thought and
wish concerning His church; as the standard of attainment to be sought by every regenerate man from the
time of his conversion, and to be sought with impatience,
from the conviction that, so long as he halts short of it,
he foregoes a blessed privilege, and fails of fully answering
the redeeming purpose. Yet surely, if the Scriptures
teach the doctrine at all, it is in this light they present it.

Such was Miss George's view of the subject. No
sooner had she subscribed her name to the covenant,
than she comprehended the largeness of its purchased
and promised blessing. She saw that salvation from
the existence of sin was as clearly contained in that
blessing, as salvation from its guilt and penalty. And,
with her energetic and intensely practical disposition,

to see was to claim; and, within the domain of Christian privilege and Divine promise, to claim is to have. There was a brief natural struggle with the demur of unbelief, "Can this be for me, who have so recently tasted of the grace of God?" But the rising doubt was silenced by the just argument, "My sole claim is the merit of Jesus: if I tarry for years, shall I have established any other, or made *that* more valid?" Her faith rose triumphant with its "Yea, Lord, if Thou wilt, Thou canst make me clean." "According to" her "faith" it was done unto her. But let us hear her own account of the transaction. The date is, August 11th, 1852, not quite three weeks after she had believed "unto righteousness," while reading Henley's Life in the shrubbery.

"Monday and yesterday, while reading the 'Life of Mrs. Rogers,' I felt that God was infinitely willing to grant me a full salvation. I could not be happy with only the fear of death removed; I could not rejoice. Yet, as no person in our Society professed to have this blessing, I felt for a moment as if it would be presumption in me to seek it. Then my conscience immediately said, 'You know better: you see clearly how Christ purchased an entire salvation; and you know well that God is as willing to give you holiness as He is to give you pardon, and, if ever willing, willing now. He is waiting to destroy all His enemies, and reign supremely and entirely.' I felt as though I dared not think about it, because my conscience told me I ought to seek it. This morning I awoke between five and six, and, as usual, fell on my knees to present myself, body and soul, to God for the day, and seek His grace. I am expecting a cousin from London to-night, utterly ignorant of religion. I feared lest all my conduct before her and others

D

should not correspond with my profession. I prayed
for grace. I felt I might have all the strength of
Jehovah, if I would but ask it, or without asking, if I
would just receive it. O, I never shall forget the time!
God offered me holiness, showing me that Christ had
purchased it for me, and I might that moment take it.
I felt that, if I refused the blessing, God's favour would
depart from me. My eyes streamed with tears. I saw
how my adorable Saviour was waiting to save every
believer fully from the power of sin, as well as from
the guilt. I said, ' Lord, I dare not refuse the blessing.
I accept of it, of perfect holiness, of full salvation.

> 'Tis done ! Thou dost this moment save,
>   With full salvation bless;
> Redemption through Thy blood I have,
>   And spotless love and peace !'

These words were immediately applied to me : ' Behold,
thou art fair, there is no spot in thee;' ' Ye are clean
through the word that I have spoken unto you.' I felt
no rapturous joy: and well I did not; for I might have
rested in that, instead of Christ, and have been cast down
after, and thought I had lost the blessing, I received
the blessing so clearly the very moment I was willing,
that no power on earth or in hell could ever make
me doubt it. I am certain that

> ' Redemption through His blood I have,
>   And spotless love and peace.'

Glory, glory be to God! I feel this evening, as I did
this morning, that I am precious in God's sight. He
loves me for His Son's sake. I am one of His jewels.
My soul is the temple of the Triune God. Now I will
be ever speaking for God, by His grace. I will recom-

mend a present, free, and full salvation to all with whom I come in contact. I feel that my God has destroyed all His enemies in my soul, and created me anew after His image. May I never, never cease to praise God!

" 13th.—At noon this day I besought God to fill me with love. I felt just as I had done previously, filled with God; not my own, but the Lord's! O, what an unspeakable blessing! I have obtained freedom from sin, a clean heart! May God preserve me!

" 14th.—I bless and praise God that He has preserved me since Wednesday. I am His. I feel He is able to keep that which I have committed unto Him. —This morning, when engaged in prayer, these words were applied to me, ' I will never leave thee, nor forsake thee.' I felt that God would never leave me, but constantly dwell in my cleansed heart, and that no man should be able to pluck me from Him, if I do not forsake Him!"

There is nothing mysterious, nothing exceptional, in the foregoing narrative. Miss George fulfilled the conditions God required, and received the blessing He had promised. She was *willing* to be made holy. She sought to make no compromise with God. There was no evil thing she clung to with conscious or unconscious deception. She surrendered her all without reserve to God, and consented that He should impress on all the seal of consecration. And great and marvellous as the work was, she had faith that God could and would effect it. She saw it to be " the hope of" her " calling." She read it on the blood-sealed title-deed of her inheritance in Christ. The two immutable things, God's word and oath, gave her assurance that it could and would be. And she staggered not through unbelief. Since she was not

straitened in God, she determined not to be straitened in
herself. She enlarged her request and faith to the
measure of the promise. She opened her "mouth
wide" for her heavenly Father's liberal gift. She
spread out her lap to make room for the "good measure,
pressed down, and shaken together, and running over,"
which He offered, and waited to bestow. And, as she
had asked and believed, so it was done unto her.

Blended in the diary with the account of her own
spiritual change, there is another narrative too interesting to be altogether omitted. About a week after her
conversion, a young relative, who had just landed from
a four years' apprenticeship to the sea, arrived on a
visit. Cousin Eden had been religiously trained, and
had lived a steady decorous life until his fifteenth year,
when yielding to the wayward impulses of youth he
forsook his employment, and turned sailor. Since then
he had indulged in all the license and profanity unhappily too characteristic of such wayfarers of the ocean.
After five successive voyages to India he was now on
shore for a holiday, and a good Providence directed his
steps to his aunt's house at Welford. It was no small
trial to the decision and courage of the young convert
to be brought thus, at the outset of her course, into
such close companionship with one to whom all sacred
things had long been the theme of banter and contempt.
At once, however, she did the best thing she could in
the case: she laid it before God in prayer, earnestly
seeking counsel and help. And soon she was encouraged to hope, not only that she would be enabled to
maintain without compromise her own Christian consistency, but that her prayers and efforts would be
successful in the reclaiming of the wanderer himself.
With no little discernment and tact did she go about

her difficult task. "I determined not to say a word directly on the subject of religion, as I knew he hated everything good, and would only laugh and call it Methodist cant. So I only endeavoured to let my light shine before him, to have everything as peaceful and happy in our family as possible, and thus to *win him over*." These tactics soon began to tell. The stubborn heart of the young sailor would have bristled up in defiance of any overt attempt " to make a Methodist " of him; but there was something in this unexpected mode of procedure that disarmed opposition. This " beauty of holiness" contrasted strongly with the rude coarse ungodliness in the midst of which he had been living. Recollections of earlier and better years awoke; and impressions long smothered, and seemingly dead, began to stir anew within him. All these favourable symptoms were watched with affectionate interest by his cousin; and her prayers increased in fervency as the answer appeared to draw near. At length on the Sabbath evening she ventured to request him to accompany her to the chapel. He consented. The Preacher's text was strikingly appropriate: "To-day, if ye will hear His voice, harden not your heart." It was enough; all resistance was now at an end; the young scoffer returned, subdued and penitent. Miss George shall give the issue in her own words :—

"Not much conversation directly on the subject of personal religion passed between us till Tuesday. Then, as we were walking in the garden, he told me all his past history, all his suffering and all his sin, his afflictions, warnings of conscience, and the like. In my heart I kept praying, and God enabled me to direct the penitent and despairing backslider to Jesus crucified. He said he was a thousand times worse than the thief

D 3

on the cross; he dared not look up to God, lest he should
be struck dead. I begged him to pray. No, he dared
not; he had not prayed for four years and a half! I
left him, and retired to my chamber to pray for him,
telling him what I was going to do. It affected him,
and he went into the barn, and, I believe, prayed there.
I gave him the hymn commencing, 'All ye that pass
by,' to read. I found him afterwards still wretched,
almost despairing of mercy. I prayed with my whole
soul night and morning, and felt an assurance that my
prayers would be heard. We often read together Carvosso's Memoirs, Mrs. Rogers's Memoirs, and Doddridge's
' Rise and Progress,' rising very early in the morning
for prayer and reading. On Wednesday we attended
prayer-meeting. At night, when he retired, I begged
him to look to God without any delay for the blessing,
for he never would have so good an opportunity. We
arranged to meet early next morning. We did so; and,
to my surprise and joy, he had obtained God's favour,
and was happy. I wept and praised God, and said I
would always trust God now, and be bold in working
for Him. On Sunday, cousin Eden told his conversion
to my class-mates, who joined us in praising God.
He has to forsake many old companions, sell all his sailor-
clothes, and give up the sea entirely—no little effort."

The conversion of her cousin was a source of great
benefit to Miss George herself. It filled her with gratitude ; it increased her faith in the prevalence of
prayer; it stimulated her to greater zeal and self-devo-
tion in the cause of her Saviour; and provided her with
help and comfort where she had looked only for
hindrance and persecution. It was at once an aus-
picious and an appropriate commencement of that life of
bold and faithful service which she from this time led.

CHAPTER IV.

CLEAR SHINING.

"Blessed is the people that know the joyful sound: they shall walk, O Lord, in the light of Thy countenance. In Thy name shall they rejoice all the day: and in Thy righteousness shall they be exalted." (Psal. lxxxix. 15, 16.)

HOLINESS is at once the best guarantee of stability, and the best equipment for service. Some Christians feel a secret hesitancy about seeking so elevated a state, lest they should not be able to maintain it in this world of hindrance and temptation. Such fears are ill-grounded. The probabilities of relapse are fewer when sanctification is entire, than while it is imperfect. There is a better prospect of continued health when the constitution is sound, than when it harbours lurking tendencies to disease. Holiness is spiritual soundness; and, therefore, to the sanctified soul the dangers of declension are diminished, though of course the possibility remains. Facts, moreover, abundantly show that these are not the characters who fall from their steadfastness, but such spiritual valetudinarians as have never ventured to test to the uttermost the Great Physician's skill.

Holiness is also the best equipment for pious labour. For holiness is *consecration*—the placing of all at God's disposal—the devotion of all to God's glory. Holiness is the "single eye," to which perplexity is made plain; the guarded tongue, whose "seasoned" words are all for edification and praise; the diligent hand, which in the morning sows the seed, and in the evening is not withholden; the loving, humble heart, which seeks not its own, but is content to sink into nothing that God may be exalted. And God exacts holiness as the condition of large and signal success. The live coal from the altar must touch the Prophet's lips, and his iniquity thus be taken away, and his sin be purged, before he is qualified to be the bearer of God's message. Barnabas was "a good man, and full of the Holy Ghost and of faith; and much people was added unto the Lord."

In Miss George the truth of these remarks was exemplified. From the time that she attained this elevated state, her course never wavered. Temptations she had, demanding a wary outlook, and stout, prayerful, uncompromising resistance. To the Christian warfare, with its weary vigils, its vexing skirmishes, its stern hand-to-hand encounters, she was no stranger. Times of depression also came, when heart and flesh were ready to fail, and when faith clung to a Saviour whose face was mysteriously hidden. There were fluctuations, too, in the intensity of her affections, and the measure of her enjoyments; in the fervour of her devotion, and the buoyancy of her faith. From these things—inevitable concessions to human frailty, and the imperfection and discipline of the present state—Miss George, of course, was not exempt: nevertheless, her career henceforward was one of exemplary steadfastness. Of her habitual state it may be said, that she lived without sinning; she did not enter into condemnation. She retained to her life's end an unbroken consciousness of the truth, that "the blood of Jesus Christ cleanseth"—now cleanseth—"from all sin." She "reckoned" herself "dead indeed unto sin, but alive unto God through Jesus Christ." She never wavered in her purpose to be the Lord's. She had laid her all upon the altar, and she never withdrew, or wished to withdraw, in whole or in part, the sacrifice.

From this crisis she was also "in labours more abundant." In the conduct of her school, which now devolved wholly upon her, she displayed great diligence and conscientiousness. From the beginning she had possessed much aptitude for teaching, and great fondness for the employment; and now both tact and love were sanctified. While scrupulously attentive to the mental improvement of the children, she made it her first care to lead forth the trust and affection of their young hearts to the Saviour. Her delicate discernment of character, her skill in simplifying truth, the influence which, by a nice combination of decision and gentleness, she easily wielded, were all put into requisition for this purpose, and not without encouraging instances of success. Thus did she carry her religion into what we may call her sphere of secular work, making it a point of conscience to be faithful in its immediate duties, yet never losing sight of those higher interests to which, in her estimation, all others were subservient. Her labours, however, did not terminate here. By many, the worry and exhaustion of spending so many hours a day in the management of a school, would have been deemed plea sufficient to exempt from all further exactions; not so by Miss George. Recreation was to her but a change of work. The close of school-duty was the signal for other and equally congenial employment. She would then sally forth into the village, health and weather permitting, on a round of pious and charitable visits to the sick and poor. She had usually a list of ten or a dozen special cases, all of which she contrived to see two or three times a week.

In these Home-Missionary labours, her faith and patience, her zeal and tenderness, were beyond all praise.
No abode was so uncleanly, no disease so loathsome, as
to repel her in disgust. A young lady of refined taste
and superior culture, rather fond than otherwise of the
elegancies of life, she was often to be found in wretched
hovels, where all senses were offended, praying by the
bed-side, or with her own hands ministering to the
wants, of some half-clad, half-starved sufferer. Very
rarely did she despair of a case. To the dying sinner,
on whom the pains of hell seemed already to have got
hold ; to the aged sinner, who had reached the eleventh
hour in all the stolid hardness induced by a lifetime of
ungodliness ; she would speak with unconquerable hope-
fulness of a Saviour's unbounded mercy ; and in secret,
with an importunity that refused to take a denial, would
she wrestle with God on their behalf. Diffident and
awkward at first, she soon acquired tact and boldness in
this kind of work. It became the best-beloved of her
employments. Nor were her poor neighbours slow to
appreciate her self-denying kindness. She was as an
angel of mercy to them in their want, and suffering,
and sorrow. Doors and hearts, which were shut in
resentment against the advances of all other religious
people, were opened to her gentle persuasiveness. And
" the day " alone will reveal what was the fruit of all
this patient labour ; and to how many of God's hidden
ones her visits gave cheer and hope, when heart and flesh
were failing ; or to how many of the dark and outcast
the words which they heard from her lips, perhaps in
their last extremity, were words of eternal life.

Other means of usefulness opened to Miss George as
time advanced ; and from none did she withhold her
hand. She had a large class of older girls in the Sab-

bath-school, for which she made it matter of conscience
to prepare herself carefully and prayerfully during the
week. Among the manuscripts transmitted to the
compiler of these memoirs, are many papers, obviously
intended to be turned to account in this way,—epitomes
of Jewish history, transcripts from works on Scripture
antiquities, and the like. Shortly after her conversion
she formed another class of young females, which met
on one of the evenings of the week, and in which
Biblical exposition and religious conversation were
blended. Add to all this, an unremitting attendance
on all the public services of religion, and the daily
devotion of a large amount of time to personal spiritual
improvement; and the whole presents the pleasant picture of a life, not spent languidly without a purpose,
nor frittered away in frivolities, but earnestly consecrated to life's great ends.

Of what that life was, however, in its daily details,
Miss George's own diary will give the best idea. She
began at a very early period, as we have seen, to keep a
record of her religious experience, and of the principal
events that affected it for good or evil; finding the practice, as all will whose eye is single in it, a very wholesome one. In this diary the fluctuations and conflicts,
the temptations and deliverances, which marked the
history of her inner life; the diligent culture, the
prayerfulness, and scrupulous self-inspection, by which
that inner life was sustained; and the faithful, zealous
labours in which it found its outward expression, are all
duly chronicled : not in the way of self-commendation ;
more often, on the other hand, in deep self-upbraiding ;
and never otherwise than as glorifying the grace of God.
The chief business of the biographer will henceforth be
that of selection and arrangement, with the interjection

of such comments and explanations as the character of
the extracts, or the continuity of the narrative, may
seem occasionally to demand.

For a few days the entries exhibit all the exuberant
joyfulness and flaming ardour which might be looked
for as the immediate consequence of so great a change
as that which she had just experienced. She walks in
perpetual sunlight; the wicked one touches her not;
"over the glory" is "a defence;" and, constrained by
her newly-found blessedness, she cries to all, "Come
near, and I will tell you what the Lord hath done for
my soul." Cousin Eden is still with her, and very
pleasant and mutually helpful is their communion. Let
the following extracts serve as a sample of much in the
same tone :—

"August 15th, Sunday.—This has been a good day.
I rose soon after five, spent much time in reading and
prayer, and felt my faith wonderfully strengthened. I
dared not doubt for one moment but that my faithful,
covenant-keeping God would fulfil His promise, and
give me many souls in this village that I have set my
heart upon, and do not intend to let rest. I am determined to honour God by strong faith; and then He will
honour me by allowing me to work for Him, and
making me useful. I felt this morning that I was as
clay in God's hands; I was His child, His will was
mine; I was His willing and obedient servant. I
prayed much for cousin Eden, and soon after seven went
down to him. We read and conversed, and encouraged
each other. At eight we went to the prayer-meeting.
God was there, and blessed us. At school all day I felt
in a very peculiar manner that God was well pleased
with all I did and said. He spoke through me: the
words were God's words; and I saw that they sank into

the hearts of my girls. When I was speaking of the great safety of God's children, and the awful danger of sinners, I saw tears in most eyes. I was only the instrument through which God spoke.

"16th.—Last night I retired with a sweet consciousness that my ways pleased God. I awoke before five, and immediately called on God. I was much blessed in private; felt unlimited confidence in God's promises. From seven to eight Eden and I spent together, reading, and encouraging one another, very profitably. I find continually new places to visit, and have now fourteen sick people on my list. God does indeed bless my efforts, and hear my prayers. One of my poor spiritual patients told me a week ago that she dare believe in Jesus. Another last night told me that all fear of death was removed, and she was happy. On Friday night she had been unhappy, and afraid to die. A third was released from earth and conducted to glory a few days ago. Yesterday her poor, old, and feeble body was committed to the dust. I visited her when in the agonies of death, and commended her spirit to God, and He helped me to deal faithfully with the three women present. O, may I sow beside all waters!

"17th.—Last evening I visited a poor man, very dark and ignorant. I asked him if he was happy. 'No, I should think not,—it's likely for a body to be happy here!' I asked him what he meant. Very grumblingly he made answer, 'Why, I don't know what to be about—nor anything: not like' to be happy.' I told him simply what would make him happy, and begged him to look to Christ now before he became weaker. He did not know that he was a sinner. I prayed with him and his good old mother, and this morning in prayer had faith that God would enlighten

E

and save him. 'Whatsoever ye shall ask in prayer,
believing, ye shall receive.'

"19th.—This morning I did not feel so much of the
presence of God in my devotions as heretofore. Still I
was much blessed and comforted. This evening I have
again seen the poor dark man I visited a few days ago.
Praise God, my prayer is heard! The Spirit of God has
wonderfully enlightened his mind: he sees himself a
sinner, needing mercy; and God, a God ready to pardon
sinners through Christ. O, may he soon be happy! I
had much liberty in conversing with him, and praying
for him. He wept much, and thanked me for coming."

The next day she speaks of temptation to irritability
in the school, and of much shame and grief occasioned
by wasting half an hour in "unprofitable conversation"
with her cousin; evidences these, if of nothing else, of
the sensitive and jealous watch she kept over herself.
Yet the day did not pass without its seasons of intense
enjoyment and consecrated toil, as witness what
follows:—

"20th.—This evening, after school, I had many
visits to pay. I went to my chamber, and prostrated
myself before the mercy-seat; and O, I could not refrain
from weeping aloud! God seemed to fill me with Himself. I never had such views of the goodness of God,
and of my own weakness; of the reality of eternal
things, and the trifling worth of things temporal. I
could have knelt there for hours, *receiving* God's blessings simply; for I wept too much to pray. I felt that
I was as much God's servant as the angels in heaven
are.* I felt that God was well pleased with me, and
would go with me wherever I went, and make me a

---

* As truly and as willingly.

blessing. Praise God! While I am yet calling, He answers; nay, before I speak, He seems to fulfil my desire.

"This evening I have had to bless and praise my God again; for poor dark M—— tells me that he believed in God for pardon last night while I was praying with him. He says this has been a happy day. What a mighty change since Tuesday!

"I desire, O my God, to offer Thee my thanks and my all, body and soul, to be Thine entirely. Make holy my every thought. May all my words and actions glorify Thee. I am Thine. Amen."

Next follows the story of a Sabbath, crowded through every moment with sacred employment, and unutterably happy:—

"22d, Sunday evening.—Glory and praise be to the holy name of God, not one good thing has failed me of all that He promised me this morning! At the morning prayer-meeting I beheld plainly by faith my Saviour stooping from His lofty throne to own and bless me. It was a blessed time. I went expecting, and was not disappointed. During the twenty minutes or half hour between prayer-meeting and school, I felt in a peculiar manner God's immediate presence. I felt that God loved me much; that my ways pleased Him. I offered myself and my services to God without the slightest reserve; and He accepted me through Christ, and assured me that I was clean; that He would use me for His glory, and speak through me to my girls, and any other persons I might converse with during the day. I enjoyed sweet communion with God; for while I was asking, He answered; and this blessed sweetness I have experienced throughout the day. My heaven is surely begun below; for God and love are heaven. Yet I have never felt so much of my own

weakness and insufficiency. I can do nothing alone,
but all things through Christ, which strengtheneth me.
This afternoon I was surrounded by great girls. Before
I commenced teaching, I was conversing with the Lord
as face to face. I was so overpowered at the thought
of the work before me, of my responsibility and weakness, that I should have sunk beneath it, had not my
heavenly Father filled me with the comfort of His
promises. Before tea I visited three families, and
spoke to many other persons; and God was eminently
with me in all. From five to nearly six I spent in my
bed-room, weeping and praising God. Words cannot
express how loving and how near I felt my Maker to be.
I wanted no tea; I had indeed meat to eat which the
world knew not of. In the evening Mr. B. preached
his last sermon. My cup was nearly overflowing all
the time. I could have gone home just then. I kept
repeating,

> ' The promised land from Pisgah's top
>   I now exult to see ;
>   My hope is full (O glorious hope !)
>   Of immortality.'

I was very, very happy; gave my all again as a sacrifice,
and prayed much for my dear girls."

The same strain of rapturous enjoyment continues for
several days. The "sensible smiles" of her heavenly
Father are upon her continually, and her heart within
her responds with deep warm pulses of filial love. Even
while about her domestic duties, her joy is so irrepressible that she cannot refrain from frequent outbreaks of
singing, till the very servant begins to suspect that she
is in possession of the secret of some strange happiness.
The one or two brief extracts which follow, the reader

must expand and multiply for himself into much of the same sort:—

" 24th.—Yesterday afternoon and evening I had a very bad headache; but, after school, God helped me to visit four families. I had much liberty in speaking pointedly to each member, and praying.

" 25th.—Last night I visited M——, one week since the day he told me he could not be happy. He was rejoicing in God's pardoning love. I encouraged and questioned him."

Cousin Eden's last day at Welford has now come. He must go forth from this quiet and pleasant anchorage into the rough world; must abandon the adventurous sea-life for the landsman's monotonous routine of labour, and give the best account of the change he can to his scoffing acquaintance. It is thus the two cousins part— never more to meet in this world:—

" 26th.—Rose at twenty minutes past five, and spent some time in prayer, reading, meditation, and self-examination. I could not be satisfied, as I did not feel so much of God's presence and love as I frequently do. I did not doubt in the least that my heart was pure and spotless, and that I pleased God; but I did not feel melted in love, as often is the case. While I was dressing, my faith increased. I felt my Father's smile sensibly. After looking to God, I met my dear cousin Eden in the parlour at seven o'clock. It was the last morning before his departure. We had indeed a blessed season. God and heaven filled my soul. I wept for joy. Eden felt the same; and we both wept, and testified of God's abundant goodness to each of us. God was very, very near. We encouraged each other, and then knelt down and commended each other to God in prayer, offering ourselves again to God entirely and for ever. Eden is expecting to meet with a flood of persecution. Be Thou, my God, as a wall of fire round about him. Enable him to confess Thee boldly before wicked, scoffing relations, and the world. As his trials and persecutions abound, so may Thy consolations. Direct his path just where Thou wilt. He knows not where to go, or what to do; but Thou wilt provide.

"27th.—God, my God, is good indeed. I feel much sweet peace. Tears of joy and love continually fill my eyes. O, the blessedness of being a child of heaven!

"Mamma is very unwell. I have had her duties to attend to to-day, as well as my own, yet have very much enjoyed the day. God has indeed blessed my soul. I visited two families before chapel, and dropped wayside words to three or four other persons, with whom I have met.

"29th, Sunday.—This has been a good day. I rose at ten minutes past five, and enjoyed my private devotions. God promised His presence should go with me. We had a good prayer-meeting at eight o'clock. I was much blessed. While I was yet calling, God answered. At school all day I felt I was perfect weakness, but trusted entirely to Christ, as a little babe to its mother. God told me what to say, and enabled me to say it. I have met with discouragements; but I pass over them all, and look to the promises. I see signs of good in some girls, and others grieve me as much. O, that all were converted! Have visited seven families, and felt it to be blessed employment. Have tried to live and act all day as though this were my last.

"30th.—Have received a note from my cousin. Poor fellow! 'He is mad, his brain is turned, he will soon repent; he has caught the Methodist distemper; has been preached to from morning till night,' &c., &c.

But he glories in it all; and so do I. Many sad and disrespectful things are said of poor cousin Elizabeth; but I feel they are false, and my God condemns me not.

"31st.—Rose at half-past five. Did not feel so happy as I wished. There seemed to be a thin veil between God's face and my soul. I believed He was well-pleased with me and loved me; but He did not commune with me so intimately as heretofore. I wept before the throne, and would not be comforted, till my God told me more clearly that He was perfectly pleased with me. While waiting before the Lord I received comfort, and felt a peculiarly humble and submissive sweetness, though not such delight as on former occasions. All the morning I felt a settled peace. After dinner I sat for half an hour in the carriage in the barn, whilst my little ones were at play. I had the Hymn-Book in my pocket, and in it found much comfort. I looked to God, and the intercourse seemed open between heaven and my soul. O, how sweet! No words can describe it. I wept with holy transport. I was humbled into nothing; God was all in all—my justification, my holiness, and my all. I could not help saying,—

'Precious the moments are and sweet,
While Jesus is so near.'

I feel Him very, very near while I write. He is blessing me with His sweet presence and love. O, what ineffable condescension for the mighty Jehovah to commune with such a worm! Make me, O my Father, just what will be well-pleasing to Thee. Keep me humble as in the dust. I feel now that I can hardly refrain from weeping for solemn joy. Praise the Lord, O my soul!"

For some weeks from this date Miss George suffered much from violent pains in the head and face. The ailment was in part constitutional, and troubled her at intervals more or less throughout her life. In this instance it was probably aggravated by the state of high emotional excitement which the joyous changes through which she had recently passed had occasioned, by the frequency and fervour of her devotions, and by the excessive curtailment of needful rest which she practised, in order to secure the more time for spiritual culture. After attacking her intermittently for some weeks, the pain became at length so sharp and disabling, that she was obliged to relax a little. Her pious activities were for a while suspended, and even her closet-duties were of sheer necessity abridged; for any severe and continuous tension of the mind was more than she could bear. Yet, in the midst of all, her soul prospered and rejoiced. Unable formally to pray, she could yet lie lovingly and trustfully in the arms of Jesus. And He, who "knoweth our frame, and remembereth that we are dust," condescended to her weakness, and supplied all her wants. She enjoyed sweet and constant communion with God. The mere uplifting of her heart to her "Father that seeth in secret," altogether apart from the intellectual or physical effort of prayer, met with an instant response, and drew down abounding consolations. Often afterwards she would refer to these few weeks of pain and incapacity as the happiest of her life.

"September 3d.—A day of peace unruffled; but head bad all the day. Was quite prevented praying or reading more than two or three minutes together. I managed to pay a few visits, and attend the Teachers' meeting. God blessed me abundantly, notwithstanding my weakness.

"5th, Sunday.—Up at five minutes past five; head rather better on waking. My soul was quite happy, and God promised to go with me through the day, and bless me. I went to morning prayer-meeting, and found it good to be in God's house. At school, all day, God was with me. In the afternoon I had a number of grown-up girls as visiters, to whom I spoke plainly. I visited two families in the evening, and one at dinner-time; spoke, read, and prayed at G——'s, and begged some of them to come to chapel. Three came, and three more young girls that I had persuaded. I hope God blessed their souls.

"9th.—My head considerably better; quite a change. Mr. Stott told me on Monday that I 'must not expect it to be well, so long as I was up eighteen hours, and only in bed six. My nervous system could not stand it.' I have retired at ten instead of eleven since, and intend to continue so doing: then I can continue rising at five."

This evening she met for the first time the class of young females to which reference has been already made. It had been formed at the request of several young persons in the village, who, though not prepared formally to unite themselves with the church, were yet willing to spend an hour of the week with Miss George in religious conversation and study of the Scriptures. The task seemed to her a formidable one, and her anxiety and trepidation in undertaking it find expression in her diary again and again as the day draws near.

She fixed upon the first nineteen verses of the 33d chapter of Ezekiel as the subject of the first lesson, and with much self-distrust invoked counsel and help from above. And she gratefully records the perfect composure with which she was able to discharge the duty, and the evident impression which her earnest and faithful

comments made upon those who were present. From
that time the class met weekly, with much beneficial
result to its members. To return to the diary:—

"18th, Saturday.—The last week I have been called
to suffer instead of to work. Praise God, I have been
perfectly happy and resigned. It was my Father's will,
and therefore mine. I have been in constant pain,
more or less, all the time in head, face, tooth, and neck,
and had withal a swollen face and sore mouth. I could
not speak at all on Monday and Tuesday, and scarcely
ever since. I have been quite unable to read, (eyes
very weak,) or pray in words. Still God's goodness to
me has been unspeakable. I cannot express it. I have
been in perfect peace. Satan has not been allowed to
tempt me once. I was quite expecting that he would
suggest that, as I could not pray, or read God's word for
so many days, I could not retain the blessing of holiness; but my all-wise, all-kind Father would not suffer
him to distress me while lying on the sofa or bed. My
soul has enjoyed sweet communion with its Maker, and
tears have involuntarily started in my eyes; but I have
been obliged to check them, and even turn from the
subject. This would be a dangerous thing to try in
health, but I received no harm. Whenever my head has
been a little stronger, then God has given me more of
His sweet presence; just as much as my weakness could
bear. Yesterday morning I was rather better, and felt
overpowered with God's sacred presence and goodness
all the morning. I could do nothing but weep tears of
grateful joy and humble love. The last ten lines of the
ninth hymn beautifully describe my feelings at that
time.* This day has been one of much sweetness.

---

* "The tears that tell your sins forgiven;
  The sighs that waft your souls to heaven:

God is with me, filling my heart with love, my eyes with tears, and my tongue with praise. O, the inexpressible bliss of being a child of God! One day last week I heard from Eden. Providence has seemed to direct his path homewards. He is now with his father at Cardiff, and has joined his old Leader's class again. What hath God wrought!

"19th, Sunday.—Enjoyed much of the Divine presence, though my pain was great. Just managed to go to school in the afternoon, and sat as pupil in my own class. Mr. Hopkins had to teach, but I thought my presence might encourage the girls. I felt such exceeding love to them. My head was as though a weight were resting on it, and all the night I could not read, sleep, think, or pray.

"23d.—Very, very happy, as every day, and fully resigned to the will of God. After school I went and lay on the sofa, and enjoyed such sweetness as I cannot describe; close communion with the Triune Jehovah. O, the infinite condescension of the Deity! Who can worthily extol it? I felt as peaceful and as happy as a little babe sleeping in its mother's arms: not a care, a trouble, or a wish, save to promote my Father's glory. It was heaven begun below. It was indeed that sweet land of rest, —

'Where pure enjoyment reigns,
And God is loved alone.'

"The guiltless shame, the sweet distress;
The' unutterable tenderness;
The genuine, meek humility;
The wonder, ' Why such love to me!'

"The' o'erwhelming power of saving grace,
The sight that veils the seraph's face;
The speechless awe that dares not move,
And all the silent heaven of love."

I gave myself up entirely into my Father's hands. I had not the slightest will of my own. I told Him that I was as willing to suffer as to do, and I felt it; and, praise God, I feel it at this moment! I desired that which would be most to His glory, and, if restored to soundness, wished only to work for Him. I felt that I should love to visit my sick friends again, to teach my girls, pray for many sinners, &c.: still, as it was, I was as happy as possible. O, what cannot the grace of God accomplish? The happiest time of my life has been the last fortnight.

"25th.—On Thursday night I met my beloved girls, read to them the first chapter of James's ' Anxious Inquirer,' and then addressed each one separately. Several shed tears, and acknowledged that the Spirit of God had been striving with them much lately. After the meeting, the pain left my head, and all day yesterday I felt none, nor to-day. I am, however, obliged to keep quite still; my eyes are excessively weak; and unfavourable symptoms return, if I do or think of anything. But all is well: I am filled with God's love. May the Lord Jehovah preserve me from sin to my life's end!

"27th.—This day, especially this morning, has been a sweet and precious time to me. I went to my chamber, and knelt before the Lord, and in a moment, before I could ask, He met me, and filled me abundantly with His love, so that I wept for joy for a long time. O, the unspeakable goodness of my God! I feel that I am wholly the Lord's, body and soul, time and talents. I am willing to be, do, or suffer anything that my all-wise Father may appoint, and desire to work for God to my life's end."

The next day's record opens with the overflow of a glad, humble, thankful heart:—"Praise and glory be to

my God for His unspeakable love and goodness to me,
a poor unworthy sinner! Why should my Father so
bless me? How many times a day I am led to ask
this question with tears! O, how blessed

> ' The genuine sweet humility,
> The wonder, Why such love to me!' "

After this exulting outbreak, the mention of Stoner's
"Memoir," which she is now reading, leads her mind
back to those long troubled years, during which she had
been an unsatisfied seeker of repose in Christ. "Many,
many times," she writes, "I have seemed within a
hair's-breadth of the kingdom of God, and yet did not
see just the way, the simple way, of trusting on the
merits and atonement of the Saviour, whether I received the witness of the Spirit or not just at the time.
Even after fuller light had come, I lived for three or
four days by faith alone, without any great joy or sensible
assurance; with nothing save my own determined trust
in Jesus. I knew I could not be lost if I continued to
trust on the merits of Christ, the atonement for sin."
She adverts then with deep regret to the waste of so
many years in unprofitable vacillation; to the misappre-
hensions of Ministers and religious friends as to her state;
and to the foolish shame which had hindered her from
disclosing to them in plain words that she was not a
child of God, and thus securing from them counsel and
help. But she was not one of those who—to adapt an
old proverb—throw away good time after bad; who
squander the precious present in slothful and despond-
ent regrets over the unsatisfactory past. The retrospect
only kindles into fresh ardour her resolution henceforth
to live for God wholly and alone; and the entry accordingly closes with the energetic prayer: "May my God

F

help me to be holy in heart and life, to be a living
testimony of His power to save from all sin, to be
Christ-like, to live each day as if my last, and to know
constantly that all my ways please Him. Amen!"

During her indisposition, though unable to visit them,
Miss George had not been forgetful of her poor sick
friends. Often, when pain and weakness permitted,
she had uplifted her heart to God, in sad yet trustful
sympathy, invoking blessings upon them. The afflicted
man, to whom reference was made in the commencement of this chapter, was especially in her thoughts
and prayers. He had been almost the first-fruits of her
zealous labours, and was now drawing rapidly near his
end. She was the more anxious about him, since other
pious people were somewhat incredulous as to the
reality of a change so sudden in one so extremely
ignorant. Even his old mother, a good woman, was
disposed, like many of her class, to require some more
palpable proof that God had accepted him, and was
removing him to a better world. Miss George's simple
faith in the Divine mercy, and the efficacy of prayer,
had set her own mind at rest upon the subject; yet it
was not without much sorrowful sympathy that she
thought how the poor man must die unattended by
almost the only friend who gave him credit for sincerity, and whose voice was familiar and pleasant to him.
On the morning of the day after the date of the last
extract, she heard that the great change had taken place.
In the afternoon she went to the house. "The good
old mother," she writes, "with streaming but joyful
eyes, said, 'My dear son's gone rejoicing home; and, bless
you, Miss, and everybody else that ever spoke to him,
or prayed for him!' 'Well, Nanny, what did he say?
How did he die?' 'O, Miss! my prayer was heard: I

had a sign. He called me to him, and, looking up and pointing, said, *Mother, do you hear the music and the singing?* Where, my lad? *O, mother! and do you see the glory? I am going!*—then died!' I was rejoiced, and knelt down and praised God for a friend safe in heaven."

Gradually, as her health amended, she resumed her old activities. Two days after M——'s decease, she is praying by the bedside of another poor creature on the verge of the grave; and, hearing a few hours subsequently of her departure, she writes, " I felt ready and willing to be in her place. All day I have meditated much on the world of bliss, and longed to be there. I am ready to wing my flight any time. May my God ever keep me thus!" Then follows,—for this heavenward aspiring was no inert, unhealthy mysticism,— "From eight to half-past this night, according to our arrangement, I have spent in interceding with God for our Sabbath-school, particularly in pleading for my own class, and *the two new Teachers*. Lord, convert them both! May I teach to-morrow as though it were my last Sunday! I am very, very happy in God."—The arrangements for an approaching Missionary tea-meeting having devolved chiefly upon her, she thanks God that in borrowing trays, selling tickets, &c., she has been " enabled to speak a word for her Master at every house." On the Sabbath, though suffering severely from a departing twinge of the old ailment, she records, respecting a meeting which had been held in the afternoon,— " I should have liked all to know how I felt; but flowing tears would have prevented my telling of the unutterable sweetness, ' the joy unspeakable and full of glory!' It was indeed heaven upon earth. I was overwhelmed in thinking of the love of God to me, and the unspeakable blessings He has given me. O, who would not be a Christian ? "

The diary then proceeds thus:—

" October 6th.—This morning I was not so diligent in redeeming time while dressing as I should have been. My thoughts were not so heavenly and devout as usual. I was planning and arranging what I would do for the conversion of different persons; but I find it best to have something purely spiritual to think of while dressing. God should have the first employment of our powers. I am intending now, by the grace of God, to recommence the practice of early rising; and I trust it will be to the glory of God, and the good of my soul. This day I have felt great peace in drawing nigh to God in private ; but, through the loss I sustained before breakfast, not such a sweet and abiding sense of my Maker's presence as usual. I have felt, however, an entire deadness to the world and all its vanities. My prayer is,—

> ' Henceforth may no profane delight
> Divide this consecrated soul;
> Possess it Thou, who hast the right,
> As Lord and Master of the whole.'

" 9th.—The last two days I have not felt in so prosperous and joyous a state. I have been troubled with wandering thoughts; not once upon sinful subjects,— still idle thoughts, not to the immediate glory of God. I have been given to see how easily I should go astray, if not kept every moment by the power of the Omnipotent Jehovah. I have feared exceedingly lest I should have grieved the Holy Spirit by unsanctified thoughts, or any neglect of duty. May God show me if I have done so ! I want to be always thinking of God, praying

to Him, and praising Him. Even when engaged in
duty, even mental duty, I may find a parenthesis for
prayer.

"Last night I was stirred up by reading a little of
good Mrs. Judson's Life. I felt great love for souls, and
an earnest longing to be made useful here at Welford.
I never shall have a better opportunity, though I am
willing to work anywhere, in any clime, so that I may
be useful, and best promote my Father's glory. I have
been thinking much about China lately. I should love to
go to be a labourer in some tiny spot of that mighty field;
but I leave the future entirely in the hands of my Lord,
whose I am, body and soul. I know that He will
direct all my paths."

Another poor sufferer, to whom this young evangelist's sympathy and prayers had often been as springs
of water to the faint, was now about to put off the
pained and wasted body of flesh.

"Just at dark, this night, I was sent for to visit Mrs.
G., who was in a dying state. I went, after imploring
the presence and blessing of the Holy Spirit, and felt that
I was God's messenger as much if He had sent an angel
from heaven to the house. The poor woman could not
speak for a long time. Her mother told me that she was
continually asking for Miss George to pray to her
blessed Saviour to come and take her. At length the
poor creature revived a little, and whispered very softly
to me that she wanted to go to glory. I said, 'Can you
give all up now? your husband and two little children?'
'O, yes, Miss; all up, all up!' I told her that Jesus
would be with her, and guide her safely through the
valley. She spoke of her pains, which were very
severe. I said, 'They will soon be over: you must
think what sad pains our Saviour bore for you and me,

and all of us; then you will not think yours so bad.'
She said, ' O, I deserve more than this: this is none too
much—no, none, none!' She then began praying in her
simple style, ' O my dear Saviour, please to fetch me;
please to fetch me! O, do, please! do send glorious angels
to take me to heaven! Come, come! O, please to come!
Come to-night. O, do come now, my dear Saviour!'
Thus she continued for a long time; then, turning to me,
' O, Miss, please to ask my Saviour to fetch me to-night!'
I said, ' Well, I'll pray presently; but first I'll read a
nice hymn to you about heaven, that happy land where
you are going, and about the happy angels.' I read suitable hymns and verses to her, and then conversed about
the realities of heaven; and, O, how near it seemed! I
would willingly have exchanged places with the dying
saint. I afterwards kindly and earnestly addressed all
in the room separately. They were weeping. The husband and mother both say that they once enjoyed religion,
but have lost it. I begged them and the sister to seek it
at once, showing them how it was the one thing needful; and then knelt down and prayed to my God for them
all. A few minutes after, another sister and a visiter
came in. After urging them both to seek a preparation
for death and heaven, I left; praying that God would
fasten conviction on their hearts, and lead all the family
to seek religion.

"I do feel that I am a vile unworthy creature to-
night, not worthy to do anything for so holy and good a
God.* I wonder He will deign to use me at all. I deserve eternal punishment, and nothing less at His hands:
yet I have now redemption through the blood of Christ,

---

* " So likewise ye, when ye shall have done all those things
which are commanded you, say, We are unprofitable servants: we
have done that which was our duty to do."

even the forgiveness of sins; nay, I dare to say, His blood *cleanseth me from all sin.* O my soul, blush and be ashamed at such love to thee! My God, make me useful; give me souls. Here I am; Thine now, and Thine for ever, body and soul, time and talents: make me perfectly holy and Christ-like.

> 'Hallow each thought; let all within
> Be clean, as Thou, my Lord, art clean.'

Amen and amen."

A few days more, and the sufferer to whom the above extract relates found glad release. Here is the final scene. Who will venture to say how much of reality, or how much of disordered yet blissful imagining, there is in these glimpses and snatches of heavenly glory, permitted to dying saints, just as they are rending asunder the veil of sense to see " eye to eye?"

" 13th.—At eleven o'clock to-day Mrs. G.'s triumphant spirit entered glory. Praise, praise the Lord! She said, 'she should have died yesterday, but when the angels came for her, she was not ready; she could not die without seeing her husband again: she waited an hour and a half, and when he came home, the golden gates, which had been standing open all that time, were shut, and she had to wait until the Lord was pleased to send for her again.' Many other delightful things she said, and, after wishing all good-bye, and giving suitable exhortations, exclaimed, with glistening eyes, ' The glorious angels are come again. I have done with you. I am quite ready. I am going now to my Father in my new home.' She then lay in a quiet, composed state until eleven, when she ceased to breathe. May my last end be like hers!"

Miss George's visits to the sick and dying gave her,

as we have already seen, many opportunities of speaking
to those who, as nurses or neighbours, happened to be
present.   Of such opportunities she was ever careful to
avail herself.   Here is an example :—

"Called to-day on Mrs. B.   She is rather better in
body, and willing to die; believes that she shall be
saved through Christ, but has not the clear witness that
she *is* saved.   For twenty minutes I talked to a neighbour who was in the house, to whom I had never before
spoken.   I nursed her baby all the time, which pleased
her, so that she was the more willing to listen to me.
She never attends any place of worship, never reads or
thinks of good things, never prays.   I spoke to her in
the most solemn and affectionate language I could command; but it made no impression.   'Ah! it's of no use,
Miss; I'm sure it's of no use me trying to do differ-
ently.'   I said, ' Then do you really mean to go on as
you are now, month after month, year after year, until
you are in hell ?'   'No, Miss: I hopes as I shall get
better some time.'   'When ? In a month ? In a year ?
Every day you live, you sin against God, and grieve the
blessed Saviour; and the longer you delay, the harder
your heart will be; and you will be cut down and sent
to hell ! '   Before I left I made her promise that she
would pray for the Holy Spirit, and come to chapel on
Monday night to hear Mr. Reacher."

About this time a sort of wake was held in the
adjacent town of Stratford, called from one important
ceremonial of the day,—"the Stratford Bull-Roast."
There are few of our rural towns and villages in which
some such periodic festival is not celebrated, to the
infinite injury of the inhabitants.   At these rustic car-
nivals, many a young man and woman takes the first
step to ruin; many a father contracts the habit which is

to turn his home into wretchedness; often religious
impressions are dissipated, and those who were not far
from the kingdom of God fall into open sin; to say
nothing of the utterly profitless waste of money and
time by the classes which can least afford them. To
Miss George's deep sorrow, many of the girls in her
Sabbath and week-day classes signified their intention
of visiting the Stratford wake. With tears and entreaty
she sought to dissuade them, and, when they persisted
in their purpose, wept bitterly before God in secret on
their behalf, and prayed that His Spirit might yet alarm
and trouble their consciences even in the midst of the
scene of vanity. But how was her distress heightened
to learn subsequently that certain members of the
Society, fellow-teachers with herself in the Sabbath-
school, had also been present at the festival! With her
wonted uncompromising fidelity, she went forthwith to
the delinquents, and told them kindly, yet plainly, what
she thought of their conduct. She pointed out how
that which may not be directly evil in itself, is made
evil by its associations. She urged the pernicious influence of their example; showing, for instance, how by
their conduct her own mouth would now be closed in
the presence of those of her school-girls who had erred
in a similar way. At first, huge offence was taken, and
a serious rupture threatened to take place in the small
village Society; but Miss George, while remaining firm
on the ground she had taken, displayed so much Christian gentleness and meekness, sustained all misinterpre-
tation with such unruffled good temper, and showed
herself so purely influenced by a godly jealousy for the
cause of Christ, that the erring members at length confessed themselves in the wrong, and the breach was
healed. Thus far it has appeared right to allude to a

circumstance very illustrative of Miss George's bold and
faithful consistency, and occupying a large space in her
diary : but only the quotation of the diary in full, which
for obvious reasons is impossible, could fairly exhibit
the thoroughly Christian-like way in which she conducted herself throughout this painful and delicate
affair; how jealously she watched her motives; how
deeply she humbled herself before God; how constantly,
in each step, she sought His guidance; and with what
calm trust she rested upon His promise.

With what care, in the mean time, her own spiritual
life was cultured, and how steadily it progressed, the
following brief extracts will show :—

" 14th.—I have felt an inexpressible composure in
leaving myself, body and soul, for time and eternity, in
my Father's hands. I have the delightful, abiding
witness that my merciful Lord receives me, and loves
me. He gives me all blessings as I am willing to
receive them. But, O! the infinite store purchased by
our blessed Saviour passes all conception. I feel a sweet
delight in being a servant, a labourer of the Lord's. I
am entirely His; ready, I hope, for all His will—to do
whatever He bids; go wherever He directs.

" Since Sunday I have been led to pray much for the
Spirit. Everything without Him seems utterly useless.
This day I have had faith in prayer. My God has seemed
to ask me to ask; telling me that great requests would
most delight Him, and that He could not deny me,
because His Son's word was pledged. ' What things
soever ye desire, when ye pray, believe that ye receive
them, and ye shall have them.' I have paid four visits
to-day, and secured promises from four young people to
attend my Sunday-class, and from some others to come
to the preaching. May God bless my efforts! I dare

scarcely be very urgent for God to own *all* my efforts, lest Satan should take advantage of it, and in some weak moment thrust that hateful, soul-destroying sin, *pride*, into my heart. I am quite as willing that God should work by other means, and that I should suffer His will instead of doing it. The abundant consolations I received when my head was bad, seem quite to have endeared to me the thought of affliction. To-night I have been comforted and rejoiced, through meditating on that sweet and comprehensive passage, 'My God shall supply all your need according to His riches in glory by Christ Jesus.' Why need I fear for anything? If I am *ignorant*, God has an infinite store of wisdom, which through Christ I may receive. If I am *weak*, God, can supply me out of His unbounded store of strength and grace. I praise God, and take courage.

" 17th, Sunday.—To-day, and all the past week, I have felt a remarkable deadness to the world. It has no tie for me, no share in my affections. I could leave it gladly any day; and I hope I shall, unless by living I can work for God. I have felt to-day as though I would do anything, of any kind, to save souls. I wish to live every day as if I thought I should die at night; to be in a state of constant preparation for heaven. But, O, how vile, how worthless am I! How can I dwell in heaven?

' Jesus, Thy Blood and Righteousness
My beauty are, my glorious dress;
'Midst flaming worlds, in these array'd,
With joy shall I lift up my head.'

" 18th.—Lately I have felt as if living on the very brink of eternity, and believe I see things as people do just when they are going to die. O Lord, may I act at all

times in accordance with this impression. May I be
holy in heart, lip, and life. May my conversation be
as it becometh the Gospel of Christ. May I glory in
nothing save the cross, and be ashamed of nothing but
sin. May I never be ashamed of Jesus, or of letting it
be known that I am a whole-length Christian !

" 22d.—This evening I had a feeling which was quite
new to me; a kind of sadness, yet a very sweet sadness.
I wept for a long time on my knees, and my God in His
fatherly tenderness poured into my soul the most
abounding consolations. I cannot tell why I felt thus.
It was not on account of sin that I wept. I longed, it is
true, for more good to be doing; for more souls to be
seeking salvation : but I felt that in my heavenly
Father I had the kindest, the most condescending, and
the nearest of friends. I reclined with John on the
bosom of Jesus. I felt that I might ask what I would,
and it should be done. I had not one tie in the world.
I told my Father that I was willing and longing to
depart, and enjoy Him fully. The thought impressed
me, ' You must work for God on earth first, and then
rest in heaven.' I said, ' Lord, I am willing to live
any length of time, so that my life may be useful, and
glorify Thee.' And I believe I shall live to work for
God, though I am willing and ready to depart any
minute. The so-called pleasures of the world are
nothing at all to me. O, the unspeakable sweetness of
lying on Jesus's breast; of reposing entirely on Him !

" 24th, Sunday.—Last night I felt much sweet peace.
This morning God indeed watered my soul from above.
I again plunged by faith into the fountain opened for
sin and uncleanness, and was washed. Praise the Lord
for His goodness ! Tears alone indicated my inexpressible emotions. I felt, while at prayer,

' The speechless awe, that dares not move,
And all the silent heaven of love.'

My Father seemed *too near for me to speak to Him;* that
is, so unspeakably near, that He saw my whole heart,
every thought and every wish; and I could only weep
tears of gratitude and love. O, why to me this waste
of love ?

" 29th.—Yesterday morning I did not feel so much
earnestness for God as I wished. At noon I humbled
myself before God, and enjoyed a profitable season in
meditating on John xv. These words were particularly
applied to my mind, ' Ye have not chosen Me, but I
have chosen you, and ordained you, that ye should go
and bring forth fruit, and that your fruit should remain:
that whatsoever ye shall ask of the Father in My name,
He may give it you.' I felt that I had indeed been
chosen of God, and blessed abundantly, when I only
deserved to be cast into outer darkness. I could rely
fully on my reconciled Father, and I felt that Jesus's
blood was still efficacious to cleanse a sinful heart.

" To-day I feel more alive to God. I have a happy
consciousness that I am the Lord's entirely. All my
desire is to live and work for His glory; I care not
where. But I want to be useful in Welford now:
these are golden opportunities. This morning I was in
imagination surveying our globe; and it seemed to me
as but one small field, what we call *distance* appearing
annihilated. I saw God's creatures living and dying all
over it, and millions perishing for lack of knowledge. I
was quite willing to labour on any spot, where I could
do most good. My short day of work will soon be over.
I would as soon spend my little all of strength and
influence in China, or Feejee, as in Welford. God's

G

eye would be over me as much in one place as another.
He knows I have offered myself entirely to Him, to
be spent in His service. I have no will of my own.
I am as willing to suffer or to die, as to live and labour,
if it be the will of God. Sometimes for a moment the
earth seems so beautiful, that I fancy I should not like
to leave it. Then I think of the glories of heaven; and
this world with its fading beauties disappears, and I am,
as it were, in eternity. O that I could always stand,
as Mr. Wesley says, ' on the edge of this world, ready
to take wing; with my feet on earth, but my eyes and
heart in heaven!'

" 31st, Sunday.—Did not wake this morning till
after seven. I must rise earlier. Spent some time in
reading my lesson, meditating on it, and prayer. Did
not enjoy sweet communion with God as I often do. I
did not feel that my heavenly Father was answering my
petitions as soon as I made them; nor was the way to
Him so clearly open. Still I hung on Christ. I offered
myself to God, body and soul, and went to school praying for the Spirit to direct and accompany my words.
We had a pleasant and profitable time. Before and
after dinner I spent time in prayer. I had to hang on
Christ. God did not meet me as He often does. After
afternoon-school, I visited Mrs. H. Her husband, a
tall, fierce-looking man, and a sad drunkard, was present.
By God's assistance I spoke even to him plainly and
earnestly. Saw good Nanny M. She still rejoices
over her son in heaven, and is very happy, adoring the
goodness of Jesus. I spoke plainly about eternal things
to the friends of one of my absentees. Visited Mrs. B.,
who was worse: she cannot trust fully in Jesus. Spoke
to her husband, who acknowledged that it was madness
to trifle with the soul. Was very faithful with Caleb,

as God helped me. I commended my afternoon's labours to God, to be accepted through the all-cleansing blood. Went to the evening service, praying that God would meet with me, and brighten my prospects of glory. Praise His holy Name, He did! I meditated much on death and heaven. My soul was engaged in prayer most of the time. My Father gave me a glimpse of His love. I plunged by faith into the open fountain, and felt that I was holy and His. I longed to die, and go to heaven. The thought of death was peculiarly delightful. This world contains not one tie. I feared I was doing wrong; but felt I was willing to live threescore years longer, if all that long time I could be doing good. But, O! I hope I shall not. I have always thought I should be tired of living here long. Yet my Father's will be done. I pray that I may live no longer than I live to God, and am useful."

CHAPTER V.

THE SHADOW OF A CLOUD.

"I opened to my Beloved; but my Beloved had withdrawn Himself
and was gone; my soul failed when He spake; I sought Him, but I
could not find Him; I called Him, but He gave me no answer."
(Cant. v. 6.)

HITHERTO the young disciple has walked in perpetual
sunshine, joy in her heart, and praise upon her tongue.
One of the most notable things about her diary, as yet,
has been its tone of exuberant happiness. But now,
for a while, the strain changes. Clouds intercept the
sunshine, and her soul wanders in the shadows—sad,
heavy, and perplexed. She complains of the absence
of her heavenly Father's "sensible smiles;" of a dimi-
nution of closeness, endearment, and lively joy in her
intercourse with Him. It is not that her faith has
relaxed its hold on Christ. She still retains a calm,
settled assurance that she is "accepted in the Beloved;"
nay, that God holds her to be wholly devoted, and free
from spot or blame. Yet she misses those palpable
manifestations of the Divine presence and approval,
those direct and blessed communings of the Spirit of
God with her own, which had until now been so often
vouchsafed her, and in the rapture of which she had
sometimes felt as if the veil were already passed, and
faith had merged into vision, hope into fruition.

To affirm that all such temporary abatements of
joyous and lively feeling indicate previous declension,
would be to judge very crudely of God's dealings, and

to condemn where He has not condemned. Sometimes, indeed, such an interpretation is the correct one. The soul has justly forfeited the glad and loving fellowship in which it walked with God. The darkness that has come over it results from a real withdrawal of the Father's smile. Either devotion has been neglected, or duty shunned, or temptation yielded to, or in some other way the Holy Spirit has been grieved; and thus He indicates His displeasure. And, in such a case, there must be detection and confession of the offence, and renewed application to the precious blood of atonement, before the lost communion can be restored.

But such seasons of comparative darkness may arise from other causes. Bodily disorder, heavy and harassing trouble, a habit of self-inspection morbidly jealous and severe, may overcast the spirit with gloom. The sun shines none the less brightly, though disease may have filmed the organ of sight; and the smile of God is sometimes none the less truly enveloping the Christian, though some of the many guiltless "infirmities," which yet "encompass" him, may have obscured his sense of it. Or, yet again, for the trial of those He loves, God sometimes Himself withholds the more palpable and delightful manifestations of His favour. He does not desert the soul; He does not love it the less; but He suspends for awhile those mysterious motions and voices of His Spirit, through which it has been wont with thrills of joy unspeakable to apprehend His complacent presence. These "hidings" of God's face we may class with the sorrows and afflictions which befall us providentially, as belonging to the course of discipline, wholesome yet painful, which our souls require for their maturing in holiness. Wise, well-timed, and merciful are all such withholdings. As in all our trials, so in this, the sorest perhaps of all, our heavenly Father afflicts "not for His pleasure, but for our profit." Let us not think so unworthily of Him, as to charge Him with the foolish caprice which often prompts the uncertain tendernesses of human affection. His love toward us has not changed; this is but another form of its expression; and if we rightly improve it, we shall be better for the trial. Faith will discern more clearly the great objects on which it should rest,—the Saviour's everlasting atonement and God's irrevocable word; and on these "immutable things" will fix a stronger grasp: we shall learn not to make the intensity of our feelings the measure of our piety, or the possession of lively enjoyment the sole criterion of acceptance and security. The sorrowful and intense desire with which we seek the renewal of the suspended intercourse is pleasing to God, and will bring down upon ourselves the blessing of those who " hunger and thirst after righteousness;" and when, at length, the darkness breaks away, the rapture of the morning joy will more than compensate for the night of weeping; and the restored communion will be henceforth more dearly prized, more intensely felt, and more jealously guarded, than ever.

So far as it is possible for others to judge, this last would appear to be the correct explanation of that phase of experience which Miss George's diary now for some weeks exhibits. It was not that by transgression, or remissness, she had grieved the Spirit. It was not that physical ailment entailed its frequent consequence of mental depression. But God was leading her through a new kind of discipline, both to prove and improve her; discipline certainly not joyous for the present, but to yield afterwards "the peaceable fruit of righteousness." Meanwhile she never intermitted her pious labours; the will of God was none the less dear and paramount, though the smile of God did not cheer and stimulate her as it had been wont: for Miss George was never one of those to whom good spirits and pleasant surroundings are essential conditions of work. But let us turn to the diary:—

"November 3d.—The last three days have not been so happy as previous ones. I have not sensibly felt my Father's smile. I have, in mercy, been kept from doubting of my acceptance, or even that the blood of Christ still cleanses me from all sin. And I will, by the grace of God, still hang on Christ every moment for a full salvation. But why can I not rejoice more?

"6th.—The last few days I have been in much the same state as at the beginning of the week. I have had strong confidence in God, but not much joy. I have had to live by faith instead of feeling. Not that I have been *without* feeling. Yesterday two or three times, while praying, I wept many tears of gratitude. My Father knows I love Him with all my heart; the world has no place in my affections. This morning, in private prayer, my soul was blessed abundantly. O, it was sweet indeed to lie in the valley of humility! I could leave everything of every kind to God, and feel no care but to please Him, and adorn religion by my becoming conduct. The thought of death has been peculiarly delightful to me lately. O, to depart and be with Jesus is far, far better than staying here! My constant prayer is, May I live no longer than I live to Thy glory! Lord, hear prayer for my beloved brothers on the sea! O, give them Thy Spirit, and convert them! Bless my school-girls. Be with me to-morrow.

"7th, Sunday.—This has been the worst Sunday I have spent for three months. My soul has not enjoyed sweet communion with its Maker, as is my happy privilege. Lord, Thou knowest I cannot rest without it. All the day, and this moment, I feel that I am wholly and unreservedly devoted to God. I am in my Father's hands, and know that, so long as I rely fully on the atonement of the Lamb of God for pardon and holiness, I cannot be denied these blessings. *I know that they are mine*, and I continually praise God for them. Yet I cannot feel the sweet presence of my God, and the delightful communion with Him, which I have enjoyed. We have had a painfully-interesting subject to-day, the rejected Immanuel, predicting the overthrow of Jerusalem, and weeping over it. It caused me to shed many tears at noon. I pity and love the poor Jews, the seed of Abraham, scattered abroad through sin and unbelief. Lord, hasten the happy day when they shall own Jesus as the true Messiah, and be willing to be saved by Him! Are they not Thy chosen people? Did not Thy blessed Son suffer and die that they might live? Are they not His kindred according to the flesh? Lord, pity and save them! May they look on Him whom they have pierced, and mourn because of Him!

"10th.—I cannot yet joy in God as I wish. O that I could tell the reason why my Father appears to be hiding His face from me! I feel that He is my Father, my best Friend. I love Him with all my heart. I can call Him to witness that nothing else is loved or prized by me. He has torn every idol from my heart, and my whole soul's desire is to love and serve Him, and walk continually in the light of His countenance. Why do I not? I believe fully that the whole Godhead is reconciled to me. But I want to feel it. If by unwatchfulness, or lightness, or unprofitable thoughts, I have grieved the Spirit, I do heartily repent, and am

sorry. My Father knows how willing I am to acknowledge my error, and humble myself. I feel I am a frail,
helpless creature, only deserving eternal wrath; but,
while I hang on Christ for full salvation, how can my
Father cast me off? *He cannot.*

" Have visited Mrs. B. She will not be here long.
Her mind is peaceful. She rests entirely on Jesus, the
sinner's Saviour, the world's atonement. She sees
clearly how pardon, and holiness, and heaven, with
every other blessing, come through Jesus's death.
Praise the Lord! O that I could do more for my God!

" 15th.—Spent a little of the day profitably in the
company of Mr. Reacher; but I find that I love retire-
ment dearly. I could live alone. Prayed much for the
light of God's countenance; but it was withheld. Many,
many times asked God to search my heart, and see if
any evil was therein.

" 16th.—Stirred up by Mr. Reacher's sermon on
Monday: 'For me to live is Christ,' &c. I felt willing
to live to work for God, and show my love and gratitude,
or to die. My whole desire was that Christ might be
magnified in me. I taught my class after much prayer;
but, O, I could not be happy while I could not feel that
God was being well-pleased with me. I had no faith in
praying for the Spirit. Afterwards I wept and prayed
very much. My heart was broken. I gave myself up
fully to the Lord, saying,

'Thou never, never wilt forsake
A helpless worm that trusts in Thee.'

" 17th.—It comforts me that the Lord knows all my
soul. My Father knows that I love Him with all my
heart; that I desire to do His will in all things; that
I am willing to deny myself for His sake; that I am

His entirely, whether He deign to smile on me or no.
I know I am unworthy a smile: He might justly frown
for ever. I feel as though I could scarcely ask the Lord
Jehovah to commune with such dust and ashes. I think
I have been growing in humility, if in no other grace.
I have been dwelling in the vale.

"19th.—Something says to me, amidst my tears,
'Think it not strange, as though some strange thing
had happened to you.' I have read of many others
who have been thus tried. Lord, help me! Thy smile
is life and peace: Thy frown is death and misery. I do
not feel that my Father frowns, yet I cannot see His
smile. Where is my faith? What should I say to any
other person in such circumstances? 'Wait upon the
Lord; cling by faith to Jesus.' Lord, help me to do so!

'Drooping soul, shake off thy fears;
Fainting soul, be strong, be bold;
Tarry till the Lord appears,
Never, never quit thy hold!' "

The next entry betokens more quietude and confidence, though she still lacks something of her former
happiness:—

"20th.—The bell is again tolling. It will soon toll
for me. Haste, happy day! Yet I am willing to stay
ever so long, and suffer ever so much, as a token of my
love to Jesus. I feel myself very undeserving. Jesus
alone has desert. If I am saved from hell to heaven,
His power and love will have effected the whole.
Lately I have seen much worth living for; to glorify
God, and labour with Him in the Christianizing of the
world. Last night and this morning my faith has been
increased. I can cling with a firmer hold to Jesus for
all I want; but still I am without my Father's smile. I
want more faith. Several days ago I had such a sense

of my helplessness and liability to sin as quite to discourage me. I could only weep and lament. I saw imperfection in everything I did or said, and was made to wonder how it was possible to live without sinning. Where is the unspeakable happiness I have enjoyed?"

But the day of deliverance broke at last. The end of the trial had been answered, and again that light was lifted upon the sorrowing disciple which created her heaven upon earth. She had never relaxed her grasp upon the covenant promises; in the midst of bedimmed light and dulled feeling, faith had resolutely held its own; she had never settled down in contentment with this lower state of enjoyment, but had unceasingly panted and struggled towards those sunnier heights on which she had once walked; and now at length she found her reward.

"21st, Sunday.—Last night, after writing here, I left to pray for the Sabbath-school, &c. Before I did so, I thought of myself. It seemed useless to pray for others, when I wanted God's smile myself; besides, I [felt as though I] had no faith. After praying some time, and resting wholly on Jesus for full salvation, I was almost broken-hearted and despairing, because the light of God's countenance was not fully revealed to me, when I heard the still small voice, the voice of my precious Saviour, more precious to me than ten thousand worlds. I forget the words specially applied to me, my soul was so overjoyed. It was the first time for nearly three weeks that my heavenly Father had held sweet converse with me. My soul was light as a hart. I was singing all the evening, and felt the sweetest confidence that my Father was looking on me, and smiling, and that He would be with me this day. O, the ineffable delight of enjoying God's favour! I

thought I would not doubt the love of God again. I
did not feel half the blessedness I have had on many
occasions past; but, after such a dry season, it was truly
refreshing. I thought, ' O, this is heaven enough!'

' Thy presence makes my paradise.'

There could be no heaven without it. Nothing could
afford me pleasure,—not the presence of angels, not the
company of our fathers who have gone before,—if my
God smiled not. I continued rejoicing till I fell
asleep.

"This morning, and all day, I have been happy. I
feel that I am the Lord's, and He is mine. I know
that the precious blood has not lost its cleansing power.
I have been much helped at school, and have dealt
plainly with my dear girls. This morning when I
opened my text-book on rising, I was struck with the
verses and words, ' Shall we receive good at the hands
of the Lord, and shall we not receive evil ? '

' Patiently received from Thee,
Evil cannot evil be ;
Evil is by evil heal'd,
Evil is but good conceal'd ;
And, through the virtue of Thy blood,
Shall turn to our eternal good.'

' All things work together for good to them that love
God.'

"This dispensation, then, I thought, shall surely
work for my good. I have received much good at the
hands of my Lord, and shall I not receive this evil,
which is perhaps but good concealed? It may make
me more watchful, cause me to value more highly the
smile of God, and teach me to comfort others in a similar
state."

The re-opened intercourse and recovered happiness continue.

"25th.—Much blessed at class. During the first prayer my Father was pleased to shed the sweet influences of the Spirit upon me, and then again take full possession of my heart. I felt perfect peace. Surely I reclined with John on my Saviour's bosom. I felt that I was on the Rock, and no power on earth or in hell could touch me. My Jesus shielded me. I felt that every sin was cancelled, every stain washed from my heart, and that my Father had nothing against me. This created perfect confidence, perfect love, and perfect peace. My pen could never adequately express the feeling.

"26th.—Attended Teachers' meeting. Felt rather light and trifling. Afterwards, on close examination in my closet, was convinced that I should not have spent the time thus, had it been my last evening upon earth. I humbled myself, told my kind, listening Father all my feelings, desired to be made humble and teachable as a little child, and ever to let my light shine before men. God filled my soul with peace and joy. I could not help singing His praises.

"27th.—At noon to-day I felt that I had been too little engaged in meditating on spiritual subjects during the morning. Satan would have me reason with him instead of with God; but I knelt down, and laid my case simply before my heavenly Father, and felt more joy and love than for some time past. All dinner-time my eyes were continually filling with tears of love, and I could not refrain from singing. These occasional smiles from Heaven help me; but may I not walk continually in the light of God's countenance? I did some

H

months ago. On close examination I discover some
things that I desire to improve in:—

"1. I do not rise early enough; consequently do not
get time enough for prayer.

"2. I am still too light and trifling. This is really
my besetting sin. I pray God to help me to be very
watchful.

"3. I am not careful enough to gather up all
fragments of time.

"4. I am not at all times conscientiously diligent
with my pupils; and I neglect, to a great extent, close
spiritual conversation and prayer with and for them.

"5. I do not deny myself as I should.

"Now, O my Father, assist Thy poor unworthy dust
for the future! Give much of Thy grace, and love, and
help. Hear prayer for the Sunday-school. Bless especially my beloved girls. O, save them! Give them Thy
Spirit. Be with me to-morrow. May it be a Sabbath
indeed!"

Peculiar spiritual discipline is often preparatory to
delicate and difficult service. It appears to have been
so with Miss George in the present instance. Scarcely
had she recovered her wonted tone of confidence and
peace, when an opportunity presented itself of turning
to practical account the lessons she had been thus painfully learning. A good man, a friend of the family, long
eminent for piety and usefulness, but labouring now under
grievous mental depression, came to reside for a while
under her mother's hospitable roof. The poor sufferer
had, of course, his alternate seasons of light and gloom;
but in his moods of despondency—and these were far
the more frequent—he believed himself an outcast from
God and hope. Now, since such a case is essentially

one of physical disease, it can only fairly be grappled
with by physical remedies. Mere argument, persuasion, and the like, will never effect more than an
occasional alleviation. All, however, that can be done
by such means, Miss George was the better qualified for
doing by her own recent experience. She could now
tell her distressed friend, reading the lesson from the
newest page of her own history, that, amidst all the
fluctuations of our own *feeling*, the rock of Christ's
atoning work remains fixed and rooted; that, whilst
faith clings to *that*, the soul is safe, though from mysterious causes light and joy may be cut off from it; that
the love of God is no capricious affection, though our
sense of it may be dulled by physical disease, or even
by the direct withholding of the Spirit's consolations;
and that the sorely-tried child shall, as sure as God is
true, sooner or later, if not in this life, then when life's
dark scene closes, wake up to find himself, not forsaken,
as he had gloomily foreboded, but securely folded in
a loving Father's arms. Such arguments Miss George
often used, and sometimes, for a while at least, with
happy effect. At the same time, she employed whatever other means, physical or otherwise, were available
to her, with thoughtful and patient kindness. Prayer,
of course, was not forgotten; the diary abounds with
vehement supplications on behalf of the sufferer; and
in more than one instance the relief followed so closely
upon the prayer, that it would be a piece of perverse
unbelief to deny the connexion. Here is one case out
of several. He is not to be envied who can see nothing.
but a fortuitous though singular coincidence :—

"December 3d.—At noon this day I received a most
direct answer to prayer. I had been dressing poor
Mr. W.'s head, and, during the time of my doing so, his

conversation ran in this style:—'My dear, good lady, I'm worse than ever. All is lost. I am a lost man, forsaken of God. It is impossible for you to wash my *heart* clean. This has been the worst morning I have ever had. I am truly wretched,' &c., &c. I frequently interrupted him, reminding him of some comforting promise, or begging him to leave himself in God's hands, and feel satisfied. He could take no comfort; said he had been weeping all the morning long, and should soon be dead; that he had now resolved to spend all the night in prayer for the witness of the Spirit,—he could not live without it. I assured him that he would injure his brain most seriously if he did such a thing; and that it was perfectly unnecessary, as God saw the sincerity of his heart, and that was the chief thing. He replied, ' Ah! my dear child, you don't know; you are very kind, but you don't know my distress. To be cast off! to be forsaken of God!'

"I retired immediately, resolving to supplicate in faith that God would help him to trust his soul on the atonement, and give his mind rest. I pleaded this promise, 'If ye abide in Me, and My words abide in you, ye shall ask what ye will, and it shall be done unto you.' I said, 'Lord, if I am now Thy child, if I may claim this promise, if I do now abide in Thee, and Thy words do abide in me, grant Thy servant peace in believing. And, Lord, do it *now*, that I may know Thou hearest my prayer. Thou art able; Thy Son's word is pledged; it must be done.' I thought to myself, ' Now, when I go down, shall I be surprised if he is happy? No, I will expect it.' I went down at dinner-time. In reply to my inquiry, he said, ' O, my friend, I am a deal better; all that distress is gone; I seem to be on the Rock; I shouldn't be afraid to die

now.' My soul was filled with gratitude. It is now nine
o'clock at night, and he has been quite happy all
the afternoon, and cannot account for it! He 'feels
another man.' O my soul, trust in the Lord!"

The afternoon and evening of the same day are spent
in paying a long-promised visit to a friend in an
adjacent village. The hostess is amiable and interesting,
but a stranger to Christ. Miss George's great object in
the visit is to do her spiritual good. The conversation
soon glides into a serious channel. " I continually
looked up to my Father in heaven for wisdom and grace
to perform my duty and His will. I related to her the
conversion and happy deaths of several persons who
have died lately in Welford. I also gave her an account
of a very close plain sermon I heard one day from a
Church Minister, from, 'But one thing is needful.' It
was just what I wanted to say to her; but I feared it
would not be received so well as if given in that way.
She appeared much affected. I lent her Mrs. Rogers's
Life to read. O my heavenly Father, grant, for Jesus's
sake, that it may be the means of her conversion!"—
Thus did this faithful servant sow beside all waters.

CHAPTER VI.

THE FIRST TWELVEMONTHS.——PROGRESS.

"This one thing I do, forgetting those things which are behind,
and reaching forth unto those things which are before, I press toward
the mark for the prize of the high calling of God in Christ Jesus."
(Phil. iii. 13, 14.)

MISS GEORGE's diary exhibits now, for some weeks,
the marks of a steadily progressive piety. Her communion with God was uninterrupted; her spiritual
enjoyments were intense and constant. But the more
her personal happiness abounded, the more keen and
sorrowful became her compassion for those around her
who were still without Christ. The unconverted members of her own family, the young people in her classes,
the ungodly in the village, were even hourly in her
thoughts. She wept before God, and wrestled in
unremitting prayer on their behalf. So vivid were her
views of the unhappiness and peril of their state, so
strong was her sympathy with Christ, so truly did she
enter into the fellowship of His sufferings, that, notwithstanding her natural buoyancy, and the calm and
sunny elevation upon which she now walked, her spirit
was often heavy and oppressed within her. A few
extracts, culled from much of the same import, will
confirm and illustrate these remarks:—

"December 6th.—I feel a sweet, childlike confidence
in God. I love to be alone with Him in prayer. When
the intercourse is open, and I can commune, as it were,

face to face with God, then I am never tired of prayer.
Lately I have loved to fall at the feet of Jesus weeping,
like Mary. It seems strange that I should love to
weep; but often when I feel that God is all in all to me,
and can trust fully to Him, and leave myself for ever
in His hands, I cannot help weeping for joy, and
gratitude, and love.

"8th.—I looked into 'Carvosso' this evening, and
read of the clear, unmistakable manner in which he
received the blessing of full salvation, so plainly, that
even Satan, bold and lying as he is, never durst tell him
to the contrary. So it is with me. Satan cannot be
bold enough to make me doubt for a moment that on
Wednesday morning, August 11th, God washed my
soul, polluted as it was, from every stain, in the all-
sufficient blood of His Son. Glory, glory be to His holy
name! 'I will bless the Lord at all times; His praise
shall continually be in my mouth.' Now I enjoy
perfect peace, when I lie down and when I rise up.
Every night I ask myself, 'Am I as willing this night to
die as to sleep?' And my heart replies, 'Yes! a thousand
times more willing, unless by living I can promote my
Redeemer's glory.'

"11th.—To-day I have been harassed with wandering thoughts. I have been reminded of last
Christmas, how I spent it, where and in whose company.
These things, for many months, I have laboured to
forget; but to-day I have felt an inclination to dwell on
them, which has much grieved me. I have many times
called on God, and to-night again poured out my soul
to the Hearer of prayer, who in mercy inclined His ear
even unto me, sinful and unworthy. I confessed my
weakness, and fled to the dear wounds of Immanuel,
and hid myself there. The intercourse was opened.

My heavenly Father forgave all my sinfulness, through my atoning High Priest. He smiled, and all was well.

"12th, Sunday.—To-night we have been holding a short prayer-meeting, with especial reference to a sermon to be delivered to-morrow night, by Mr. Reacher, to young people. My soul has been melted within me. Heaven and my listening Father were near indeed. I could address a present God. I could weep for hours over my beloved girls. O that they were saved! At different times to-day, when pouring out my soul before God on their behalf, these words have been sweetly applied to me, 'He that goeth forth and weepeth, bearing precious seed, shall doubtless come again with rejoicing, bringing his sheaves with him;' also, 'Let us not be weary in well-doing; for in due season we shall reap, if we faint not.' Praise the Lord! I will believe it.

"14th.—Yesterday, all day, my soul was in a very prayerful mood. I was especially drawn to intercede for my young friends, my brothers, and some young members, and unconverted teachers. At night Mr. Reacher gave us an earnest and affectionate sermon on the choice of Moses. I had occasion to thank God, and say, 'Verily He hath heard me.' Some of my school-girls were greatly affected; and one man was convinced of sin, and seemed very broken-hearted. Mr. Reacher gave tickets after service. My soul was happy. But, O, the burden of souls! I feel as if I could weep and pray day and night for them. This day I consecrate myself afresh unto the Lord, 'whose I am, and whom I serve.'

"15th.—I feel more than ever the burden of souls. O Lord, save souls! I could weep my eyes dim for sinners, for all those I love especially. O that I were.

more useful! 'Deliver me from blood-guiltiness, O God, Thou God of my salvation!' At prayer-meeting to-night, and ever since, my feelings have been indescribable. I have been truly happy in the love of God, though mournful and sad on account of sinners. A heavenly serenity has pervaded my soul,—the peace of God, which passeth all understanding. I seem to sink into nothing before my adorable Saviour, who is all in all to me. He allows me, as it were, to lean on His breast. He sees my whole heart. O that my God would keep me humble, prayerful, watchful, and obedient!

"19th, Sunday.—I have been burdened this day with an almost insupportable weight. At noon, when weeping and waiting before the Lord, I was in a measure comforted by an application of these words, 'Cast thy burden upon the Lord, and He shall sustain thee.' My burden was souls. It seemed to me that I had been labouring at school for nothing. I then visited an afflicted man, who, I fear, is resting in a false peace. A grown-up daughter and rough-looking young man were in the house. I prayed earnestly for him and the others, and read the parable of the rich man and Lazarus. But, O, how I felt as I thought, on leaving, 'Ah! it's of no use: they will not be wise!' I went to my closet, and poured out my full heart to the Lord. I wept bitter tears. Never did I so plainly see the utter uselessness of my feeble efforts, unless accompanied by the Spirit. This afternoon I had but six at school, when fifteen or twenty might have been present. I could not help weeping with those six. I was as affectionate and earnest, I think, as if it had been my last Sunday. O my God, convert them! I must leave them with Thee; Thou knowest all my heart. Save

those for whom I desire to pray. I throw myself into
Thy hands for ever."

The Christmas holidays now commenced, and with
them came a total change of interests and employments.
There is always spiritual danger attending such transition periods from one mode of occupation to another.
Habits of devotion, which had been formed to fit in
with the duties that have now terminated, become
unsettled, and new ones, adapted to new circumstances,
do not at once become natural. There is danger of
distraction, also, in the novelty of the employments
that have succeeded to the old routine. And often
moments of vacancy occur, when the mind is prone to
wander to things profitless, if not forbidden. Miss
George experienced this, and for the first few days
there is a slight tone of complaint in the entries of the
diary. But she soon recovered herself. She was too
jealously watchful, too earnest and devout, to suffer per-
manent loss; and, on the whole, this vacation was a
time of much spiritual enjoyment and profit. Thus she
writes on Christmas-eve, in the overflow of her heart :—

"24th.—Though the hour is late, I must record the
unspeakable goodness of my God, my Father, and my
Friend. O, the delight of loving God!—of being able to
say, 'My Father, Thou knowest that I love Thee with
all my heart!' I have just been spending a most
delightful season in secret communion with God.
Tears of love and gratitude overflow my eyes. O that
sinners would come to Jesus, and be happy! Words
can never express the sweet fellowship my soul enjoys
with its Maker. O, what infinite condescension on the
part of the Lord Jehovah to reveal Himself to such a
one! I join the bright angelic host, and sing praises
to God in the highest, that ever such a glorious Saviour

came to die for me. Praise the Lord, O my soul; and all that is within me, bless and praise His holy Name!"

In the course of these holidays, Miss George paid a visit of some days to an aged Christian couple, resident in a neighbouring village, who had long been wayfarers in the path of holiness. Several months before, while she was yet a prey to inward doubt and conflict, she had been their guest; and the confident and happy fellowship of the present visit contrasted brightly with the self-reproach and embarrassment she had felt on the former one. Joyfully and thankfully she told her friends of the change that had transpired; how happy she now was in the favour of God; how she felt that He held her without spot or blame; and how light and pleasant she found the yoke of His service. At the same time she herself derived profit from the visit: for Miss George was ever willing to be a learner. She had no such pert conceptions of her own superior intelligence as to make her deem the counsel of older and more experienced Christians superfluous. To her other religious attainments had been added the grace of humility; and, whenever she met with those who were veterans in the Christian warfare, she was glad to sit at their feet, and hear them talk of past perils, snares, and deliverances, and to gather for her own soul's sustenance the ripe fruit of their varied experience. In the present case, she speaks of long and frequent conversations on the subject of personal religion, and gratefully acknowledges the "establishment" and "comfort" thence derived. She returned to Welford overflowing with trust and love, and fired with a more ardent resolve than ever wholly to devote herself to the service of God. The old routine of duty was soon

resumed. In attention to her little school, in daily
visits to the sick and poor, and the diligent culture of
her own piety, the winter days flowed pleasantly on.
Thus the diary chronicles God's goodness, and her own
enjoyments :—

"Jan. 8th, 1853.—Visited my poor sick friends, who
had been 'desp'ate unked' all the week without me.
Found all rejoicing in God. I did indeed rejoice with
them. I read hymns and prayed at each house.

" 9th, Sunday.—Usual duties. Enjoyed the presence
of God all day, and at times was unspeakably happy.
Visited some sick folk with Mr. W.

"11th.—Lost in wonder when looking back on the
past. I love to trace the finger of Providence; and, O,
how wisely has God provided for me! Little did I
imagine this time last year how things would change.
Then all my brothers were in England, my sister Louisa
at home, and many other friends about me, dear and
heart-stealing. But glory, and praise, and thanksgiving
be unto Thee, O Thou most High, my Father, for Thy
unspeakable goodness in doing what I could not do,—
tearing my friends from me, that I might seek all my
happiness in Thee! And Thou art *true, true satisfying
and lasting happiness!* Thy nature and Thy name are
love. I feel it so. Praise the Lord, I am wholly the
Lord's. I take Thee, O my Father, Thou knowest, to
be my God for evermore; and Thou dost accept of me
as Thy child. Thou dost wash me in Thy Son's all-
cleansing blood, and clothe me in the robe of His
perfect righteousness.

"12th.—Have visited four sick people. Mrs. B.
seems at the point of death; but she is happy. She
waved her hand to tell me so. A few days ago, she
told me she was fixed on the Rock, and willing to live

or die. I believe she will be a star in my crown of rejoicing. To her nurse, a stranger, I talked closely and earnestly, exhorting her to begin at once to pray, and seek the pardon of her sins.

"15th.—The last three days I have been filled with praise all day long. O, the happiness of the child of God!

"17th.—Yesterday was a happy day to my soul, though I wept much for poor sinners. After school and visiting, I was weeping in great distress, when some precious promises were applied to me with peculiar sweetness.

"23d.—Visited a dying woman two or three times, and other people.

"26th.—I have felt a peculiar confidence in God, that He will make me perfect in all His will. I feel that I am every whit the Lord's. I pray to be made as holy as it is possible for any fallen being to become in this world. I pray for the perfection of humility. May I, O my God, be a monument of Thy power to save fully on earth!"

What a gush of the "joy unspeakable and full of glory" have we in the next entry! Surely heaven stooped to earth in that chamber that day.

"27th.—Last night, after prayer-meeting, I retired a few minutes for prayer. I was calling to mind how my prayers had actually entered heaven, and been heard and answered by the Lord Jehovah, the King of kings; and I thought, 'Well now, God must be as willing to hear *praise* from my lips as prayer. Surely He can listen to me, though He is surrounded by ten thousand times ten thousand and thousands of thousands of bright and happy spirits, who are giving Him perfect praise.' I then, on my knees, *praised* God

I

the Father, God the Son, and God the Holy Ghost;
saying, 'Blessing and honour, glory and power, be
unto Him that sitteth upon the throne, and unto the
Lamb for ever! Glory be to the Father, glory be to
the Son, glory be to the Holy Ghost!' At that solemn
moment words cannot describe my feelings. The veil
between heaven and myself seemed very thin. The
eye of my faith could pierce it. I saw the Lamb in
the midst of the throne, and my Father on the throne,
bending His ear to my feeble but sincere praise, and
assuring me that He was as fully pleased with my praise
as with that of the redeemed spirits before His throne,
—that the notes were the very same. I felt that God
looked upon me with perfect complacency. Glory be
to Thee, O my Father, that Thou shouldst thus reveal
Thyself to a worm of earth! I felt a full confidence
that God was willing to grant what I had been so
earnestly praying for all the day; namely, that I might
be restored as fully to the image of my Divine Master
as was possible for a fallen mortal. I believed, and
believe now, that God will do it. I am fully resolved,
by His assistance, to deny myself in anything that I
know would prove a hindrance to me, and to give
myself up wholly to God, to be stamped with His own
blessed image. I appeal, with all solemnity and
humility, to the Triune Jehovah as my witness. This
is the language of my soul, O Lord, Thou knowest.

"29th.—Alfred's birthday. Led to intercede for
him, and William, and Joseph.*

"30th, Sunday.—Praise and glory be to my God for
another very happy Sabbath! All day I have felt a
holy earnestness, and a peculiar nearness to Jesus, occa-

---

* Her emigrant brothers.

sioned by reading the first three chapters of Revelation. At school, in private houses, and by the way-side, I have, with all the earnestness I could, invited poor sinners to partake of the Gospel feast. O Thou eternal and ever-blessed Spirit, accompany every word I have this day spoken for God with Thy blessing!

"Feb. 6th.—This has been a good week on the whole. The last day or two I have not spent so much time in private prayer, through not using sufficient self-denial. I have been led to see that self-denial is a very essential part of religion; that there cannot be much religion without it. If I had risen earlier, and secured thus an hour for private devotion, I should have been far happier. Still my peace has been uninterrupted. I can look to God at all times, and ever feel an inclination to do so.

" 8th.—Mr. Reacher preached this evening a beautiful discourse on 'fellowship with the Father and His Son Jesus Christ.' O, how sweet to feel it by experience! I held delightful communion with the ever-blessed Jesus during the sermon. I felt that I was graciously permitted to sympathize with Him in His compassion for sinners.

"9th.—Visited eight families with Mr. Reacher. I do want daily to be more God-like, to leave all half-Christians behind, and go on to possess all the grace that Jesus has purchased for me. Grant, Lord, that I may be such a Christian as will do honour to Thy Name, show forth Thy power, and promote Thy glory. May others see in me what Thou art willing to do for a poor lost sinner. Stamp me with Thine own image.

"13th, Sunday.—The last week has been a blessed one. O, these are happy days! My soul has been filled with praise and love. Yesterday, especially, I

had glorious and delightful intercourse with my God.
No cloud came between. From reading the Revelation, of late I have derived such clear and blessed views
of the heavenly state, that my eyes and thoughts have
continually turned thitherward. Many delightful
seasons in prayer I have had, and have felt more faith
than usual for the gift of the Spirit on my Sunday-
scholars, my brothers and cousins, my sick patients,
the members of Society, certain persons I am specially
praying for, some backsliders, and all the world. I
have so many things and people to pray for, that I had
need to deny myself of much sleep to secure time. My
heart is enlarged. It takes in all the world. How I
love the poor Jews, God's chosen people! When will
the times of the Gentiles be fulfilled? When shall
these unbelieving scattered ones look on Him whom
they have pierced, and mourn? Hasten, Lord, the
happy time! I have had to praise and glorify my God
for the blessed intelligence that the Heathen in several
towns of Western Africa are casting their idols to the
moles and the bats. Glory to God! When shall all the
Heathen be given to Jesus for His inheritance? O, let
Thy kingdom come! This day has been a strange day. I
have had much sorrow as well as joy, and I should think
every true Christian must have. The holy Jesus wept
over Jerusalem. And, O! I could weep day and night
for Welford sinners, and all sinners. This has been a
holy day. I have no words to describe it. The world
knows nothing of it. Glory, glory, glory be to God!
When *on the mount*, I have, like Peter, wished that I
might tabernacle ·there; so delightful, so holy, so
heavenly have been my feelings. O, I have longed to
depart out of this sinful world to be with my Jesus!
But this is selfish. He dwelt here three-and-thirty years

for my sake, and suffered all the time; and shall not I be willing to suffer with Him? O, yes! Yet I cannot help 'weeping over Jerusalem.' O that men would know in this their day the things belonging unto their peace! I have felt a most delightful assurance all day, that I have been doing my Master's will, and that I shall not lose my reward, whether sinners listen or no. Yet this does not satisfy me. I want poor blind sinners, for whom Jesus died, *to be saved*. At school I have felt a holy nearness to God and the Lamb. I have only just had to close my eyes, and see

'Without a cloud between
The Godhead reconciled.'

I have visited three families, and the last a 'respectable' one. I was led in of the Spirit; for no thought was further from my mind till I passed the door. They had company; eight persons were at tea. I felt not the least shadow of embarrassment; all was gone: the matter seemed so awfully important, that to be earnest was no cross at all. I checked the trifling conversation they commenced, and told my message, feeling that Jesus had sent me to deliver it, and was listening to what I said, and indeed telling me what to say—how to silence every objection. Sabbath-breaking, neglecting the house of God, private prayer, &c., were the topics of conversation. The tears involuntarily came into my eyes, as I told them why I was so earnest. I left them speechless, excuseless. How delightful to be employed for God!"

Miss George's conduct in this last instance was a deviation from our customary Christian strategics. We have no objection to visit with our tracts and counsels the cottages of the poor; but there are certain conventional proprieties which keep the houses of our more "respectable" neighbours safe from our inroads. If a

domicile happens to be graced with a knocker or a bell,
though it harbour as much ignorance and ungodliness
as any hovel in the nearest alley, we hardly feel ourselves warranted in crossing its threshold on a directly
religious errand. And some there are, without doubt,
who will be ready to think that, in the present instance,
Miss George suffered her zeal to outrun her discretion,
and overstepped the bound-line of a certain modest
propriety, within which all our efforts to save souls
from hell ought to be conducted. Her apology, if indeed she needs one, lies in the intensity of her feelings.
Religious truth had stirred the very depths of her
being; and those who would censure her, with their
conventional surface-piety, are not qualified to appreciate or judge her. We do not stand upon proprieties
when we seek to save our fellow-beings from the ship-
wreck, or the burning house. And to Miss George, on
this Sabbath, eternal realities were so awfully near and
vivid, that any method by which souls might be rescued
from the wrath to come seemed justifiable. Those who
feel absorbingly on any subject, will often be impelled
to actions which mere bystanders will pronounce
eccentric or improper.

Visiting, however, was not always very pleasant or
encouraging work, as some of the subsequent extracts
will show :—

" 18th.—Visited a second time an old church-goer,
who surely believes that going to church and being
conversant with the Prayer-Book will entitle him to a
place in heaven. The daughter said, ' Father, Miss
George is come to talk to you a bit.' ' O, let her talk
away then,' was the polite response. He is constantly
praying to die. I endeavoured to show him that he was a
lost sinner, an *old* sinner, and that without repentance

he must perish. Poor man! he asked how I knew he was a sinner? what had he ever done wrong? and many such questions. I assured him that going to church regularly, and reading the Bible,—things good in themselves,—without a change of heart, would never save him. He replied, in melancholy wise, 'Then there won't many be saved!' True, old man! I told him that God was keeping him on a sick bed for two years out of love to him, because He wished him to be happy hereafter. 'T'aint a sign,' said he. 'Then what do you think would be a sign that God wished you well?' 'Why, to let me die, and ha' done wi' it.' In vain did I try to show him that he was not ready to die, unless he wished to go to hell. I used the plainest forms of speech possible; but all seemed useless. O Thou Holy Spirit, that hast enlightened my mind, shine into his dark heart! Let there be light!

"20th, Sunday.—A mournfully happy day! I cannot help grieving for poor blind sinners. I have felt a holy, delightful serenity of soul: could 'see Jesus' all day. My efforts seem to be productive of no good. My beloved girls, for whom I feel so much, seem as careless as ever. Lord, give me faith to believe that *Thine own truth* must do good.

"Visited several families, one in particular worthy of mention. I had heard of the death of a child in the week, and, though I had never been in the house, thought I might be welcomed if I trod on the heels of death. I thought, too, that perhaps an opportunity might occur of affording temporal relief, the parties being very poor. I was immediately conducted to the little bed, on which lay the remains of the little girl, aged eight years and two months. The mother wept distressingly. The dear child had been well the day

previous to her death, and nothing was more unexpected.
I offered the best consolation I could offer a poor
ignorant sinner, assuring her that I believed the child
was in heaven, and that God, who loves His creatures,
had done this as 'a call' to her and her husband to
repent. I prayed with her by the bedside. She
requested me to speak to her husband; and accordingly
I went down to him. Neither of them could read;
neither ever attended any place of worship, ever
offered up a prayer to God on any occasion. This they
candidly confessed, and pleaded gross ignorance as their
excuse. I was astounded at a question the mother put
to me. 'O, Miss! I want to ask you a question. You
believe my child is in heaven?' 'Yes.' 'Well then,
if we should be in *t'other place*, do you think we shall
be able to know Annie?' I took out my Testament and
read, 'And in hell he lift up his eyes, being in torments, and seeth Abraham afar off, and Lazarus in his
bosom.' I took the opportunity of speaking of the torments of the man in hell, and what he cried for when
he saw and knew Lazarus. I dealt plainly and kindly
with them, and intend visiting them again. O, the amount
of ignorance is extreme in some Welford families!"

In the next case we see the hard unregenerate heart
in trouble, and sullenly "kicking against the pricks:"—

"21st.—Visited a family, where I had heard that a
man was ill. O, the ignorance I found! I asked the wife,
in as friendly a manner as possible, if she had begun to
think about her soul. 'I ha' got summut else to think
about besides that,' was the rude reply. 'I dare say
you have, but nothing of so much importance.' 'I
don't know that,' she said. I asked her if she knew
that she was a sinner. She said most rudely, 'I knows
there never was nobody born yet, but what was.' 'Well,

I am glad you know that: some people tell me they do
not. Now, don't you think you should begin to think
about dying, and getting ready to go to heaven?' 'O,
I ha' got troubles and trials enough to think about.'
'But do you think that excuse will be sufficient when
you have to stand before God? Can you tell Him that
you had so many other things to do, that you were
obliged to neglect your soul?' To this she replied, very
abruptly, 'Yes! I'd as lief speak the truth before Him
as anybody else.' I could get no ground. Afterwards
I said, 'Now, if you were to be taken dangerously ill
this evening, and the doctor were to say there was no
hope, that you could not live till morning, should you
feel happy?' 'Yes, I should.' 'What would make you
feel happy?' No reply. 'Would you think you were
going to heaven?' 'Yes, I should.' I said, 'O, Mrs.
M—, you are certainly deceiving yourself, if you really
think so. I will just tell you a few words out of God's
Bible. *They* are really true. *Except a man be born
again, he cannot see the kingdom of God. Except ye repent,
ye shall all likewise perish!*' I requested her to lay her
work aside, and I prayed as simply as possible. My soul
was very happy; for I was working for Jesus,—teaching
what He had done for poor sinners.

"March 4th.—A delightful season this morning in
prayer. My soul was drawn out to pray for all the
world. I cannot confine myself to my friends, or to
England. I look on the history of the world, from the
beginning to the present, and weep over the wickedness
of it, and rejoice over the inexpressible goodness of God
in giving His Son to redeem it. When praying for all
the world, my soul is always blessed. Some sweet
prophecies in Isaiah encouraged me this morning. I
hope and pray that I may see the day when the Jews

shall be converted, and the fulness of the Gentiles brought in. O Lord, work elsewhere as Thou hast been working in Western Africa: then will the world soon be converted unto Thee. I have been led to pray for England especially, that God would withhold His judgments, and still grant us our religious and civil privileges; but, O, how are the blessings of Gospel-day slighted! Lord, save wicked England, and save the world. Destroy Antichrist." *

For some weeks now she is in a state of much depression; so little visible result follows from all her zealous labours. Some, of whom she had entertained good hope, "draw back to perdition." Vows made on a sick bed are forgotten on the return of health. Several of the cases on her visiting-list are most difficult and disheartening. Her school-girls, and other friends

---

* " Behold that fragile form, of delicate transparent beauty,
  Whose light-blue eye and hectic cheek are lit by the bale-fires of decline.
  All droopingly she lieth, as a dew-laden lily,
  Her flaxen tresses, rashly luxuriant, dank with unhealthy moisture;
  Hath not thy heart said of her, Alas! poor child of weakness?
  Thou hast erred; Goliath of Gath stood not in half her strength:
  Terribly she fighteth in the van as the virgin daughter of Orleans,
  She beareth the banner of heaven, her onset is the rushing cataract,
  Seraphim rally at her side, and the Captain of that host is God,
  And the serried ranks of evil are routed by the lightning of her eye;
  She is the King's remembrancer, and steward of many blessings,
  Holding the buckler of security over her unthankful land :
  For that weak fluttering heart is strong in faith assured,
  Dependence is her might, and behold—she prayeth."
                                                    TUPPER.

nearer and dearer still, are as careless and unstable as
ever. Even from cousin Eden bad news has come: he
has left his home a second time, to go and dig gold in
Australia. Her heart, so tender in its compassion for
sinners, so quick in its jealousy for the Saviour's honour,
is sorely afflicted by these circumstances. Yet she
neither charges God foolishly, nor sinks into inactive
despondency. She examines herself rigorously. May
not blame, after all, lie at her own door? Has she not
been wanting in faith, in ardent and persevering prayerfulness? Has she wrestled with God as she once did,
and laid so vigorous and sustained a grasp upon His
promises? She discovers much room for amendment.
"I have resolved," she writes, " to live nearer to God.
I believe I do not dwell in God as I once did. Yet I
cannot tell: my experience has been very different. I
have had such extremely humbling views of myself. I
have resolved, by God's assistance,—1. To retire early.
2. To rise early. 3. To pray oftener, indeed always.
4. To keep my eye fixed on Christ continually; to let
nothing divert me. 5. To deny myself constantly in
little things, and frequently ask myself, ' Am I this
moment doing the will of God?' Lord, help me! I
want to realize all the blood-bought blessings that
God has in store for me. I would have the end
for which the Saviour came into the world fully
accomplished in me. I have great hungerings and
thirstings after righteousness. To be cleansed from
sin is a great and glorious blessing; but that cannot
satisfy me. I leave *that* altogether amongst those things
that are behind, and press forward after something far
more glorious. God's word shows me that there is
much that I have not received. I am continually
longing to depart. I fear I do wrong. Yet I am will-

ing to live and suffer with my Saviour, if by so doing His glory may be promoted, and my crown brightened."

And still the sick, poor, old, and dying find in her a true evangelist. Her heart was heavy, yet her labours were not slackened. She acted on the principle,—Duty is ours, results belong to God. Some of the scenes described in the next few entries were not of a kind to inspire her with heart and hope.

"26th.—Visited Mrs. M., the woman who spoke so very rudely to me some days ago. [*Vide* p. 92.] Two days after that time, she had a married daughter brought home ill, with two children. Since then I have visited her frequently, and by little kindnesses have softened the lion into a lamb. The poor daughter, a fine-looking young woman of twenty-eight, has, from the nature of her disease, been exceedingly stupid and inactive. She soon took to her bed, and appeared rapidly falling away. I talked to her of Jesus, and prayed for her; but all seemed useless. She did not fancy she should die, and did not feel able to pray or repent. On Thursday last I visited her, with a very heavy heart. To speak seemed cruel; her head was in such dreadful pain. Yet how could I leave her? I told her that perhaps in a few days she would be worse still, and quite unable to pray. She had no power or inclination to exert herself in the least. I saw the infinite necessity of seeking religion in health."

This poor creature died on the very day on which this entry is dated. Miss George was present: no change for the better had taken place.

"29th.—Yesterday I visited M——, father of the young woman who died on Saturday. He was ill in bed, considerably worse, and apparently near death. I found him truly in earnest about his soul, and wishing people to pray with him. I exhorted him, as best I could, to look to Jesus. O that sinners would be wise in health, and serve God then!

"After that I went to see Miss H., who had expressed a wish that I should visit her. It seemed a call; and therefore I obeyed, though it was a cross. I prayed with her by her request. May the Lord fully enlighten her mind, and save her! O, what a merciful friend is affliction! how often it makes sinners begin to pray! I spoke to two or three besides Miss H., and on returning felt much happier in having done something for Jesus.

"Visited an old man whom I never saw before, but had heard to be an old sinner. I thought, as I entered his filthy little abode in the dusk of evening, 'If ever this man get to live in one of the mansions of glory, it *will* be a change.' He was seventy-nine years old. He gave me a welcome when he knew who I was, and told me how well he had known my papa, grandpapa, and others. He could not ask me to sit down, unless it had been on the filthy ground. I soon came to close questions, and asked him how he should feel if death were to visit him that night. O, unprepared! He had served Satan threescore years and ten. I was as earnest and faithful as possible, endeavoured to picture to him his wife (who has been in heaven thirty-four years) and children at the judgment, placed on the right hand, and himself on the left; and the sentences! He invited me to come again, and said several times that he very much liked my discourse. O that Jesus would render me a blessing to Welford sinners! Now is my time for work. I retired, and prayed for them all; for my work is never done till I have prayed over every case in private. I want faith, mighty faith!

"This morning I spent mostly in visiting and plead-

K

ing with and for sinners. It is my most delightful
employment.

"1.—The ignorant old Churchman. [*Vide* p. 90.] I
see no change. I thundered the law at him as well as
I could, trying to alarm him; but all in vain. 'Do you
pray?' 'Yes, I says the Lord's Prayer and the Belief
every morning and night.' What is to be done? All
his perceptions are blunted. The poor daughter begins
to fear that *I* cannot change him.

"2.—Miss H., a backslider, whom I saw for the first
time a fortnight ago. I entreated her then to return to
her Father, and to come to chapel or church, both of
which she had neglected for twenty-six years. To the
astonishment of the village, she went to church on
Good-Friday and last Sunday. This morning I have
been imploring her to seek salvation at once. I
requested her that, on her knees, she would read
Luke xv., and pray earnestly.

"3.—A young man who has been ill, and sought and
found religion during his illness. He is getting better,
and still clinging to Jesus. He retains his knowledge
of sins forgiven. Praise the Lord! I was rejoiced, and
told him of the dangers and temptations he must
expect, read and prayed.

"4.—Mrs. B., the woman who lost her little girl
suddenly. She is careless, and excessively ignorant.
Talked to her of death and judgment.

"5.—Mrs. W., another poor woman, who can read,
and knows what she ought to do, but does it not. I
entreated her to begin at once to repent and pray for
pardon. She thanked me.

"6.—A very old woman, eighty-two or three, and as
ignorant and deaf as old. I shouted to her of Jesus, the
old sinner's Saviour. 'She hoped the Lord would pardon

her sins before she died.' She spoke of the crucifixion, alluding to Good-Friday. I asked, 'Did Christ suffer for His own sins? Had He ever sinned?' 'Well, I dunno as He had. I don't remember just now anything as He had done.' Again, 'Are you not sorry that you did not begin to serve the Lord before?—that you did not love and serve Him when you were young?' 'How does you know as I didn't?' I told her easily enough how I knew.

"7.—A change. An old man, whom affliction has brought to Christ. On the evening of Christmas-day, when I was praying with him, and reading,

'Arise, my soul, arise,' &c.,

all doubt was removed. He had retained his confidence in God. O, praise the Lord! I have since laid the cases of these seven before God. I have others to see this evening, and my class to meet. Lord, help me!

"April 3d.—The last few days I have tried to live nearer to God. I have not been so joyous as I used to be. I see so clearly my vast imperfections; what I might be, and what I am not. I can continually rejoice in God as my Saviour, but am restlessly anxious for the conversion of sinners. I can truly say, with the Psalmist, 'Rivers of water run down mine eyes, because they keep not Thy law.' Many times a day do I weep over sinners, my brothers, my cousins, my scholars, my sick and old people, all Welford, and all the world; the poor Jews especially. Jesus often comforts me in my sorrow.

"5th.—Last night, on retiring to rest, I had a precious season in prayer. I enjoyed sweet nearness to Jesus, and could have stayed for hours. I lay in His arms as free from care or trouble as an infant sleeping on its mother's breast. O, that I could ever feel so!"

She then goes on gratefully to record the unanimity and powerful Divine influence which she learns to have prevailed at the Circuit quarterly-meeting; intelligence which gratifies her the more, as she had devoted a great portion of that day to special intercession on behalf of the meeting, and of the work of God in the Circuit.

For a few weeks now she speaks of frequent and harassing temptations, occasioning much distress, and some degree of spiritual detriment. The tempter seems to have sought to exaggerate her general sensitiveness of conscience into a morbid and injurious jealousy concerning things indifferent. She has commenced reading a work that deeply interests her, an Exposition of the Book of Revelation. Hardly can she take it up, but the thought is as if thrust into her mind, "You are more anxious to increase in knowledge than in piety; you would rather read than pray." Often she is so vexed and distressed by the reiteration of the charge, as to be compelled to lay aside the book, and resort to her Bible, or fall at once to prayer. Further, she has been reading an article in a religious periodical, rebuking the intemperate and offensive zeal of those Christians who, in their efforts to do good, forget the "whatsoever things are lovely." The rebuke was just enough in itself, but it did not apply to her, whose bold fidelity was so finely tempered by the courtesy and tenderness of Christian love. She begins to question, however, whether she may not have erred in this way, and that the more readily, as her mind is already depressed by the apparent ill-success of her exertions; and certain by no means respectful comments on her conduct have lately floated to her ears. Dreading above all things to injure the cause she loves best, by aught at variance with the gracefulness of the Christian character, she now desists a little from the faithful directness with which she had been wont to urge the claims of religion on all within the range of her influence. But it is a law of our spiritual nature, that a feeling debarred from exercise and manifestation will soon itself diminish in intensity, just as, in the case of the Hindoo Fakeers, those limbs of the body which are kept immovably fixed in one position become at length dead and useless. Miss George soon found, therefore, that her love of souls, and zeal for the glory of her Saviour, no longer allowed to be practically operative, began to lose something of their wonted fervency, and that the general tone of her piety was suffering proportionably. This opened her eyes to the true direction of the course she was taking; she saw how subtly the tempter was ensnaring her, entangling her in a greater error through over-fear of a less. With much compunction she resumed her former habits, and with them soon recovered her former fervour and happiness. She had not transgressed in heart; but, through excessive self-jealousy, had erred in judgment; and He, who has promised that if the eye be single, the whole body shall be full of light, corrected the error, and led back her feet into the right path, before they had been caught in the cunning snare of the evil one.

To return to the diary.

" 21st.—Throughout yesterday my mind was greatly harassed by Satan. He tried in every way to rob me of my peace. Though convinced of my Saviour's favour, I could not *feel* His smile, nor obtain an immediate answer from Him: and prayer does not satisfy me; I must have communion. In the evening I had to visit some sick old men; but could not go unless I could *feel* that Jesus was sending me. I was agonizing in prayer,

K 3

and the time was nearly gone—the tea-bell had rung unheeded—when Jesus appeared. He told me that He was well pleased with me; was my Brother, Saviour, Friend; that I was to go forth in His great name, fearing nothing. O, how unspeakably delightful is such language to a poor troubled child! With feelings like these I could go anywhere, speak to anybody, high or low, rich or poor. I went forth rejoicing. This morning Jesus is precious to my soul, and encourages me. Lord, help me! May I walk before Thee, and be perfect.—Now, in all this I have not had the slightest doubt of my heart's being cleansed from sin. I have had constant faith in the blood of the Lamb.

"May 14th.—During the last week or ten days I have felt an increase of holy earnestness. Jesus has been unspeakably precious. I have been enabled to take up the cross, and speak more boldly to sinners. During the last few weeks I have frequently visited the old Churchman. On Thursday last he exchanged worlds,—himself unchanged. O, the infinite importance of seeking the Lord in youth! That man's faculties and emotions seemed completely blunted. He could neither see nor feel his danger. He appeared given up of the Spirit. I could not pray with any hope for him.

"On Thursday evening I visited one of my girls, who was ill with a fever. She had expressed an expectation that I should call. I talked to her of Jesus; and the mother seemed astonished when I told her I knew my sins forgiven, and had no fear of death. She wished it were so with her. May God affect their hearts!

"16th.—Yesterday was a happy day. Jesus was present and precious continually. My soul was calm, resting sweetly in Him. I have now finished Barnes's ' Notes on Revelation.' It has been blessed to me. I have never before seen it to be such a privilege to be a Christian. I have resolved to be a more faithful witness than ever; to be in the world, but not of it; to glorify my Master continually. O, the amount of happiness the Christian may enjoy if he will! I have been contemplating the blessed state of the redeemed in glory, and longing to be there. I do not, however, wish to die yet; for I have never done or suffered anything for Christ.

"20th.—Praise the Lord for His goodness! Lately He has filled my soul with His love. Whenever I pause to meditate on His mercy and kindness, I am constrained to weep tears of gratitude and love. At the means of grace this week I have felt Jesus very present and precious. Indeed all the day long I have had sweet peace. Satan has been less busy; or, as I have kept nearer to my Leader's side, he may have been afraid to approach. Glory be to God!

"27th.—Sunday was a happy and glorious day. I beheld my Jesus smiling all day. I rejoiced in His unspeakable love, and was exceeding glad. Many times the last few days have I been affected to tears when contemplating the exceeding love of Jesus. This morning one of my beloved school-girls passed out of time into eternity, leaving behind her a testimony that she is gone to inhabit one of the mansions prepared for those who love God.

"29th, Sunday.—This day have visited the bereaved parents of my dear young friend, and seen her lifeless body. I looked upon it with joy, though tears would start. My dear Mary is an angel now. This delightful thought has filled my soul with a strange commixture of feelings. I have wept many times, and wished I could join her. No, I must wait awhile. O that I

could daily live with heaven as much in view as to-
day! Mary died without sigh or death-groan. She
was joyfully waiting for her call, and often had delightful views of the glories of the eternal world. She
many times gave expression to her happiness: 'she
could not weep,' she said, 'because she was so happy!'

"June 9th.—At class to-night I was filled with
happiness and love. Mr. H. said, 'Sister George, tell
us how happy you feel to-night.' I burst into tears,
and could say nothing. I recovered a little, but could
not tell of the exceeding love of my God. I feel so
thankful that God has wrought such a glorious change
in me. I do seem dead to the world; it has no charms
for me; my affections are in heaven.

"16th.—The past week has been one of perfect calm
and holy striving. The love of God has filled my soul.
At the means of grace, public and private, I have
rejoiced with joy unspeakable. 'Bless the Lord, O
my soul; and all that is within me, bless and praise
His holy Name.' My soul has lived in heaven, and I
have been continually longing to be dissolved.

> 'O let it not my Lord displease,
> That I would die to be His guest!'

I cannot rest on earth, when such glory awaits me in
the skies. My sole desire is to glorify Jesus, my
precious Saviour, who has done so much for me, every
day, every hour. But, O, my innumerable imperfections
and weaknesses!

"22d.—I praise the Lord for His goodness. My
peace has truly been 'as a river' the last week. As
soon as I have knelt at the throne of grace, my heart
has been melted by Divine love. Last Sabbath was a
glorious one. In the afternoon, while reading some

religious biography, I was led to examine myself, and then saw what God had done for me. My evidence of being fully saved was clearer than ever. I can truly say that sin is slain in me. I always feel a calm settled confidence in God. My own will is entirely lost in His. I never feel any temptation to impatience or fretfulness. The very things that used to irritate and annoy me most, cause now not the slightest feeling of the kind. My continual prayer is to be made meek and Christ-like. I wish that Christ may constantly be magnified in me, whether in doing or suffering, living or dying. On Sunday night, when giving myself afresh to God in private, my soul was filled with praise. Jesus was unspeakably precious. I could only exclaim, amidst floods of tears, 'My Jesus! My Saviour! My precious Jesus! My Father! My own Father! Glory be to Jesus, my precious Saviour! Glory be to Thee, Thou blessed Spirit, for ever and ever!'

"28th.—Last night Mr. Reacher preached from, 'Thy Spirit is good; lead me into the land of uprightness.' I felt that I was already walking in that lovely land, and feasting on the ' milk and honey' that continually flow there. I was filled with rejoicing at the goodness of God to me. Lord, keep me ever near Thee! O that that 'good Spirit,' who has striven with me for so many years, and enabled me to repent and believe, may go on to perfect me in all the will of God!

"July 3d, Sunday.—The last few days have been happy ones; solid, settled peace.

"Wednesday.—Enjoyed sweet communion with the Spirit.

"Saturday.—Glory to God for His continual love and goodness! He keeps my mind stayed on Him, and so 'in perfect peace.' How sweet it is to love Jesus, and to be loved of Him! Praise the Lord, O my soul!

"10th, Sunday.—The most blessed Sabbath I have spent for some time. I have felt God's day to be an inexpressible delight. Rose before half-past five, and from six to seven enjoyed a sweet season of communion with God. My cup ran over. I had power to plead with the Holy Spirit for His continued presence and help throughout the day, and now I will praise Him for His goodness. He has been very near all day. I felt in the morning that He was my Friend, who had loved me all my life, and done so very much for me, and that He would grant my desires. And I have been filled with the Spirit all day, and enabled to warn and exhort some bold hard-hearted sinners, who never attend any place of worship. I read tracts to them on Sabbath-breaking; and one wicked profane woman seemed to listen to what I said about the possibility of knowing our sins forgiven, and living ready to die, &c. She actually came to chapel afterwards.

"Monday.—Happy all day. In the evening was detained from chapel; but God blessed me at home.

"Tuesday.—So filled with the Spirit all the evening, that I was constrained either to weep or sing.

"17th, Sunday.—My soul increasingly happy in the love of God. Praise the Lord, O my soul! The way to heaven gets brighter every day. I love to meditate on its glories: it keeps my soul far above these earthly things.

"21st.—Each day of this week has been one of great delight. I feel that I am only just beginning, as it were, to live to God. I see before me such a degree of holiness to be attained by mortals, that I seem only just setting out. I want to be made blameless before God and man. I have given myself afresh to the good Spirit to finish

His work in me. I am now willing, and invite Him: He used to strive when I was unwilling, and by frequent carelessness seemed to repel Him.

" 25th.—Yesterday (Sunday) was an unspeakably happy and glorious day. I felt in the most sensible manner the presence of the Triune God, the Father, Son, and Spirit, all my own, *my* God. Praise was on my lips all day. I am conscious of a growth in holiness. The Spirit is answering my oft-repeated and earnest petitions, and taking me into His own hands to make me perfectly holy,—faultless before God and man. Glory be to God for ever ! "

During the three months which the last few entries cover, Miss George's cup of happiness was full. She possessed the deep peace of the fixed heart and single eye. There was the utmost harmony in her nature, as in the chords of a well-tuned instrument. Diligent in works of mercy for her Saviour's sake, she drank rich draughts at that well-spring of happiness, to which only Christian sacrifice and labour can open the path. She watered others, and in doing so was herself watered. Temptation was not suffered to vex her. Those sensible tokens of the Divine presence and favour were constantly vouchsafed her, which were to her "better than life." These were the Delectable Mountains, with their clear air and happy sunshine, their rest and recruital, and prospect, dim and distant, but rapturous, of the Celestial City. Such quiet restful intervals in the toil and conflict of the pilgrimage are sometimes permitted to the Christian, and are to be enjoyed with thankfulness, yet not to be mistaken for the final rest.

Reviewing this period, in a letter to a friend, Miss George writes: "These have been the best three months I ever had. I could not possibly tell you what I have enjoyed of the love of God. The more grace I needed, the more was given. I have had nothing approaching to a doubt or fear for a moment. I have not only felt perfect settled peace, but joy in the Holy Ghost continually. For weeks together I have been so triumphantly happy, as to be compelled to sing or weep."

During the greater part of this time, one of her married sisters was on a visit home for the recruital of her health. That a greater shyness and reluctance to converse directly on the subject of personal religion is often felt by near relations than even by total strangers, is a fact of very common observation. For a long while this feeling raised a shadowy barrier between the two sisters, so that little or nothing was spoken on the subjects really uppermost in the minds of both. Miss George feared that her sister's piety was languid and drooping: she longed to communicate the deep rapture which so often broke in tears from her eyes and singing from her lips; but the words froze upon her tongue when she attempted to utter them. At length, dreading above all things lest she should grieve the Spirit of God by refusing to take up this cross, she burst through the restraint. There was a long conversation one Sabbath night, in which the sympathies of the sisters met and mingled. Elizabeth told the whole story of her own entire devotion and serene enjoyment, set forth to her sister the same happy state as a glorious possibility for her also, probed kindly but firmly her conscious and regretful short-comings, and urged her to more earnest prayer and endeavour. The impressions made in that solemn midnight conference were deep and lasting. The ice had thawed in such sisterly communion, and henceforth without restraint they could speak to one another of the subjects on which they felt most strongly.

And great was Miss George's joy to receive letters from her sister after her departure, stating that both herself and husband were now earnestly seeking to comprehend Christ's "unsearchable riches," and to know the love "which passeth knowledge."

Twelve months had now elapsed since the day when Miss George first attained herself to that blessed state, into which she now sought to guide and beckon others. Thus she commemorates its return:—

"August 11th.—On this day, the anniversary of the memorable day on which God made me holy, slaying sin in me, will I consecrate myself afresh to God. O, my Almighty Father, I take Thee still for my own Father, Guide, and God! Help me to love and obey Thee always, and may I constantly enjoy the sweet testimony that my ways please Thee. Jesus, my Brother and Friend, I still am Thine! O, may I witness for Thee in this sinful world more faithfully than I ever have done! Do Thou be always present in my heart. Holy Spirit! I am Thine; Thou hast saved me. Carry on Thy work. Beautify me; purify me without and within, till I am blameless and without fault before God and man. Accept of Thy unworthy creature, Thou Triune God! Stamp me with Thine own image. Help me to receive all Thy goodness waits to give. May I ever be pressing forward—forward! Amen."

CHAPTER VII.

THE SECOND TWELVEMONTHS.—ACTIVITY.

"Salute Tryphena and Tryphosa, who labour in the Lord. Salute the beloved Persis, which laboured much in the Lord." (Rom. xvi. 12.)

FOR some time since the last date, the diary exhibits chiefly the active phase of its writer's character.

"August 17th.—I felt on Monday for a little time as if I might settle down and do nothing. But no; I thought of the words, 'What doest thou here, Elijah?' and, as I had time, felt that I must go out. In visiting, my own soul was much blessed. Sitting by the bedside of a poor deaf old man, a disciple of Jesus, I felt that my Saviour was looking on me with pleasure, because I was visiting 'one of the least of His brethren,' and He regarded it as being done unto Himself. I was wondering if my visit was of any benefit to the old man, when he broke the silence by saying, 'It seems to cheer me up, and do me a deal of good when you comes to see me, Miss.' O, I cannot express what I felt! The tears came in my eyes. The words seemed to come from Jesus. I felt it to be an unspeakable privilege to be used by Jesus as a messenger of comfort to the dying saint. They who neglect visiting the sick lose many precious blessings. And, O, what will it be to hear from the glorious Judge at last, 'Inasmuch as ye did it to one of the least of these My brethren, ye did it unto ME!'

"27th.—The last week has been all calm, settled peace with God. O, praise the Lord for His goodness! Riding from Stratford this evening, I was exulting in the love of God. I felt that God looked upon me as spotless, because arrayed in Christ's perfect righteousness. My love to Jesus was intense. I could only praise Him with all my heart. The Spirit is daily working within me a righteousness which will *fit* me for the paradise of God. Jesus's righteousness is my *title*.

"28th, Sunday.—Jesus was unspeakably precious to me this morning, while praying for all mankind. I enjoy a most delightful *rest*. No words can describe it. My tears have flowed several times this day when thinking of the great and glorious deliverance God has wrought out for me.

"A few days ago I visited a sick woman, the wife of a small farmer. She received me very kindly. She is a Churchwoman, trusting in the sacraments and church-going for salvation. She knew the Scriptures well, and repeated, amongst other passages, 'Come unto Me, all ye that labour and are heavy laden, and I will give you rest.' I asked her if she knew by experience the meaning of that text; if she had ever felt sin to be a burden; if she had ever been labouring and heavy-laden. 'No,' she said, 'she never had.' Yet she told me she was quite composed in the prospect of death. Poor blind woman! I told her how I had felt myself; and that no person could go to heaven without holiness. I also told her the steps to its attainment,—repentance, faith in Jesus Christ, &c. It was all quite news to her. She seemed pleased, and promised to begin praying that God would show her her sinfulness, and the necessity of a change of heart. The last time I visited that

L 2

house, five or six years ago, when I was collecting for
the Missions, that woman ordered me out in the most
abusive language, and threatened me severely if ever I
stepped over the threshold again."

It may be as well to pursue this narrative without
break. After the lapse of a week or two, she visits the
sick woman again. During the interval the disease has
steadily advanced, and now the vital flame is flickering
low in the socket. But the few words spoken at the
last visit have been seeds of light and life. "I found
her," writes Miss George, "as the neighbours had told
me, 'saying beautiful prayers.' I said, 'You are much
worse: you will not be long here.' She replied, 'No,
I shall not: I may perhaps live through the night, or
I may not.' I said, 'I hope you are very earnest
about your soul: you have not a moment to spare.'
'Well, I hope I shall be ready any moment when the
Lord shall come. I hope soon to be with Him.' 'On what
do you build your hope?' I asked. 'On Christ, the only
Rock: He is a Rock, and I am building upon Him. He can
save me.' 'Do you know that you have been a sinner?
that you have broken God's laws, and exposed yourself
to His wrath?' 'Yes,' was the answer. 'Well; and
do you know there is but one way by which you can
possibly be saved,—by coming as a poor, lost, hell-
deserving sinner, and trusting in Jesus, who has died in
your stead, been punished for *your* sins?' This she
knew well, and repeated scriptures and prayers in proof.
'Do you think that God has forgiven all your sins for
Christ's sake?' 'No, I don't think He has; but I trust
in Him.' During this conversation she wandered many
times; her arms and hands were restless, and everything showed me that a few hours probably would find
her in eternity. O, the exceeding solemnity of the

scene! 'Is she saved or no?' I asked myself. 'It is the eleventh hour. She is actually dying. What can be done?' I lifted my heart in prayer to God earnestly, if ever I did, that if she was deceived, He would enlighten her. I told her, though it seemed cruel to speak at such a time, that prayers, scriptures, sacraments, and church-going would never save her; that she must look to Jesus alone for present salvation. I left her at a late hour, and resolved to pray for her. I went to Mrs. G., and asked her and her husband to pray that God would receive her. I felt faith and power; the thought of the thief on the cross, and other scriptures, gave me encouragement. At eight o'clock in the morning the tolling bell told me she was gone. She died at four A.M. Mrs. G. tells me she also was greatly encouraged in prayer. I have heard no particulars yet; a pious woman sat up with her."

Now follows the practical lesson from the scene :—

" I hope now, by God's grace, to be more diligent than ever with *the living*. O, the infinite necessity of being prepared for death! The dying hour is not the time to seek preparation."

For a few days about this time, the diary indicates some relaxation of diligence. Insufficient causes are suffered to interrupt her visits to the sick and poor. One evening, in particular, it was upon her heart to go to see the poor old Christian mentioned a few pages back, who was now drawing rapidly near his end; but some other occupation intervened, and the visit was deferred. Early the next morning the toll of the passing bell smote at once upon her ear and conscience. On going out into the village, her worst fears were confirmed. Poor old D. was dead. This cut her to the quick. The old man's wife and children were ungodly

and with these only about him, no Christian voice near
to whisper the promise, or offer the prayer, he had to
wrestle with the last foe.   The thought of this was
distressing enough; but to her the worst aspect of the
case was the faithlessness and ingratitude she had
shown to her Saviour.   This humble saint, thus bereft
of human comfort in the mortal agony, was one of
Christ's friends; and neglect of the disciple was failure
in love and devotion to the common Master.   Thus she
reasoned and felt.   Those words smote upon her heart
in reproachful tones, "Inasmuch as ye did it not unto
one of the least of these my brethren, ye did it not to
Me."   Overwhelmed with sorrow, she sought the
privacy of her chamber, and wept long and bitterly.
Several pages of her diary are filled with passionate
self-reproaches.   "I never, never can forgive myself,"
she writes.   "Through my wicked negligence I have
lost a glorious sight,—to me the sweetest sight on
earth,—the death of a saint; but it is not that which
grieves me.   I cannot think of *that*.   I feel too vile, too
unworthy to have been present.   The thought that
grieves me is, *that I have slighted Jesus*.   I feel as Paul
felt when he said to Jesus in the temple, ' When the
blood of *Thy* martyr Stephen was shed, I also stood by
consenting unto his death.'   I sinned against Jesus a
thousand times more than against His dying friend,
though *that* was bad enough.   O, that I had not been so
foolish on Saturday !   O, my Saviour, may I never,
never, so long as I live, thus offend Thee again !   I am
unworthy, unworthy; but if Thou wilt suffer me to go
forth to comfort Thy followers, or tell of Thy love to
poor sinners, may I always henceforth set a proper
estimate on the privilege ! "   She did not long mourn
uncomforted.   In all her abasement and bitterness of

spirit her faith relaxed not its hold on the atoning Saviour, and before closing the entry she speaks of recovered peace. A few days after, she records—

"A blessed and glorious day; the best I have had for a month. The whole day my soul was filled and melted by Divine love. I was unspeakably happy. Tears were continually filling my eyes, and praise my tongue. I resolved, by God's grace, to be 'a vessel sanctified and meet for the Master's use.' I believe all this blessing came upon me in answer to the prayers of some good person or persons, and I often think so; for, when I am least expecting it, sometimes I am especially blessed."

For a few weeks now her piety seems to have sunk a little from the elevated tone it had sustained during the last three months. It was, indeed, to be expected that the lively rapture of that period would abate somewhat; that temptation, graciously averted for a while, would return to harass, if not to overcome; that this buoyancy of spirit would be succeeded by more sombre moods; that God, who had suffered her to rest for a time under the cloudless radiance of His smile, would yet again exercise her faith and patience by wise chastenings, even perhaps as aforetime, by the mysterious darkening of His countenance. All this was to be looked for as in keeping with the disciplinary character of the present life; and in all this there would have been no occasion for self-reproach. But, in the present instance, there was more than the abatement of spiritual enjoyment; there was temporary spiritual declension. She had recently lost a friend, to whose larger experience she had been wont to look for counsel, and from whose distinguished piety she had derived incentive and example. Amongst the Christian

associates who remained, there were some who thought
her righteous over-much; and she now began to question whether she were doing right in diverging so far
from the beaten path which the bulk of religious people
about her trode, and were content to tread. These
eccentricities of faith and zeal, in which she indulged,
were they absolutely required by the law of Christ? Or
were they self-imposed—a species of "will-worship,"
in which pride as well as conscience mingled? Other
professed Christians lived complacently enough without
making themselves thus singular; and why should she
seek to differ from them? Was it then, after all, that
she was saying in her heart, "Stand by, for I am holier
than thou?" At the same time, conspiring with these
specious suggestions to draw her aside from the narrow
path of labour and self-sacrifice, certain special worldly
allurements were presented to her; and, for the moment, her eye lingered, her step faltered. But it was
only for a moment. Her heart was still fixed; the will
of Christ her law, and His approval dearer than life.
Her faithful soul turned to Him, and cried, "Whom have
I in heaven but Thee? and there is none upon earth
that I desire beside Thee." And He, faithful also on
His part, was soon by her side to instruct and rescue
her. There was a sharp brief struggle, and complete
triumph. Her soul escaped like a bird from the snare
of the fowler. She saw through the subtle sophistry by
which the tempter had sought to deceive her; she
turned resolutely from his baits of earthly pleasure;
she girded up her loins, to pursue with fresh vigour the
path she had chosen, determined to look for rule and
precedent, not to the maxims and lives of the professing
church, but to the lively oracles and the great Exemplar.
The following extracts from the diary will show how

her piety recovered its former tone of health and
happiness:—

"October 11th.—Last week I was increasingly earnest. On Sunday especially I was deeply humbled
before the Lord. I was in the very valley of humility,
where I ought to be. I felt that the blood of the Lamb
cleansed me from all sin; but yet I could not joy in the
Holy Ghost. I could only weep and pray. I felt that
the Spirit had been grieved by my want of holy devotedness; by my not lending an attentive ear to His
inward monitions, when they were opposed to flesh
and blood; by my suffering any object to come between
my soul and the face of my God. How needful to be
willing to be 'led of the Spirit,' and to live not to
please ourselves, even as our blessed Saviour pleased
not Himself! I think the following a good definition
of ' an idol : '—

> 'Whatever passes as a cloud between
> The mental eye of faith and things unseen,
> Causing that brighter world to disappear,
> Or seem less lovely, or its hope less dear;
> This is our *world*—our *idol*, though it bear
> Affection's impress, or devotion's air.'

How easy to get such an idol!

"Yesterday and to-day I have been much blessed in
reading old letters in old Magazines. Last night my
soul was filled with holy confidence. My Father said,
'Thou art all fair, My love; there is no spot in thee!
Thou art cleansed from all thy filthiness and from all
thy idols.' 'Walk before Me, and be thou perfect.' I
felt sweet perfect peace, though not such holy rejoicing
as I did. O, I am ashamed of myself! May the Lord
hide me in Himself! I flee to Him. Glory be to my
own God for His exceeding goodness! He fills my soul

again with His love. He has my whole heart, every
whit. I feel weaned from the world and worldly
things. It is very delightful to rest alone on my
Jesus. My soul is filled with praise, and my eyes
with tears. It has been a mighty struggle; but I am
again entirely lifted above the world, and all desire to
please self.

"17th.—This evening our Minister preached on
Peter's fall and restoration: the words, 'And when he
thought thereon, he wept.' I felt it very good. I
could open my soul, and say, 'Lord, Thou knowest all
things, Thou knowest that I love Thee.' Jesus was
very, very near. I could see Him as Peter did, and see
Him *smile*.

"22d.—Glory be to God for His goodness! He
makes me very happy. He is a precious Friend. I cast
on Him my every care. I desire to please Him 'in all
things,' and to do nothing on which I cannot ask and
expect His blessing. I am getting by heart some of
Paul's writings,—the Philippians. I love the Epistles.
Holy Spirit, guide me into all truth! This evening I
dedicate my whole self afresh to God, a living sacrifice.
My God accepts me. I have faith in the blood of
Jesus. I feel a greater determination to press forward.
May the good Spirit lead me on.

"26th.—The last few days I have been constantly
giving myself up to God. I have had solid peace,
though not lively enjoyment. But I am looking to
Jesus. I feel determined to keep thus looking to Him,
and believing on Him for a complete salvation. I will
not look at self, as that will do me injury. Satan is
tempting me severely; but let him suggest what he
may, my God knows that my whole heart is given up
to Him; that all my desires are heavenward, that I long

to be changed into His image, and to magnify Him continually.

"28th.—Meditating on the passage in Mark xi. on prayer, I saw that I ought to believe more. I was led to intercede for myself and others, and enabled to exercise stronger faith. God gave me a blessing, but not till I believed for it. I asked, ' nothing doubting,' for more spiritual light and wisdom. I said, ' Lord, I now comply with the terms : I believe Thou must, Thou wilt give the blessing.' Thus I believed: *not looking within to see if I was becoming wiser.** I looked steadfastly to the promise, and very soon felt such a holy nearness to God as I have not felt for a very long time. I saw, almost as distinctly as when I first believed, God my Father, the Almighty Jehovah, with every possible blessing and good purchased by His Son and treasured up in Him, waiting to impart whatever the hand of faith would claim. He said, ' Ask what thou wilt, and it shall be done unto thee.' ' Fear not, only believe.' ' What things soever ye desire, when ye pray believe that ye receive them, and ye shall have them.' I prayed for a deeper impression of the Divine image on my soul, and I believe that God gave it.

---

* This is a point of great practical consequence. In prayer, we should look *outwardly* to such facts as, the Divine presence, the atonement and mediation of Jesus, and the promises ; not *inwardly* to the state of our own emotions for the purpose of ascertaining whether we are now receiving the blessings we seek. Afterwards it may be well to examine our own spiritual state, and discover whether we have prayed rightly and so successfully, or amiss and so with failure. But, in the act of devotion itself, our great concern is to fulfil the conditions of successful prayer ; and the one primary condition is *faith*, and faith is fed and fostered by a steady looking to the promises. In those promises, therefore, our minds should be absorbed.

"Nov. 9th.—My soul has been blessed in the prayer-meeting. Was encouraged to go on looking unto Jesus, and sighing for constant communion. Have derived much assistance from reading old letters of Mr. Wesley's. If he were on earth, I would write to him. Perhaps he has a knowledge that his writings profit my soul: if so, it surely increases his happiness. I wish I could converse with people as holy as he was; but Jesus can make up to me for the want of human help. I lie at His feet, waiting to be taught and guided into all truth. I want all His love."

The following extracts from a letter bearing the same date as the above, will explain more fully the assistance derived from these old letters of Mr. Wesley's, and throw back light on other passages of her recent experience:—

To the Rev. John Reacher.

"MY DEAR FRIEND,

"LATELY I have been reading a number of letters in old Magazines, which have been made a blessing to me. They are *spiritual mirrors.* In one that has recently come to my notice, from Mr. Wesley to a young lady, I think I see the error into which I fell some time back, though I knew not of it. How many wiles Satan has, particularly for the inexperienced! The words are these:—'O, beware of voluntary humility, of thinking—Such an one is better than I, and why should I pretend to be more strict than she? What is that to thee? Follow thou Me. You have but one Pattern: follow Him inwardly and outwardly. If other believers will go step for step with you, well; but if not, follow Him.' Of course, as you say, if my eye had not been 'diverted from Christ to men and things,' I should not have begun to look to men for examples. When, however, I began to reason that I was more strict and singular than others, who were more useful than myself, and consequently, as I argued, much better, I did not think that I was doing wrong. It seemed, indeed, then, as if I must have been acting hypocritically. Well, I hope I shall learn wisdom by experience!

"I am looking for great things, and I think my faith has increased. I have been led to meditate on that passage in the 11th chapter of Mark, which speaks of mountain-moving faith. I hope to obtain it; but it is very hard work to believe what—without faith—would be an *impossibility*, and to believe without *doubting in the heart* that the thing is [shall be] really done.* I dare say you have found it so often. But why should we doubt? We believe our trusty friends. If we believed as John used to do, (1 John iii. 22; v. 15,) what mighty wonders we should see! *Some* have done so. Lord, increase our faith.

"I have but one desire and one aim,—to live very near to God, that I may glorify Him by a holy and consistent walk and conversation.

"E. A. GEORGE."

One day, about this time, Miss George was permitted to enjoy a singularly glorious manifestation of the Divine presence. She has recorded the circumstance at length in her diary, and in more than one of her letters. It made a profound impression on her mind, and exerted

---

* Not that Miss George interpreted the passage literally. She did not expect or covet the faith that wrought miracles; but a faith strong enough to grasp with calm unwavering reliance any and every promise of God's, even where to human appearance, *impossibilities* stood in the way of its fulfilment.

M

a beneficial influence on the whole of her subsequent
career. Her own narration is as follows :—

"Nov. 11th.—Yesterday, after a day spent in one continual looking up to Jesus for richer blessings, I went
to class. I felt the Lord drawing near, and was led to
praise Him abundantly. I looked steadfastly unto Him,
and while so doing the Leader addressed me. I expressed myself as 'having but one aim and one desire,
to be made perfect and complete in all God's will.' Mr.
H. said he 'hoped my faith would continue to increase,
and that I should get into the holiest place, and ever
keep there.' My eyes were closed, and my heart fixed,
when I seemed to be taken into heaven, though I was
perfectly conscious that I was in the chapel. This I
know, that I was admitted into the immediate presence
of God, the Father and the Son. I am at a loss how to
express what I experienced so as to render it intelligible.
I felt that I knew what Stephen meant when he said,
'I see the heavens opened, and the Son of Man standing
on the right hand of God,' only that I was with Jesus, with
God. I would have complained of weakness, imperfections,
unworthiness, &c., but I could not. *A veil was thrown
over them all*, and I was assured and re-assured that I was
holy and without fault before God. This I was compelled
to believe. I felt in an inexpressible manner that God
Himself was as perfectly pleased with me as if I had
never sinned at all; that He altogether forgot my sins,
and admitted me to His friendship and communion as if I
had been a holy being from the beginning. At length
I was obliged to cease speaking, and passively to accept
all God's love and favours. I simply said, though my lips
never moved, 'Lord, why dost Thou thus condescend to
bless and commune with me?' The reply was, 'It is
no more condescension than it is to bless a glorified

spirit: all is of mercy; and thou art as precious while on earth as thou wilt be when in heaven.' I can now understand the feeling of perfect complacency that saints enjoy in heaven. They are not suffered to feel shy distrust or backwardness, because they have been rebels: all are children, dearly beloved children. I am sure I enjoyed a foretaste of heaven, though I am at a loss how to describe it intelligibly. What I have written was not half that transpired. Jesus told me that heaven was mine, that He was mine, that the earth was mine, that all things were mine. He had purchased everything for me, and had appeared unto me to show me how I might obtain more and more holiness. I might have all that I needed; for everything was mine. I was His love, His sister, and His bride. He had pardoned me, sanctified me, and sealed me, and left me on earth to glorify Him. All that could give comfort and promote child-like confidence, my Saviour, whose love was unspeakable, said to me. He answered every question, met every excuse, told me never to doubt, but always to believe that He would ever be with me, and all that He had was mine. While in the chapel and walking home, I seemed to have every blessing I asked or needed. Glory be to God, this was no vision, but a reality—all of it! The blessedness has continued all this day. O that this delightful intercourse may ever be kept open! Surely it was talking with God as a man with his friend—face to face."

This is a remarkable incident, yet by no means unexampled in the lives of eminent Christians. With such ecstatic revelations God has been wont in all ages to bless those who have intensely loved and closely followed Him. And over and above the present rapture they create, such seasons have their uses in the economy

M 2

of the Christian life. The very remembrance of them
is ever after a solace and incentive : and, as the percep-
tion of some form of ideal beauty, or the perusal of some
work of consummate genius, elevates the standard of
taste, so that henceforth the insipid and the grovelling
cease to charm; so do these rare glimpses of the glorious possibilities of the Christian life awaken in the
bosom a salutary dissatisfaction with the dull average
of religious enjoyment and attainment, and stimulate to
the pursuit of a loftier ideal.

There is, however, one feature in Miss George's
narrative, on which a cautionary remark or two may
not be out of place. It will be observed that she speaks
of the communion which she held with God, as if it had
assumed a conversational form. She refers her requests
or difficulties to Him, and the impressions which then
arise in her mind she interprets as His direct replies.
Nor is it on this occasion merely that she does this: such
expressions as, "God told me," "God assured me,"
"The words were applied," have occurred with notice-
able frequency in these records of her private devotion.

To deny that the Spirit of God does thus directly
operate on the spirit of the Christian, would be a
scepticism opposed both to Scripture and experience.
The great object of the Saviour's mediation is to bring
"far off" man "nigh" to God, to make his soul the
scene of the Divine Spirit's presence and agency, and to
create within it spiritual senses and affections by which
this sacred Presence may be joyously and vividly felt.
There is such a blessing, within the compass of Christian
promise, as "the communion of the Holy Ghost."
Every true believer in Jesus is familiar with the voice
of that blessed Comforter and Guide, of whom the
Saviour said, "Ye know Him; for He dwelleth with

you, and shall be in you." And it is to such as walk
most closely with their God, that the suggestions of
this Divine voice are most frequent, and its tones most
clear.

Nor would it be fair to throw suspicion on the
genuineness of the communications which Miss George
believed herself, in the present and other instances, to
have received from God. This is one of those hidden
things of the spiritual life, with which a stranger inter-
meddleth not. It is only where some inconsistency
occurs between such individual suggestions and the
infallible teaching of the word, that we, to whom it is
not given to discern the spirits, are competent to say
decisively that they are not of God. Of such inconsistency there is no trace in the extracts given above from
Miss George's diary. There exists, therefore, no reason
for denying the validity of her belief; while, on the
other hand, her eminent piety, her diligent study of the
Scriptures, and the absence of enthusiasm from her
general character, are so many strong presumptions
in its favour. Still it is no superfluous caution to
remind the reader that all such impressions are to be
jealously scrutinized, and tried by that one infallible
criterion which God has given us. The written word
is higher and more authoritative than all inward lights
and notions. It is man's supreme court of appeal on
all questions of Divine teaching. Though " an angel
from heaven" were to tell us aught plainly out of
harmony with what is therein revealed, he must not
be credited. With this unerring standard of spiritual
truth must all mere impressions be compared. And if
they accord not with "the law and testimony," then are
they not from above. Though they have come to us in
our loftiest moods of devotion, they are to be discarded

as temptations, the more perilous because the more plausible. Generally speaking, indeed, such impressions, when genuine, are conveyed through the medium of the word; it is merely that a fuller meaning unfolds in the doctrine or promise, or a more powerful influence imprints it on the soul. The cases in which the word is not used as the vehicle of the suggestion are probably exceptional; and even then, as has been already said, there can be no inconsistency between the two. Let this be steadfastly borne in mind, and there is then no danger in holding it as a very precious and comforting doctrine, that our heavenly Father does, by the agency of His Spirit, move directly on the thoughts and hearts of His children. It has been by the removal of this safeguard that this doctrine has been so fearfully abused; and that fanatics have sought a warrant for the wildest errors and the gravest crimes in their own pretended lights and impulses. And lest by any means Miss George's mode of speaking on a subject, on which exaggeration is so easy and so perilous, should be misinterpreted, these cautionary remarks have been introduced.

The singular blessedness which she this day enjoyed threw its light forward on her path for a long time subsequently. She had received a new impetus in her religious course, and for a while

> "Ran up with joy the shining way."

Thus the diary continues :—

"12th.— This day I have been praying for what Stephen enjoyed. 'He was a man full of faith and of the Holy Ghost.' If I had this exceedingly mighty faith, I could glorify God better.

13th, Sunday.— A glorious day! I was very near

heaven all day. In school I knew not what to do, or how to speak. I wanted to be in private, that I might sing, weep, and praise the Lord as I would. I was blessed in visiting; but O for mighty faith! At night, when alone, God gave me power to wrestle as I never did before. I wanted two things: to be filled with faith, and with the fulness of God. God blessed me greatly. I could have prayed and praised all night long.

"14th.—A blessed day. Was all day long employed immediately in my Master's service. Visited many families, and God gave me words for everybody, high and low, rich and poor, young and old. At night, in private, my whole soul was filled with praise. For an hour I continued praising God, and wished I could but stay all night. I had the spirit of prayer. I was determined to be just the saint God is waiting to make me. I am wholly the Lord's. May God preserve me!

"17th.—Glory be to my God for His exceeding precious love! He fills my soul. Last night, whilst reading to myself before prayers, I was so unspeakably happy, that I longed ardently to be gone. Heaven was in my soul. This day I have been labouring to believe, in spite of unbelief. I will not rest till I am filled with faith; but I have learned that this blessing is not to be given me in a moment. I must use what faith I have, and that shall be increased till I am full of faith, and can claim all the promises.

"19th.—Yesterday I had sweeter communion with Jesus. I felt that He loved me in a manner I never did before. My faith remained strong, though high mountains rose before it. In the evening, these words were very forcibly applied to me—words that I had never thought of, or scarcely noticed: ' Who art thou,

O great mountain? Before Zerubbabel thou shalt
become a plain.'

"The last ten days God has taught me more than I
ever expected to know in my life. I prayed that the
Spirit would lead me into all truth, and I am sure He
has done so. He has shown me the meaning of
numerous passages of Scripture that I never understood
before, and which no human teacher could properly
explain. This morning I gave myself up to God, to be
led and taught everything. I was willing to be as a
little child. I felt Jesus very precious; but, during
the after-part of the day, I have experienced what I only
had faint glimpses of before; namely, *union with Christ*.
I fancied I knew what the words meant before; but I
am sure I never did. This day Jesus has taken me to
Himself in so remarkable a manner, that I cannot find
words to explain it. He has made me one with Himself. I am in Him, and He in me. Instead of seeing
Him as at a distance, beholding me with complacency,
I feel Him *with me—in me*. He has been conversing
with me all day, as my Beloved, calling me His sister,
His love, and bride. I have not had to pray exactly,
but Jesus has been with me, saying, 'I can deny thee
nothing: even thy desires whispered in My ear must be
granted.' O! is not this knowing ' the love of Christ,
which passeth knowledge?'

"24th.—The Lord shows me, by what I enjoyed on
Saturday, the abundance of happiness He has in reserve
for me. I believe He can give as much every moment
as He gave then. This I did not know or did not
believe at the time; but the eyes of my understanding
have been opened to see more of the power and will of
God toward them that believe. I see that there is no
end to the degree of holiness that may be obtained on

earth. *I ask the highest.* The Lord has done much for
me. I was running the race; but He has taken me up,
and carried me a distance in a little time, and set me
down again to go on running. Praise His Name, He
has set me down nearer heaven! I have felt this week
as I never did before; as if I were already exalted
with Christ, already crowned and sharing His glory.
The feeling is best expressed in the words,—

> ' Sit in heavenly places down,
>   While yet we in the flesh remain ;
> Now partakers of Thy throne,
>   Before Thy Father reign.'

It is sitting ' with Christ in heavenly places ;' but I
quite believe that what I now know and enjoy is but a
foretaste of what the Lord will speedily reveal, *if I am
faithful.*"

It is singular to observe with what literalness at this
time she looks for the fulfilment of individual passages
of Scripture in her own experience. The words of God
were very real to her. These, and no vague mystic
" impressions," were, after all, the true aliment of her
soul's life. Thus she writes, a few days later :—" I
fully believe it possible for me to feel *the Saviour presenting me to His Father blameless,* every moment in the
day. To-day I have seen my Father God well pleased
with me; not as I commonly do; but Jesus has presented me to His Father and my Father as blameless
and holy; and my Father has smiled on me, and been
willing to admit me to His communion, seeing the end
accomplished in me, for which He gave His Son."*

---

* "If a man love Me, he will keep My words: and *My Father will
love him, and We will come unto him,* and make Our abode with
him." (John xiv. 23.)

About this time, as recent extracts show, the subject
of *faith* was much in Miss George's mind. In particular,
the extent to which faith was legitimate in prayer for
the salvation of others, occasioned her much thought
and perplexity. She read in her Bible, "What things
soever ye desire, when ye pray, believe that ye receive
them, and ye shall have them." Did this, or did it not,
make it incumbent upon her, in interceding for the
conversion of others, to believe absolutely that the
thing would be done? She came to the conclusion that
it did; and that if she could only strongly and perse-
veringly maintain such faith, in every case, however
seemingly impracticable, she should yet see the desire
of her heart. In a letter to a friend, bearing date Nov.
26th, she asks: "In praying for the pardon or full
salvation of a person, may I believe that the Lord will
do the work *instantly*, or only that He will do it some
time? Mark xi. 24 means, 'Believe that ye do *now*
receive.' I can believe thus for myself; but may I for
another? Is Jesus bound to do the work, if I do my
part aright, namely, *believe?*" Here she assumes it as
certain that the thing will be done: the only question
she considers as open respects the *time*.

These sentiments go a little further than either
revelation or reason will warrant. It is true there
have been multitudes of instances in which intercessory
prayer has been crowned with success. There are few
earnest Christians who could not tell of friends and
neighbours, on whose behalf they had long wrestled
with God, and who, though for a while stubbornly
resistant to all spiritual influences, at length relented,
yielded, and joined them as fellow-wayfarers in the
path to heaven. And these numerous instances of
success supply the basis for a strong *probability* that in

each like case prayer shall have a like prevalence. Yet
it is not to be forgotten that the strong cries and tears
of pious and pitying friends have sometimes *not* availed
to storm the obstinate ungodliness of the sinner. One
thing only is certain, that our prayers shall secure to
those for whom we pray large accessions of spiritual
power. For the sake of our intercessions, God will
show towards them a more pitiful forbearance ; will
surround them with outward circumstances more conducive to piety; and will ply them with more powerful
and long-continued spiritual influences.* This assurance our *faith* may grasp strongly; and beyond this
there is, for the encouragement of our *hope*, the high
probability that these influences will, sooner or later,
bear down resistance. But to affirm that certainly in

---

* The following remarks on the subject of ministerial power,
occurring in Mr. Arthur's "Tongue of Fire," appear pertinent to
the subject in question :—" When we speak of ministerial power, we
are never to be understood as implying that any amount of power in
the Minister will *necessarily* subdue his hearers. What may be fully
relied upon as the result of power dwelling in the Minister, is, that
he will make every hearer feel that a spiritual power is grappling
with him, and bringing him either to yield to the voice that warns
him, or to set up a conscious resistance. ' Almost thou persuadest
me,' is the language of one who can scarcely prevent himself from
yielding to the force that is impelling him towards Christ. Felix
trembled, and said, ' Go thy way for this time; when I have a convenient season, I will call for thee.' Here is a man consciously
under the impulse of a power which is urging him to a result that he
dreads; and, to escape its influence, he adopts the ordinary plan of
' putting off for a while.' But the very awakening of this conscious
resistance, the setting up of this struggle in the breasts of men, is in
itself a proof of power; and he who can do this, although he will
have his Agrippas and his Felixes over whom to mourn, will
undoubtedly have numbers of others over whom to rejoice."—
Page 267.

every case, provided only that prayer be importunate, and
faith unshrinking, resistance shall be overborne, would
be to make an assertion inconsistent with fact, reason,
and Scripture. With *fact;* for Paul mourned vainly
over undecided Agrippas and disorderly walkers; and
there was a Judas amongst the friends of the Son of
Man. With *reason;* for such a sentiment is irrecon-
cilable with human free-agency, making one man's faith
and earnestness absolutely determine another's salvation.
With *Scripture;* for, in the case of the nearest of
human relationships, the Apostle puts it as matter of
hope only, not of certainty, that the patient devotion of
the believer shall subdue the resistance of the unbe-
liever. "For what knowest thou, O wife, whether
thou shalt save thy husband? or how knowest thou, O
man, whether thou shalt save thy wife?"

Miss George, then, was in error in endeavouring to
believe, as if it were matter of absolute assurance, that
each soul she prayed for would ultimately be saved.
The "all things whatsoever" of the promise are limited
by necessary qualifications, which she overlooked. That
the Spirit of God would powerfully influence the subjects of her intercessions, it was at once her right and
duty to believe; that those influences would sooner or
later prevail, presented itself indeed as a strong probability, but no more,—a stimulus to hope, not a guarantee
to faith. Had she thought correctly on this subject, she
would have been saved much of the depression and
self-reproach which she occasionally fell into, when
her prayers and efforts met with apparent ill-success.

There are several persons mentioned, frequently by
name, in her diary, for whom at this time she specially
interceded, and whose conversion, in accordance with
her convictions, she strove confidently to expect.

Amongst these are three that peculiarly elicit her sympathy, and apparently for no other reason than that they are the unlikeliest of all. The first is an old man, whom she has visited twice a week for more than twelve months. He is paralytic and bedridden. For a long time during his affliction, he refused to see any one save the Clergyman: at length, Miss George contrived to gain admission; and now, for many months, the Clergyman and all others have grown weary of visiting him, and she alone is left to care for his soul; except, indeed, that Sabbath after Sabbath, in the village-church, "the prayers of the congregation are desired for ————." The fluctuations of his state sorely try the faith and patience of his young visiter; for sometimes her hopes are raised by his penitence and earnestness, and at other times dashed to the ground again by his hard apathy, and fits of outrageous passion.

A second case is that of a woman, who once enjoyed religon, but unhappily relapsed; and now, sick in body, and apparently declining rapidly to the grave, has sunk into a state of morbid depression. Here spiritual distress has become complicated with physical disease, and, as in other instances of the same class, the only effectual deliverer is death. Of this poor sufferer we shall hear again.

The third case has come more recently under her notice. In one of the lowest and vilest " yards" of the village, she has found, in ill-health, a woman to whom she had spoken one Sunday in the summer, and who had, in consequence, made her appearance in the chapel, to the surprise of everybody. (*Vide* p. 98.) The woman has the repute of being one of the worst in that bad neighbourhood; profane, abusive, and violently passionate. But affliction has subdued and softened her, so

N

that now she listens to instruction very meekly, confesses with tears of penitence her past wickedness, and
earnestly vows to lead a new life, if longer life be
vouchsafed to her. Here, then, is a hopeful case; but it
has its shady side. The wrathful and vindictive spirit
which has so long possessed this woman is not cast out
without a struggle. As strength revives, there are
returns of the old paroxysms. One terrible scene took
place under Miss George's own eyes. They had talked,
read, and prayed together; the woman was humble
and subdued; all was cheering; when suddenly some
trifling provocation, a mere children's quarrel in the
yard, roused a perfect tempest of passion, which for the
time swept away all restraints. It was long before she
recovered sufficient calmness to listen again to her
visiter, who, with a charity that hoped all things, sought
to show her how sinfully she had acted, and did not
desist until the chafed spirit was once more humbled
and sad.

For these three souls Miss George poured forth incessant prayers, struggling to maintain through all discouragements, as she thought herself right in doing, a
steadfast assurance of their ultimate salvation. And
still her faithful earnestness redounded at all events to
her own spiritual profit. How steadily she grew "in
grace and in the knowledge of Christ Jesus" her Lord,
let these extracts from the diary testify :—

"Dec. 1st.—The last few days death has seemed very
inviting. My Jesus has been very precious; but the
more I enjoy of His love, the more I desire to be with
Him, that I may see Him as He is, and be like Him.
This night, at class, I could do nothing but weep for
joy. I have been to see a little dying boy, and longing
to lie in his stead.

'O 'tis better to depart,
'Tis better far to die!' ' "

Then follow some verses of her own—the out-gushing of the happy emotions that at this time filled her heart.

" Fain would I drop this cumbrous clay,
And mount above the skies;
Could I but hear my Saviour say,
' Arise, my love, arise!'

" There's nought below to which I cling;
Earth has no tie to me;
My raptured soul is on the wing,
Celestial joys to see.

" A crown already mine I view,
It glitters from afar;
I soon shall wear it as my due,
Bedeck'd with many a star.

" Even now by faith with Christ I reign,
And by His side sit down;
His mighty power hath made us twain,
In soul and spirit—one.

" This blissful union may I feel,
Long as on earth I stay,
Seal'd by the Holy Spirit's seal,
To full redemption's day.

" Strong in the Spirit's might, may I
My humble path pursue,
With patient zeal to sinners cry,
' My Saviour died for you!'

" Thus may I live the life below,
That angels do above;
The power of godliness to show,
The power of Jesu's love!' "

" 7th.—This day received a note from my Leader, begging an interest in my prayers. This humbles me,

N 2

and makes me fearful lest I should not glorify God. I
ought to pray, and that with full assurance of faith, so
as to secure a blessing. Mr. H. says he is cast down
beyond measure; so distressed that he can only sigh and
weep before the Lord, and wish himself far away. I
have written him a note, to the best of my ability, and
had faith in committing him and his burdens into the
hands of Jesus.

"8th.—Have been to class. Mr. H. said that last
night he was so greatly blessed and encouraged, that he
could not express his extreme happiness. His tears
were turned to joy. He said Jesus had been far more
precious than he had ever before conceived; and that
praising God was such sweet work, that he could
willingly have praised all night long. Glory be to
God!

"14th.—The last week has been a good one. Glory
be to the Triune God! I cannot express the happiness
my soul enjoys, and has enjoyed. The Father and the
Son are so near, so precious. I am sitting down with
Jesus in heavenly places, and enjoying all His love. I
cannot help longing to be with Him altogether.

> 'Let it not my Lord displease,
> That I would die to be His guest.'

I feel it does not displease my God at all. It is His
sweet approving smile that excites the desire. Glory
for ever be to Jehovah, my Father; and to Immanuel,
my Brother; and to the blessed Spirit, my Sanctifier
and everlasting Friend!

"In the 'Christian Miscellany' for this month I see
my little piece, 'To Young Ladies;' also, 'I don't like
Class-Meetings,' which was in the 'Youth's Instructer'
last month. May the Lord bless them."

The last paragraph alludes to the practice which she had now commenced, and continued to the close of her life, of occasionally contributing to religious periodicals, especially to such as were most popularly circulated through the Christian Society to which she belonged. One or two tracts also came from her pen. It was one other mode of "doing good," for which she had "opportunity," and therefore she embraced it. Her little pieces are chiefly narrations of incidents that she had herself witnessed, or words of advice and caution on points of practical piety: they make no pretension to literary merit, yet are always simple and earnest, and some of them exhibit not a little skill in the art of telling a story. She usually wrote under the signature of E. A. G.

"27th.—Eight days since I recorded on this paper the unspeakable goodness of God. Now that I attempt to do so again, my eyes fill with tears, and my heart swells with praise. I adore the Triune God. O, if I were in heaven, I think I could give nobler praise. I am here but a babe. I can only lisp: my soul longs to speak out worthy praise.

"On Thursday, Saturday, Monday, and Wednesday, I visited an old woman, Mrs. W., at 'the Bridge.' She has been ill eleven weeks. I heard of it about a month ago, and felt that I ought to go to see her, but really had not time to take so long a walk, with all my other duties. I prayed that the Lord would spare her. Two or three times afterwards, I heard that she was at the point of death, and wondered if anybody visited her: still it was not convenient for me to go. At length, on Thursday last, I heard that she was still living, and resolved to go immediately. The poor creature, though I had never spoken to her before, thanked me beyond

N 3

measure for coming. She said, 'My dear friend, I feel
that the Lord has sent you to care for my poor soul:
therefore, I love you, and Him too.' I asked her if she
knew that she was a sinner. She replied, 'Can you tell
me anybody that is not?' 'Well, if you know that you
are a sinner, and feel it, I suppose you are very sorry
for having grieved God!' 'I always am sorry when I
do wrong; I have been all my life long.' I asked her
what hope she had of heaven, as her friends thought she
was quite fit to die, and so did she herself. She said,
'Why, the mercy of God, to be sure: my dear friend,
don't you know the Lord is merciful?' 'Yes, Mrs. W.,
He is very merciful; but He is just too.' I endeavoured
to show her that no 'beautiful prayers' could save her,
unless she looked to the Lord Jesus Christ, who had
atoned for her sins. I believe the idea was quite new
to her.

"On my next visit, I conversed on the same matters,
and showed her that heaven was a *gift*, and not a
reward as she thought, and that her sufferings could
not atone for her sins; for she would exclaim, 'O, when
shall I have suffered enough?' Before I left, on a third
visit, she uttered the name of Jesus; which made me
weep for joy. I was almost overcome with the love of
God. Yesterday I found her very penitent; praying,
'Lord Jesus, have mercy on me!' I said, 'Do you
think He will have mercy on you?' She burst into
tears, and said, 'He died for me!' 'Yes, praise the
Lord, He did die for *you*, that *you* might be saved.'
She said, weeping, 'He must love me, or He would not
have died for me; and God must love me too, or He
would not have given His only-beloved Son to save me.
And if They both love me so, I am sure They will save
me.' All this she said with such perfect confidence,

that I could not speak for gratitude. I told her of the Holy Spirit of adoption which God gives His children, and which I enjoyed. She could not understand it; but, blessed Spirit! Thou wilt make it plain. I returned, praising God, and fully compensated for my journey through the snow.

"On Monday afternoon I went two miles to see an old man that I heard was near death; very deaf, and very wicked. I should have gone a year ago, but several persons told me that I could not make him hear, —that a man could not. I felt, however, that I ought to go; and went, though all said, 'It's a hopeless case, Miss;' first praying that I might be able to sound the name of Jesus in his ear, if nothing more. I took in my pocket grandmamma's silver trumpet, and, after shouting for a long time to no purpose whatever, produced the trumpet, knelt down and held it to his ear, putting both my hands round the opening to prevent the sound escaping. I shouted tremendously, 'Do you pray to the Lord Jesus?' The last sound caught his ear. 'Jesus!' he said, weeping, 'Jesus came to save poor sinners; and I am praying to Him to save me.' I made him hear, 'Jesus died for you,' and several other words; and have a good hope that he will be saved.

"31st.—Have been to see Mrs. W., and have secured an opportunity of speaking to her wicked drinking husband. He was in her chamber. I spoke of hell, heaven, death, the love of God, the uncertainty of life; to all which he listened patiently. Then I spoke to him in a parable. He listened till I came to the 'Thou art the man,' when he rose quickly and departed, saying, 'I shall not think of having any more discourse of this sort.' I pray that the good Spirit may sooner or later bring the 'discourse' to his memory, and that it

may be seed cast upon the waters, to be seen after
many days."

It may as well be added here that the dying woman
lingered yet for some weeks; that she was often visited
by her kind and faithful instructress; that she gradually attained to clearer light and firmer trust, and at
length died in peace. Farther on in the diary are
entries to this effect:—"Poor Mrs. W. said to-day, 'All
my prayer is that I may have faith to receive the
precious benefit of the death of the Lord Jesus.' Lord,
grant her request!"

"Last Sunday visited Mrs. W. again. I felt greater
love for her than I ever did before, though I always feel
it a great privilege to visit her. She could resign
everything into the hands of God, all her tremendous
troubles; and rest alone on Jesus. She says she believes
God's anger is removed, and she has no fear of meeting
Him. I fully believe she will be saved. I bade her
good-bye, and commended her spirit into the hands of
God. I felt great tenderness while so doing; could not
help weeping. I think she cannot live till I can go
again." A week afterwards: "Mrs. W. died on
Thursday last."

In such labours of faith and charity the year came to
a close. One of the first entries in the diary for the
new year is a long and remarkable one. Twelve
months before, she had drawn up a dozen resolutions,
embracing chiefly points of practical godliness. They
are singular, as showing how elevated was that standard
of Christian conduct which she proposed to herself.
She now deliberately reviews the past year, rigorously
tries herself before God and conscience by her own
resolutions, and, according to the result of the investi-
gation, pleads guilty or not guilty under each count.

It is astonishing, considering the stringency of her rules, how few are the breaches for which she has to condemn herself. One portion of the year's experience the reader will find made the subject of particular comment,—those few weeks, namely, of partial declension referred to some pages back; and her own calm and scrutinizing retrospect confirms the sentiments there expressed. Here is the extract in full :—

"Jan. 2d, 1854.—Have been writing to William in Australia. O that the Lord would convert my beloved brothers! One day last week especially I was led to pray for them, when my Father manifested such love to me as I seldom feel. I was pleading the promise, ' Delight thyself also in the Lord, and He shall give thee the desires of thy heart.' I had great faith and confidence in commending them to the Lord, and was almost assured that they would be saved. My Father seemed to say, 'Only ask Me, and I must give it: confide in My word.'

"I have been led to take a retrospect of the past year, and am surprised at the goodness of God to me. For everything that I have said or done according to His will, I give Him the glory; and for every weakness and imperfection I fly to those precious wounds of my Saviour.

'Lo! from sin, and grief, and shame,
I hide me, Jesus, in Thy name!'

Last January I made several resolutions which the Lord has enabled me to keep in great measure. They were as follows :—

"1. Never to go where I had no need.

"2. To speak on personal religion to every individual with whom I should come into contact, if possible; to

be instant ' out of season' as well as in season; to sow
beside all waters.

" 3. To endeavour to spend the year 1853 as if I
were sure it would be my last, and as I should wish I
had done in the hour of death. That I might do this,
I resolved to try to spend each day in the year as if my
last; to do nothing I would fear to do on my dying
day.

" 4. To ask every night whether I was as ready and
willing to die as to sleep.

" 5. To live with death, and heaven, and the glorious
realities of eternity, continually in my view.

" 6. Never to speak or hear evil of anybody, nor to
engage in any unprofitable conversation.

" 7. To keep the strictest watch over my *thoughts;*
never to allow myself to think on any subject that
would draw my mind from Christ; especially never to
day-dream, or dwell on the past, though ever so full of
interest; never to look into the future, but to live
to-day.

" 8. In all my visits among the sick and poor, to say
what I had to say, and after prayer to leave; never to
indulge a habit of trifling, but to speak to sinners as
though I never should have another opportunity.

" 9. To do everything to the glory of God; to feel
that I am the Lord's witness and disciple; and that all
my work is to deny myself, and do His will.

" 10. To watch against, and, in the strength of God,
to try to overcome, every known fault; that I may be
blameless and harmless, the child of God without
rebuke.

" 11. On no occasion whatsoever to attend any means
of grace, or visit any person, (whether sick or well, rich
or poor,) or read the Scriptures, without before and

after imploring the blessing of God, as the case may
require.

"12. To write no *unnecessary* letter, none on which
I cannot ask God's blessing; not to write for the praise
of men, but in all things to seek the glory of God and
the good of souls.

"For a long time I believe God enabled me to keep
these rules almost inviolably; but at one period in the
past year I became less particular, more like other
people. This arose from the snares of Satan. I reasoned thus:—I am not so useful as such and such
people that I well know; I have not souls for my hire,
as they have. Yet I am ten times more particular in
my conduct, and in listening to conscience, than they
are. Is this needful? Will they not accuse me of
hypocrisy, and say, 'Where is the extra good you do for
all this?' Besides reasoning thus myself, I was reasoned
with also in this style. This led me to abhor myself as
I never could describe. I fell into the evil which Mr.
Wesley terms, 'voluntary humility.' I felt unworthy
to write to or converse with any Christian. I fancied
that, by my particular and conscientious conduct, I had
acted as though I were better than other people. Alas!
it was a sad error. I soon found that, without constant
watchfulness over my thoughts, and instant looking to
Jesus, I could not enjoy any sweet communion with
God. I could only pray; and my prayers were nothing
but humble acknowledgments of unfaithfulness, short-
comings, &c., &c. Always, before that, I had prayed
in perfect confidence, child-like, feeling that my Father
was well pleased with me, and that He allowed me to
converse freely with Him, and that Jesus did the same,
as my Brother and Saviour. And, I praise my God, I
have done so since. I stumbled thus for three weeks,

but it was four or five before I quite rallied from the effects. Since that time I have lived up to my twelve rules better, but not without occasionally breaking some of them. I will look at them singly for the year. The

"1st. I think I have never broken.

"2d. With three or four, or, at most, not more than half-a-dozen exceptions, I have kept this. I have dealt faithfully with hundreds of persons about their souls. I think no one could be aware of the possibility of keeping this rule, without trying it. In the morning I pray that I may speak for Jesus to everybody; and, when I leave the house, it is with *this very intent*. I feel ashamed that I have ever broken it. I need not once: it has been trusting to my own strength too much that has caused me to do so. Lord, help me this year!

" 3d. The first part of the year I kept this, and have ever had it in view more or less. But I have not kept it as I might have done. I see that I might have redeemed more time from sleep to spend in prayer.

"4th. My answer has been, 'Far readier,' nearly all the year round. I think I forgot it that stumbling time. God took from me the desire to depart and be with Christ then.

" 5th. Very seldom broken.

"6th. Broken occasionally, but always with deep remorse and humbling.

"7th. Kept with great strictness till August or September. Sometimes, since then, I have been too careless about the matter. I do not day-dream, or dwell on the past or the future; but I have not been so careful as I ought to be to think only on profitable things.

"8th. I feel very little condemnation, if any.

"9th. I am not aware of having broken this rule.

" 10th. God has given me help in doing this. Still I have faults not yet overcome. Lord, help me to slay them!

" 11th. I am not conscious of having broken this as it regards visiting, or the means of grace, or private reading. I know that before and after family-prayer I transgress sometimes.

" 12th. Kept. Though to keep this rule has occasioned great self-denial and determination. I once found myself indulging in an unnecessary correspondence; but, on strict examination, discovered that the whole and sole end was not the glory of God: therefore, I resolutely gave it up, though it was a pleasure.

" Wherein I have been enabled to keep these rules, I give God all the glory: and wherein I have broken them, I am sorry; and pray that I may have greater grace this year, and may learn from the experience of the past. Lord, I am Thy servant. I give Thee my all,—my body, soul, time, talents, hands, head, feet, influence,—all! O, use me for Thy glory! May I be sanctified and fit for Thy use. Amen and amen."

The last of the foregoing resolutions relates to her correspondence. Of the steadfastness with which it was kept, a few extracts from her letters, written about this time, will furnish the best evidence. They will show how the strong master-passion flowed out into all the acts and relations of her life.

To the Rev. John Reacher.

" *Dec.* 28*th*, 1853.

" My life is praise; and, glory be to God, it shall be praise! Lately my communion has been with the Triune God. And, O, how sweet has the converse

9

been! I enjoy such holy intimacy with the Three Persons as I cannot describe. Only to *think* of it fills my eyes with tears, and my soul with humble adoration. I can only say, 'Glory be to the Father! glory be to the Son! and glory be to the blessed Spirit!' and long for the period when I shall be for ever with the Lord, and praise Him as I would.

"I feel that I am every day living in the spirit of sacrifice. I am entirely given up to God, and live accepted through the Beloved. With you will I renew my vows to be for ever the Lord's.

"My dear friend, I hope that the ensuing year may be to you a very holy and happy one; that you may be very useful in winning souls to Christ. You cannot labour in vain, if Jesus sends you forth with His word, and you deliver it, seeking only His glory. This is just what I feel when visiting. I feel that Jesus sends me, as directly as if He sent an angel on a message to earth or elsewhere. And I will not go unless I thus feel. I always say, 'Lord, what is Thy will concerning so and so?' or, 'What shall I say to such a person?' When I get the word, I simply *deliver* it; and then ask the Spirit to apply it, or, as Mr. W. says, 'harrow it in by prayer.' "

To Mrs. Laugher.

" Jan. 30th, 1854.

"I HAVE had much visiting to do all the holidays,—visiting, I mean, amongst the sick and dying. I have not been from home at all, as mamma has been so very unwell, and I have had so much to engage my time and attention in the village. From my sick-list three have very recently been removed to Abraham's bosom; which is a sweet satisfaction."

After alluding to the return of her pupils, she continues : " It exercises all my ingenuity to know how to keep them employed, and to arrange their studies. I feel it an important work, one that will tell on eternity.

> 'Every work I do below,
> I do it to the Lord.'

I feel as much need of prayer before I enter the school-room as before entering a class-meeting or Scripture-class. It seems a delightful privilege to have the opportunity of teaching the children Gospel truth. They are all the children of thoroughly worldly people, whose whole religion, I fear, consists in *going to church once on fine Sundays.*"

After a grateful reference to that memorable 11th of August, 1852, whence she dated her entire devotedness to God, she adds : "Yet then I was but a babe. I am conscious of having been growing ever since. Glory be to God for the blessings He has given, the mysteries He has revealed since then ! I was then only just beginning to live. The blessed Spirit has since been leading me on in the land of uprightness, guiding me into all truth, teaching me the meaning of ' being crucified to the world,' of ' communion with God,' of ' union with Christ,' of ' having our conversation in heaven,' of ' sitting with Christ in heavenly places,' of ' going on to comprehend with all saints what is the breadth and length, and depth and height, and knowing the love of Christ, which passeth knowledge.' My soul has been expanding, my faith's capacity has been widening. I think there is no limit to the holiness that may be attained on earth. Even after a perfect meetness for heaven has been given, the soul may not only live near heaven, but, as it were, *in* heaven, and feel the Son ever presenting it to the Father blameless. Let us go on to learn all the mysteries and beauties of holiness.

"I live *to-day* only: thinking each day, 'This may be my last: how would I act if I knew it were?' The thought of death is always peculiarly delightful to me: that is why I so love to visit the dying. I feel an ardent desire for the salvation of souls. I could do or suffer anything that they might be saved, and Jesus glorified. How gratitude ought to stimulate us to cry for sinners!"

To the Rev. John Reacher.

"Feb. 1st, 1854.

"THE new year! Ah! what will it record? I only attempt to live *to-day.* If I would spend a year well, I find I must spend each day well. May time record many well-spent days!

"I believe I experience an increase of 'calmly fervent zeal' for the salvation of perishing sinners. The last month the burden of souls has lain heavier on my heart than for a long time past. I have conversed with many persons who are calmly sleeping on the verge of hell: I can use no milder language. Their folly has led me to cry mightily to God; and the love of Christ has constrained me to use all possible earnestness in exhorting and warning them. I believe they think me beside myself sometimes, when I tell them I am determined to be clear of their blood. 'Deliver me from blood-guiltiness, O God!' I shall have to meet these Welford people at the bar of God. O, I wish that the things of eternity were as open to them as to me! At the same time, I praise God alone for awakening *me.*

"Since school commenced I have not enjoyed such constant nearness to the Saviour as before; but my heart has been right, and I hope to do better. My attention is fully occupied with my inquiring little ones. I feel it a great privilege to be permitted to teach them Gospel truth. I believe the parents must be sceptics, from the manner in which the children reason, compelling me to prove every statement I make. 'How do you know it is true? Are you sure? How did men know what to write in the Bible?' are questions they put to everything. Yesterday, I think, they asked me fifty questions about heaven and angels, and glorified saints, enough to puzzle a divine. 'Is it true they wear long white gowns there? And do they put crowns on their heads? Where do they get the gold from? and the wood to make their harps? Then, if they don't have real crowns and harps, why does the Bible say they do?' May the Lord make me a blessing to them! I am working for eternity."

To Mrs. Laugher.

"*Feb.* 17th, 1854.

"MY DEAR OLD FRIEND,

"YOURS was given me at half-past ten; but I was compelled to deny myself the pleasure of opening it till after school,—an annoyance connected with all my letters now.

"I hope, my dear Matty, you will have grace to follow the leadings of the good Spirit continually: then you will do all things well. What need for constant, hourly self-denial! We may 'walk high in salvation and the climes of bliss,' if we are only willing and obedient; but, to do so, we must crucify self, and follow the Spirit's teachings implicitly. What a blessed

and precious Guide! What a positive proof of His
love to us does our past experience afford! He wooed
us when we resisted His gentle voice, for years perhaps:
then will He not now lead us into all truth, if we
beseech Him? How sweet is communion with the Holy
Ghost! What holy intimacy we may enjoy with the
Triune God, if we will,—deeper and sweeter than we
can now conceive! O, may we go on to be 'filled with
the knowledge of His will, in all wisdom and spiritual
understanding!' May we 'know what is the exceeding
greatness of His power to usward who believe.' May
we continually 'sit with Christ in heavenly places.'
And, O, may the Spirit reveal to our understandings
the full meaning of those words! How perfectly holy
it is our privilege to be! How plain are the Scriptures
on this point! Let us pray that we may be preserved
blameless, until we take our seats above. Let us save
ourselves reproaches in the hour of death, for not having
lived 'up to our privileges.' Now is the time. Lord,
grant us grace to cleave close to Thee!"

These letters have carried us considerably beyond the
date of our last extract from her diary. The energetic
vow of consecration which closes that extract was not
a mere form of words; but her life, during the early
months of this year, evidenced its deep sincerity. The
suspension of school-duties for the Christmas holidays
gave her increased leisure for the kind of work she best
loved and was most happy in. Cases multiplied on her
visiting-list, and her ardour and diligence abounded yet
more and more. A very passion of pity for souls, and
devotion to the Saviour, took possession of her; and all
she could do was too little to satisfy the yearnings of
her heart. It may give more interest to the narrative

to group together some of the cases which at this time especially drew out her sympathy; condensing the materials which her own diary furnishes.

A young lad had left the village Sunday-school some years back, to go into service in another locality. Here he had run wildly into sin, and become so utterly careless of everything higher than coarse sensual indulgences, as even to forget how to read. Returning to his native village, he became desirous of recovering this lost acquirement; and for that purpose began again to frequent church and chapel. Never, in his worst moments, had he been able utterly to stifle the impressions which survived from his early religious training; and now they returned with tenfold force. Still he was too weak to check himself in his evil courses; and his heart was the seat of a miserable strife between the tyranny of sinful passion, and the perpetual protest and revolt of an awakened conscience. At length disease smote him; and, during a somewhat protracted decline, he bitterly repented, sought, and found forgiveness. Report pronounced him already dying, when it first brought to Miss George's ears the intelligence of his sickness. She at once, however, resolved to visit him. She spent with him portions of two successive days, though the nature of his disease rendered all approach to him offensive in the extreme. She found him very weak, very humble, and very happy. Thus she writes of her second visit :—" I read the hymn beginning, ' Arise, my soul, arise.' He repeated the last verse after me; and then, his face lighted up with a beam of heavenly glory, clapped his poor hands together with rapture, and exclaimed many times, ' O, how happy! happy! happy! happier than ever! happier than ever! O, how happy!' He pointed upwards, and waved his

hands,—'Heaven! heaven! I shall soon be there.' I
fed him with some jelly, and thought to myself, 'O, may
it ever be my lot

> After my lowly Lord to go,
> And wait upon His saints below;
> Enjoy the grace to angels given,
> To serve the royal heirs of heaven!'

I wished him good-bye; saying, as he held my hand,
'William, I feel envious. I think you will be in heaven
first, and I should like to go as well.' He replied,
smiling, 'I hope you will soon follow, Miss.' It
seemed very grateful to my ears, unless the will of the
Lord were otherwise." The next day, the reclaimed
prodigal went home to the Father's house.

Another case of late repentance.—A young female,
the daughter of ungodly parents, but well instructed
herself in the truths and obligations of religion, is
suddenly stricken with inflammation in the lungs; and,
from his first visit, the doctor gives "no hope." There
is alarm and agitation in the soul of the dying girl;
for hitherto, in spite of light and conviction, she has
withheld her heart from God. Miss George visits her
unremittingly during the few days of her rapid decline,
and wrestles in secret with God on her behalf. Gradually she takes a juster view of the Divine method of
salvation, and plants a firmer hold on the great sacrifice
for sin. Faith soothes her agitated spirit, and there is
hope in her end. The entries in the diary are but brief
memoranda:—"Tuesday.—Saw Miss ——. She is
very, very ill. She has more light than I anticipated.
I believe she will be saved. Her parents are in heathen
darkness, and as frightened as possible for me to see
her, lest I should disturb her mind. Saturday.—Saw
Miss ——, and said what I could to instruct and

encourage her. I could pray for her believingly, and for her dark parents, with strong crying and tears. Wednesday.—Visited Miss ——. She is trusting in Jesus, and seems to see the way clearly. She says, Jesus, who saved the dying thief, will not cast her out. Friday.— Miss —— dead! How short an illness has hers been! May it be made a blessing to her father and mother!"

Another case that lay much upon her heart at this time was that of a woman whom a combination of moral and physical causes had brought into a state of religious despair. Miss George says of her: "She has been a miserable desponding Christian all her life, notwithstanding that all her sons have been converted to God, and she has had so much that demanded rejoicing and praise. I have often told her to trust more to God, not to bear her own troubles, or meet them half-way, &c.; but in vain. *She would be worldly-minded.*" The issue is, that now, being seized with sickness, she has fallen into a state of morbid despondency. They who in the cares and troubles of every-day life allow themselves in a habit of ungrateful, fretting, complaining distrust, are but ill-prepared for the heavier shocks of calamity. "Nothing that I could say," writes Miss George of her visit to this miserable woman, "had the slightest effect. She seemed not to hear me, and could not take any encouragement. I quoted the promises most applicable to her case; but in vain. 'Ah! Miss George, they are not for me! Not one promise is mine. O, how wicked I have been! how false! I have always been a hypocrite. I had the form of godliness, but denied the power.' All these things, and many more, she said in a tone of utter despair. Her body is in a very weak state, and I imagine will not last long. The horrible burden seems too much for her. With gloom and bitter remorse she

said, several times, ' O, what a happy woman I might
have been! but now I am lost! If I would but have
cast my burdens on the Lord, and committed everything
into His hands, I might have rejoiced in His love,
instead of mourning all my days. But I would go after
the world. I would not let the Lord act for me. I took
matters out of His hands; and now it is too late.'
I prayed with her afterwards. She held my hand
between hers for a long time, and smiled for a moment,
but then sunk down into her usual gloom." This state
of things continued for some weeks; the body getting
weaker, and no breaking-up of the thick clouds that
darkened the soul. The case deeply moved Miss
George's sympathies. She often visited the poor desponding, decaying woman, and did the best she could
to comfort and encourage her. At the same time her
diary records many periods of especial intercession,
and is thickly interspersed with prayers written in full,
singular for their vehemence and importunity. She
requested another pious female, her most congenial
religious associate in the village, to unite with her in
wrestling with God on behalf of their unhappy neighbour. At length, by slow degrees, hope and peace
visited the dejected heart; and, some weeks further on,
there are brief entries in the diary to this effect:
" Mrs. —— is in a more comfortable state of mind,
though not happy." " Last Sunday Mrs. —— was made
quite happy, though she is more desponding now."

An old man, whom she had periodically visited for
some years during a tedious decay, and to whose mind
she had been the means of imparting the light and peace
of Christian truth, was now drawing near his end. She
had hoped to be able to cheer him by her presence to
the last; but small-pox had entered the cottage, and

carried off a child from the very chamber in which the
old Christian was dying. The danger to herself Miss
George would have braved; but it was neither prudent
nor right to run the risk of carrying the infection to her
little pupils. It distressed her deeply, however, to think
of that solitary death-bed. " I do not make trials of
many things," she writes; " but this has caused me to
shed many tears, and given me many head-aches. I
have thought of the apparent cruelty of it: he would
think that I loved my own body better than his soul.
Yet the Lord has known my perfect willingness to visit
the poor man, and has sympathized with me, and blessed
me. I have been consoled by the thought that God can
work without sending me, and have therefore been
instant in calling upon Him." Thus tender and Christ-
like were her sympathies. To be hindered ministering
consolation to a dying saint in a hovel is one of the
heaviest " trials" she has known. A day or two after
she writes again: " Poor Old B. died at two A.M. No
creature has been to speak to him during his affliction.
I feel a clear conscience, but a heavy heart. I am fully
satisfied that he is in heaven. I had power to pray for
him in the full assurance of faith. I shall see him
again. A friend, who called a day or two before his
illness, tells me that he exclaimed, ' Bless the Lord, O
my soul; and all that is within me, bless and praise His
holy Name!' He must have been happy, as he was an
enlightened man."

Many other instances of her zeal and diligence are
presented by her diaries at this time, which cannot be
woven like the foregoing into connected narrative. Let
the following stand as a specimen. It is the record of
one day's labours.

" Feb. 11th.—Visited old A. B——, a pattern of

contentment. I wish her excellent qualities could be known. Her name deserves to be had in remembrance. Some time, I think, I will write a tract about her. I love to listen to her wisdom, and feel my own ignorance. Visited an old man and woman; the former a careless old sinner, the latter an old backslider. May the Lord own my efforts! Saw Miss H., a backslider. In prayer I felt much the willingness of the Lord to receive her, and could not help weeping. She seemed affected, and has promised to be in earnest. May this seed never perish!"

Meanwhile she was not negligent of the culture of the inner life. She knew that good works are the fruit, and not the aliment, of a living piety; that it requires for its sustenance meditation, devotion, and the habit of faith; and that to be absorbed in labours for others, and relax care of one's self, is but to broaden the channel, while suffering weed and sediment to choke the spring. Hence, interspersed with those entries in her diary which tell of outward activities, are others which show how diligent she was all the while in maintaining the inward life of faith; how close and hallowing was her fellowship with God; and, though shaded at times by the intensity of her compassion for sinners, how bright and joyous was the aspect of her piety. The following extracts, extending over the early months of this year, will confirm these remarks:—

"Jan. 23d.—Yesterday evening the Lord blessed me abundantly. At class, after preaching, I felt it especially good. My Saviour presented me to the Father blameless.

"30th.—The last week I have been engaged in school-duties again. I have nine pupils. I feel the need of much wisdom and discretion. I feel that I am

working for eternity. O that I may please the Lord
in all I do! I feel it a great privilege to have the opportunity of imparting Gospel truth to the children of
godless parents. Last week I was enabled to live with
eternity in view. O that I may ever do so!

"Feb. 5th, Sunday.—This morning the Lord was
very precious to me in school. He blessed me, accepted
me, and declared me fair and without spot. I have felt
this day increasingly earnest to do good, and improve
my opportunities of usefulness. Lord, make me a
blessing to all this village!

"12th, Sunday.—At night, in chapel, and before
starting, felt great power and faith in praying for the
Spirit to bless the service. Was assured that good
would be done. Was myself hungering and thirsting
after more deep and true holiness."

In the next entry, she gives incidentally her weekly
plan of prayer:—"At noon, on Monday, for my brothers.
—On Tuesday, my scholars.—Wednesday, the Society
here.—Thursday, the universal church.—Friday, the
world.—Saturday, all Ministers and Sabbath - school
teachers.—Sunday, the villagers, and especially any
particular cases. I always keep in my Bible a list of all
the sick that I am visiting, especially those for whom I
bind myself to pray without ceasing, and of any persons
who request me to remember them. I pray daily for
all on the list, for many of them many times in the day.
This I consider to be the sweetest privilege and honour
I have; one I cannot have when in eternity.

" 17th.—I have but one desire,—to enjoy more intimate fellowship with God, to please Him in all things, to
be preserved blameless till death. My God will be
faithful, if I am. In prayer I have had stronger faith, or,
more correctly, *no unbelief*. I have felt, when interceding

P

for a revival, or for my brothers, or sick people, that
God heard, and would surely answer. I need not doubt,
nor could I.

"22d.—On Monday night, while Mr. Stott was dwelling on a favourite subject of mine,—viz., the Christian's
true dignity,—I was unusually blessed. I sat with Christ
in heavenly places, and realized the truth of the scripture, 'All is yours.' I felt, suddenly, that everything
was mine,—earth, heaven, God the Father, God the Son,
God the Spirit; that Jesus had purchased all; and
that, because I simply believed in Him, all was given
to me. I could ask no more: I needed no more. I
could not describe my feelings: it would have been a
great relief to weep. I was not particularly joyous;
but amazed, almost overpowered. The weight of blessing seemed so immense that I could scarcely breathe.
I could do little but draw deep sighs. This prostration
of strength continued for hours, more or less.

"26th, Sunday.—My whole soul is hungering after
more righteousness. I want deep holiness, more intimate communion with God. Father, give me 'all things'
evermore. Thou hast given me Thy Son, and in Him
is all fulness. O, help me to realize this glorious and
mysterious truth! I have been reading over the 8th of
Romans, and weeping for gratitude to God for the
change He has effected in me. O, the times, the many
times I used to read that chapter on my knees, and
pray that its truths might be fulfilled in my experience!
I knew well the meaning of the 7th chapter; now I
know the meaning of the 8th. Glory be to God!"

Some of the expressions that follow will require a
word or two of explanation. Domestic troubles had
begun to gather thickly upon Miss George and her
widowed mother. Some of these will have to be more

fully spoken of by and by; and others are of a nature
that cannot, in detail, at least, be made public. Suffice
it to say here, that the misconduct of one who ought
to have been the prop and pride of a home, which death
and removals had so sadly thinned, had darkened it with
worse than grief; that the effects of his evil courses were
beginning to be seriously felt by his sister in the withdrawal of pupils from her school; and that now, to
crown the whole, the news had just reached them that
the house they tenanted was sold, and that, to meet the
convenience of the new landlord, they would have to
vacate it the following Michaelmas. The sombre back-
ground of these actual and threatening calamities
throws out into brighter relief the undisturbed trust and
serenity which continue still to mark Miss George's
religious experience.

"March 2d.—At prayer-meeting last night my soul
was greatly refreshed. I felt Jesus sweetly near and
precious. I lay in His arms as a babe on its mother's
bosom,—*free from care.* I felt that He was my Brother
and Friend. It was delightfully applied to my mind,
' This is perfect love, which casteth out fear.'

"9th.—I can leave all our affairs in my Father's
hands. He will do all things well. Yet I cannot bear
the thought of having to leave this house. We have no
idea at present where we shall go. Lord, direct us!
May no step be taken against Thy holy will! Teach us
Thy will: Thou art our God.

"20th.—The last few days I have had a delightful
realization of Jesus as my High Priest before my
Father's throne. I have been sitting with Him on His
Father's throne. Glory be to God for this exceeding
great blessedness! We need not die to find heaven. I am
sure that I can say, with truth, that I have been living

within the veil. I have had liberty to enter into the holiest by the blood of Jesus. O, may I be filled with the fulness of God! Lord, teach me fully what that means."

There is an uncouthness of expression about what follows, but the meaning is obvious enough. She feels her union with Christ to be a something so intensely real that all ordinary modes of describing it seem trite and feeble.

" 26th, Sunday.—This afternoon going down to school, I was led to groan for more holiness and oneness with God. Jesus gave me to feel that I was indeed united with Him; that I was actually *one* with Him, a part of Him; that earth was not my home, but I was, as it were, let down to do something for Him, after which He would draw me up. It was like letting the hand down to do anything, and then taking it up. The realization of this is very delightful, though the words seem mysterious and unmeaning. In the school I felt sweetly my union with Christ, that He employed me as His spokesman; speaking through me as through a mouth-piece. I could scarcely refrain from weeping for happiness. As to temporal affairs, I felt what I can never express. I rejoiced in being hedged in and kept in the dark, and thus having the opportunity of leaving all in Jesus's hands. Though we must leave Vine-House in about three months, and know of no house at all suitable and at liberty anywhere, I was as happy, and as sure of being provided for, as if I had a thousand at my own disposal. I do not expect long to remain so free from tribulations as I have been. These have been my golden days. I never expect or wish to be happier; I mean as to temporal things: I hope to love God more. I have never had any illness in my life. And when I read, ' What son is he whom the Father chasteneth not?

If ye be without chastisement, whereof all are par-
takers, then are ye bastards, and not sons;' I wonder how
it is that I have no chastenings. Deep waters may be
before me, though I see them not. Lord, prepare me for
all Thy will. Sometimes I feel anxious to know whether
we shall have to leave Welford or not, that I may
settle my mind on something. I have no choice at all.
The Lord's will is mine. I only wish to do some good,
and glorify Him.

"31st.—I find that my soul is growing. I am
stretching out my hands and heart to God for a deeper
work of grace, and watching more narrowly my
thoughts, words, manner, and actions. I enjoy a most
sweet rest in the arms of Jesus. Lord, make me complete in Thy will!

"April 4th.—Yesterday morning I resolved to set a
constant watch over all my thoughts as well as words.
I began early, and found Jesus very near to help me.
Till school I managed well, and the whole day was a
considerable improvement on the past. I feel that, to
grow in grace, I must keep my eyes steadily fixed on
Jesus, and let no cloud of useless thoughts intervene.

"I fear my feelings towards Mrs. —— are not what
they should be. I seem as though I could not go and
sit down and have a friendly conversation with her.
Not that I wish her any harm; but I fear I am tempted
to look upon her as the sole cause of our having to leave,
instead of always feeling (as I do at times) that she is
merely the instrument, and that God, my Father, in
His infinite wisdom and love, must be ordering it for our
good, and His glory. I have never put myself in her
way but once, lest I should speak unadvisedly to her.
Lord, may I be very jealous of Thy honour!

"5th.—Last night, after my Scripture-class, I held

P 3

sweet communion with Jesus; and, when in bed, my
soul was filled with His love and praise. I could leave
everything in His almighty hands. This day He has
been very precious to me, kindly removing every doubt,
and fear, and anxiety as to the dark future. Glory for
ever be unto Thee, my beloved Redeemer, my own
Jesus, for Thy love and favour! How sweet and open
the converse my soul has enjoyed with Thee! Jesus
will withhold no good thing from me. He will make
my way plain before me. I have been resting on His
bosom, enjoying all His love.

> 'O, 'tis more than tongue can tell,
> Glorious and unspeakable.' "

In the Lord's prayer the catholic petitions take the
precedence of the private; we ask for the hallowing of
God's name, and the establishment of Messiah's kingdom,
before we seek daily bread and personal forgiveness.
Surely Miss George entered into the spirit of that prayer
on the occasion she now records. She shows too that
she rightly apprehends the conditions of providential
guidance. They who are most unselfishly devoted to
God's work are securest of God's counsel and protection.
"Seek ye first the kingdom of God, and His righteousness; and all these things shall be added unto you."
"Delight thyself also in the Lord; and He shall give
thee the desires of thine heart."

"10th. — On Friday night I attempted to pray
respecting our difficult domestic circumstances, but was
utterly prevented by the words,—

> 'Make you His service your delight,
> Your wants shall be His care.'

Jesus seemed to say, ' Ask Me no more: I will provide.
Delight yourself in My service, and you shall know no

want.' I said, with grateful tears, ' Then, Lord, I will ask no more. I will leave everything in Thy hands, and delight myself in Thy blessed service.' I then found liberty in praying for the extension of my Saviour's kingdom, for the conversion of C——, and my dear sick people, &c. How good the Lord is!

" 16th, Sunday.—I have not been so recollected as I could wish during the past week. On Monday morning I rose early for the purpose of praying, reading, &c.; but actually gave way to useless day-dreaming, which surprised and hindered me much. It was not till in prayer at noon that I recovered myself. I pleaded that word, ' Casting down imaginations,' &c., ' and bringing *every thought* into captivity to the obedience of Christ.' I was delivered, and have been on my guard since. On Thursday, I was permitted to sympathize with the ' Man of Sorrows.' I accompanied Him to the supper-chamber, and thence to the garden; and beheld His mysterious agonies, when the Lord was laying on Him the iniquity of us all. I found it very blessed to share His sorrows. On Good-Friday, and since, I have enjoyed some precious times. I have only to bethink myself, and I find my soul in the presence of its Beloved. But I want habitual recollectedness. Lord, help me!

" 21st.—I am utterly astonished at the goodness and love of Jesus. I am so very unfaithful, and yet, the moment I look to Him, I find sympathy and love. I am deeply conscious of having failed to speak for Jesus in several instances lately; and, when I fall on His bosom weeping, He reproves me by a ' kind upbraiding look.' I deserve darkest frowns. Yet He forgives and comforts me. Glory for ever be to His blessed name!"

The return of her birth-day brings with it many humble, grateful thoughts of past and present :—

" 27th.—My birthday.   Twenty-three years this
day since I commenced my pilgrimage.   What shall I
say?   Shall I try to recount the mercies of God?   I
cannot.   Shall I try to enumerate my own sins?   Alas!
I cannot.   But the cleansing blood, glory be to God!
the cleansing blood washes them all away!   I can
sing most heartily the hymn beginning,—

> 'God of my life, to Thee
>   My cheerful soul I raise!
> Thy goodness bade me be,
>   And still prolongs my days;
> I see my natal hour return,
> And bless the day that I was born.'

O, the glorious change that has taken place in my
feelings and circumstances!   For many years I cursed
the day that I was born.   My life was utter misery;
sin made me so unhappy.   It is a wonder that I am
alive.   Often has the fact that my soul was immortal
prevented me from destroying the life which was an
almost intolerable burden.   Then would I have hard
thoughts of God, and say, 'Why did He give me a
soul?   I wish I were a sheep or bird, then I would
drown myself at once.' "   She then remarks how little
comprehension and sympathy she met with in those
who had the management of her childhood.   But, in
truth, as we have already seen, they were not so much
to blame; for Elizabeth had been a strange child, full
of quick sensibilities, exacting much demonstrative
kindness from those she loved, jealous of all apparent
partialities toward others, yet hiding her feelings
under such a covering of reserve that none suspected
the wounded affection and morbid sense of wrong that
rankled beneath, and often found vent secretly in floods
of tears.   She adds: " The sad things I learned from

experience when little, have been of great use in teaching me how to treat children.   Nothing to me is more
pitiable than to see a little child burdened with mental
anguish, whether from unkindness or loss of friends, or
what not."   Then returning from this digression : " I
praise the Lord that my life was spared, because I have
the opportunity of loving Jesus, and trying to glorify
Him.   My birthdays have ever been days of weeping
and sorrow, on account of the many years I have spent
without the favour of God.   O that I could redeem
my misspent moments past !   O that I had known
what fellowship with Jesus was years ago !   What have
I lost that I might have enjoyed !   Lord, I do now
with all my heart consecrate myself afresh to Thee.

> 'Take me, body, spirit, soul,
> Only Thou possess the whole.'

Grant that I may be conformed to Thy blessed image,
and reflect Thy glory.   May Thy whole will be accomplished in me.   May my light shine before others.
That I may have the abiding witness that I please
Thee, help me ever to attend to the inward monitions
of the Spirit, my Guide.   Let me ever rest in Thy
beloved arms, my Brother, my Friend, my All in all.
Amen."

Meanwhile the perplexity and trouble still continue;
nay, appear now to be reaching their height.   The old
home must be left at Michaelmas, and beyond that all
is uncertain.   One or two schemes have been suggested,
but, after anxious debate, are laid aside.   And meanwhile there is not a little to ruffle and vex,—what with
the unkindness of some, and the idle gossip of others.
But this is not the worst.   Simple trouble, coming direct
from the hands of God, is light to bear, compared with

the trouble that is occasioned by sin, especially if it be
the sin of those who are to us as our own flesh and
blood. And there was this bitterest element in the cup
of which the widow and her daughter had at this time
to drink. There were times when the soul almost sank
in the deep waters; yet the grace of God was sufficient.
"I do praise God," writes Miss George, under date
of May 7th, "for His grace. In the midst of most
provoking circumstances, I have felt a perfect calmness
of soul; not a shadow of irritation that I am aware of.
I do not think that I have spoken hastily, or had an
unkind wish or thought. This is not nature, but grace;
not the old man, but the new." And again, a fortnight
later: "We are still encompassed with difficulties; but
God is good. My confidence is unshaken. On Monday
morning, Jesus was so unspeakably precious to me, that
I rejoiced 'with joy unspeakable and full of glory.'
My trials seemed gone. Jesus carried them all; and I
do try constantly to leave them in His hands. He is
my precious Redeemer, my All in all."

The active phase of her character is now again for
some time uppermost in the diary. Her troubles have
not made her selfish. Burdened as she is with private
anxieties, she can yet go out of herself; her compassion
and sympathy are strong and tender as ever, and she
relaxes in no respect her charitable toils. Some of the
cases which now arrest her attention are worthy of a
detailed record.

The old paralytic, of whom some account was given
in a preceding page, (133,) has at length exchanged
worlds. It had been no very pleasant or hopeful task
to visit the poor man, with his failing faculties and
palsied speech, as will appear from this brief remi-
niscence: "I shall never forget his expressions: they

were so short and oft-repeated. As his speech was so
seriously affected by his stroke, he could say but a few
words at a time, and those with great difficulty. I
think, for the first twelvemonths, the only prayer I
ever heard him offer was, 'God a'mighty, ha' massy on
us!' This he used day and night; and in vain did I
try to teach him, 'God be merciful to me a sinner!' or,
'Lord, save, or I perish!' I tried the verse, 'Create
in me a clean heart;' but he could only say, 'Clane
heart! clane heart!' This I have heard hundreds of
times during the last year. Other expressions were,
'The blessed Lord! the blessed Lord! Lord Jasus
Christ!' very, very often repeated." Yet once or twice
a week, for almost two years, had she knelt by the bedside on which this poor stricken body lay, with its
piteous broken cries. She saw the old man die, and
had hope in his death. "I felt great love for him,"
she writes; "and had always much confidence in
praying for him. I fully believe he is with the Saviour,
and will hail me when I ascend to that bright clime."

Here, however, is surer ground for rejoicing:

"May 19th.—I have had my heart gladdened by
knowing that Martha C., a poor half-clad cripple in our
Sunday-school, obtained the pardon of her sins while
seated in my class, last Sunday morning week. She
sat on the very spot that poor Mary Hunt [a young
school-girl who had died in Jesus twelve months
before] used to occupy; and says she was meditating
on Mary's happiness, and thinking how they used to
pray together in an old house, when she believed to the
saving of her soul. Glory be to God, we do not pray
and labour quite in vain!—In the 'Miscellany' this
month, I have written an account of William Tinson,
who died in January last."

The next entry tells its own tale:

"22d, Monday.—Yesterday was a day of humiliation
and profit. I had a heavy cross to take up, and felt
that I should grieve the Spirit if I conferred with flesh
and blood. It was to reprove a shopkeeper for selling
sweetmeats, &c., on the Sabbath-day. Last Sunday I
was deeply grieved to see the school-children going in
parties to spend money." She then speaks of the
natural shrinking she felt from so bold a step, and the
expedients she used to screw up her courage to the
requisite pitch. "I had to forget all else, and meditate
steadily on the sanctity of the Sabbath, the evil influence on the children, &c. I read a sermon of Mr.
Wesley's, on 'Reproving Sin;' and prayed most
earnestly that the Lord would enable me to take up the
cross, and give me such words as He would please to
bless." The difficulty was all the greater, as the man
was a notorious infidel. Three times in the course of
the day she passes the shop, but her heart fails her.
In a parenthesis, she adds, "I think God permitted me
thus to feel my weakness, because I have shunned many
crosses lately." At length, the fourth time, seeing a school-
boy enter the shop, "In spite of myself," she writes,
"I stood at the gate till he returned, reproved him for
his sin, and then went up to the door. Never did I so
entirely trust in the Lord. I told Mr. —— why I had
come, and how deeply I had been grieved, &c. He
heard me seriously and reasonably, and instantly replied,
'it was no harm; every man had a right to do as he
pleased.' I said, 'Not so: we are God's creatures, and
He has a right to give us what laws He pleases; and if
we violate those laws, we render ourselves obnoxious to
His displeasure.'" The reply to this was somewhat
sullen and defiant. A conversation ensued, in which

Miss George could gain but little ground, as the very foundations of belief were so overturned in the man's mind, that there was scarcely anything left to build an argument upon. She strove, however, to touch home his conscience,—the best plan in such a case. Far from offending him, her bold consistency commanded his respect. " I left, saying, ' Now, Sir, I shall have a clear conscience, whether you continue the practice or not.' He replied, ' Yes, Miss George, you have done your duty in reproving me faithfully. It all lies with me now.' I do pray heartily that God will bless the reproof, and all the glory will be His alone. He spoke in me and by me : I did not trust in Him in vain."

A few days after this, she heard of the illness of a woman, whose character had been such as to occasion her a moment's hesitancy as to the propriety of visiting her. At length she resolved to go, and thus records the result of her visit :—" I found her far worse than I had anticipated. She was perfectly exhausted, and had been longing for some one to visit her, and had even won-dered that *I* had not been. She manifested every proof of evangelical repentance. I could not doubt but that she was sincere, even though she should grow careless on recovery. I had just been writing a piece on ' Broken Vows:' therefore I rejoiced over her with trembling. I knew that nobody would believe her to be sincere. She told me that for many hours she had expected death momently. All her sins, all her ingratitude to God, all her neglected privileges, rose in array before her : she had not one ray of hope. Hell yawned before her, and then she said to her husband, ' O, William ! I am going; but where? I have no hope at all. Nothing but hell is before me. I am too ill to pray, even if I ever dare look to God again.' The doctor was

there, and a woman; but no one to pray for her, or to
speak to her. She called to mind the numerous warnings God had given her, and all His slighted mercies,
and felt that she really deserved hell. In that awful
extremity, she vowed that if God would, in His wonderful mercy, spare her life but a few hours or days, she
would spend them in prayer. She revived a very little,
and the medical attendant told her that extreme danger
was past. She slept a little, and dreamed that she saw
in the distance a path, with many people walking in it,
but it was very exalted, and far from her reach. She
knew that path led to heaven; and unless she could
get into it, she could never reach that blessed goal.
But how to get into it she knew not: so she asked a
person to tell her the way. A voice replied, 'Christ is
the Way: look to Him.' She awoke, and was a little
comforted. She believed the dream was from God, and
that there was hope for her. At once, as she gained
strength, she tried to cast her languid eye and broken
heart on the sinner's Saviour, and wrestled for help.
Her husband, an ungodly man, read a chapter to her,
which the Lord blessed; and a poor nurse said a word
or two, which were caught with delight, because they
spoke of hope for the returning sinner. Nobody had
been to visit her, and she was still in distress when I
called; but her mind was greatly eased. She believed
the Lord would pardon her. She admitted all her
former self-righteousness and hypocrisy, and hid nothing. I directed her to the Lamb of God, who had
died for her; pressed on her the duty of asking and
expecting pardon; read suitable scriptures, and prayed.
She seemed to receive me as an angel of mercy, and
begged me to come again. I went the next day: she
had more hope, and had not lost her earnestness. I

told her of the numerous sick-bed repentances I had witnessed; of the vows I had heard, and seen broken; and reminded her of her own vows on the sick-bed in bygone days. She admitted all; but declared that, by the help of God, she would never leave Him. At each subsequent visit I found her gaining strength, and just as earnest and humble as before. Filled with adoring gratitude, I have been led to pray much for her in private. To-day I have visited her: she is better, and very happy. She is certain the Lord has pardoned her since Sunday. She has no fear of death, and is sure of heaven, through Christ. I believe the work is genuine. Lord, keep her!"

The next entry speaks of the oppression of "three heavy burdens." Her own private troubles, however, have nothing to do with any of them: all arise either from the sorrows or the sins of others. One source of distress is the open apostasy of a member of the church, whose unsteadiness has before this occasioned her many bitter tears, and drawn forth many faithful remonstrances. A second is a case of terrible affliction, which just now transpires under her own eyes, and to which we shall have presently to advert. A third is the anxiety she feels on account of the woman referred to in the above extract. It has been as she foreboded. Venturing to mention the circumstance to one of her Christian friends, on whose charity she thought she might best reckon, she has met with no credence: so thoroughly had the woman's previous conduct broken down the confidence of all who knew her. She is now absent from the village, on a short visit for the recruital of her health; and Miss George awaits her return with much doubt and trembling. The result is even better than she had dared to hope. "To-night," she writes, "my joy and gratitude have been unspeakable, to find that Mrs. ——— has returned, has sustained no loss, but is increasingly happy in the love of God; and has been to chapel, and met in class. Glory be to God for an open reward to secret prayer!"

Again, a few days after: "This afternoon saw Mrs. ———. She was still going on well, and said she had begun to have family-prayers read by her child. This is not all: with a·change of heart towards God, has come a change of feeling towards her neighbour. She has learned now the peril of the soul, and the price of its redemption, and longs restlessly to communicate to others her newly-found happiness. She told me that she had felt unspeakable concern for a very wicked old man who lived near her, and who was taken ill. She had had no rest for thinking of him and praying for him, and earnestly wished some one would visit him; but supposed nobody would venture to do so, as he was so very wicked, and had never attended any place of worship, or read the Scriptures. It greatly relieved her when I said I would go.

"The old gentleman was sitting against a table down-stairs, as he will not go to bed. He was very brightly coloured with jaundice: so I told him he would probably very soon be gone. 'Well, Miss, I pray to the Lord to take me.' 'And where do you expect to go, if the Lord does take you?' 'Well, I hope to rest; for I've had no rest here.' 'Do you expect, then, to go to heaven?' 'I don't know, Miss; I don't know where the Lord will be pleased to send me.' 'You should not pray to die: you cannot go to heaven till your heart is changed. The Bible says, *Except a man be born again, he cannot see the kingdom of God.*' 'Ah! that'll be hard for me to learn now. It does say

so? Then, if that's it, I a'nt ready to go to heaven.'
'No, indeed, you're not ready.' 'Then I don't know
what to do, or which way to begin: will you please to
tell me?' 'Do you know that you have been a sinner?'
'O, yes: I've been a terrible sinner!—a *terrible* sinner!'
'Then, the very first thing you must do is to *repent*.
God says, *Except ye repent, ye shall perish.* Are you
sorry for sin?' 'Yes, I am very sorry. I have never
done one good thing. I have been all for the world;
and now I'm afraid it's too late. I can't learn all them
things now. I fear I shall have to go as I am,—all in
the dark.' 'Jesus Christ came into the world to save
poor sinners, the vilest, the oldest, the most ignorant;
and He is willing to save you. He says, *Him that
cometh to Me I will in nowise cast out.* He died for all
your sins; and, if you ask God earnestly, He will pardon
you, and make you fit for heaven.' 'I'm unaccountably
obliged to you, Miss; for I didn't know anything about
it.' I was astonished to find the old man willing to
listen and learn. Every word I spoke seemed to give
light. I believed the change was in answer to the
prayers of Mrs. ——. He begged me to call again, and
to pray for him."

The next day, accordingly, she visits the old man
again. He has thought much upon the glad strange
tidings he had heard; the heaven-sent light is plainly
struggling through the dense darkness of his mind.
"He was very thankful to see me, held my hand all
the time, and said, 'I'm desp'ate obliged to you for
coming to teach me. I knows a good deal more about
it since you came to tell me. I only wants the Lord to
have mercy upon me, and forgive me, if He will. I'm
a great sinner.'"

And now other Christian friends came to see the poor

decaying man, and talk to him of the old immortal
story,—how the Son of God came to save sinners.
Very few, and easy to be understood, are the essential
saving truths of Christianity. Simple childhood and
doting old age alike may comprehend them. Intellects
that seemed impervious to all light, have sometimes
brightened at the story of the Cross. Poor old Hiles
soon grasped the one fact, that Jesus Christ had suffered
and died to save him. He knew little or nothing beyond
this. Conscience, quickened by the Spirit of God, had
told him that he was a sinner, and smitten him with
compunction and fear on that account. Thus far, there
seems to have taken place a preparatory work in his
heart, traceable to no human agency, save, indeed, to the
prayers of the good woman on whose sympathies he was
first laid. In this state Miss George had found him on
her first visit. And when she told him of the sinner's
Saviour, his heart had leaped within him; for the announcement precisely met his need. Jesus Christ had
died for *him:* he knew no more; his poor imbecile mind
was, perhaps, incapable of fastening on another fact.
But *this* at once assumed for him all the vividness of
reality. He received it in the simple, undoubting faith
of life's second childhood. It filled him with wonder
and love. The pains, and tears, and death of the Son of
Man became as true and palpable to him, as if he had
with his own eyes witnessed them. And the torpid
affections of his old heart broke up, and flowed forth to
the feet of this dear Saviour. It is refreshing to read
how, in his rude native dialect, he gives utterance to his
amazement and gratitude. He knows none of the
trite phrases in which Christians generally talk of their
religious sentiments; but his feelings gush forth in the
language of his every-day life. He speaks of Christ

Jesus just as he would have done of any earthly friend whose kindness had equally touched his heart to its depths. In what follows, Miss George's notices of this case are presented consecutively:—

"June 25th, Sunday.—After chapel I visited Hiles. He was worse,—in bed; but said the Lord Jesus was very good. I was much amused at the extreme simplicity of his remarks. 'I have got wonderful judgment,*—wonderful judgment, since you came to talk to me. I understand all about it now. The poor Jesus, poor cratur! suffered such unaccountable things, and all for *me!* That's where it is; that's what surprises me.' Again: 'I reckons that the poor dear cratur done wonders! done wonders! Don't you think so, Miss?' 'O, yes! indeed He did do wonders to save you and me.' 'Yes, Miss, that's where it is: what a wonder!'

"Monday.—He remarked, 'I feel now as the Lord Jesus has heard my prayers, and the prayers of all you dear people that have talked to me and prayed for me; and I feels quite happy. I should be willing for Christ to come and take me clane away. *I should be along w' Him.*'

"Tuesday.—Called with Mr. O.: Hiles was delighted to see us, and told Mr. O., 'Since Miss George and all the dear good folks have been to see me, and tell me these wonderful things as I never thought to know, I seems quite a new man. I only want to please the dear Lord Jesus, and for Him to have marcy on me. I thinks as He has forgiven my sins, because I feel so easy and comfortable as I never felt before. And the

---

* Judgment, i. s., light, understanding.

dear good Jesus has put some hearing into my head, so
as I can hear now better than ever I could. That
shows us the dear Lord Jesus has got regard for me. I
feels that He loves me.'

"Wednesday.—I called. Amongst the various things
he said, were the following. He held my hands all the
time, and frequently clasped me in his arms, as I leaned
down to make him hear. 'I'm very weak, and it hurts
me to talk, but it seems as if I can't do too much. I
must tell you how good God is to me, to spare me all
this time, and not to let me die in the dark, but to send
you dear craturs to see me. I should like *every living
soul alive* to know that I heartily repents of my past
life.' 'And what would you do if God were to raise
you up?' 'Miss George, my dear cratur, I shall never
get well again; but if I was to, O, there'd be such a
turn—such a turn in my life, as never was know'd in
all the whole world!'

"Thursday.—' Miss George, I believe the Lord Jesus
have pardoned my sins, and I'm very happy. I loves
you, and I loves to see you come; and somehow, ever
since you come to tell me these things, I seems to be in
heaven.' I read the hymn containing,—

> ' My Jesus to know, and feel His blood flow,
> 'Tis life everlasting ; 'tis heaven below.'

' Ah! that's it! that's just it! He knowed all about
it.'—Truly ' the entrance of Thy word giveth light ; it
giveth understanding to the simple.'

"July 6th.—Old Hiles said to me one day, 'Miss
George, I never set no store by the poor dear Cratur'
(that is, Jesus) ' till now ; but now I shall set a desp'ate
sight o' store by Him. Everybody ought to.' The
good man is very ill, much weaker, but happy in the

Lord. 'The testimonies of the Lord are sure, making wise the simple.'"

Two more weeks of suffering and decay, and the end came. Poor old Hiles quietly fell asleep, to wake, doubtless, in the presence of that Saviour who had "done such wonders" for him, and whom he had learned to love, though late, yet so well. He was peaceful, hopeful, loving to the last. To Miss George his last words were, "I'm going home, Miss. I shall soon be at home. I gets nearer every day." Was not this a brand plucked from the burning?

Amongst the "burdens" which, a few pages back, were mentioned as specially oppressing her spirits, was a case of terrible affliction, of which some further notice was promised. The circumstances were as follows :— There was living in the village a poor woman, bed-ridden, and wasting away, by a slow and loathsome disease, to inevitable death.* She had once enjoyed religion, but subsequently lost it, and since her affliction had fallen into a state of lethargic hopeless melancholy. For two years she had kept her bed; her husband was a drunkard, and ill-used her; her little children, what with the mother's illness, and the father's wickedness, were sorrily cared for. It was a sad case, and had touched deeply Miss George's sympathies; so that, through the whole period, she had visited the poor sufferer two or three times a week, ministering what help and comfort she might. And now it was plain that the end drew near : she was deeply concerned, therefore, to find that the gloom was settling more densely than ever on the soul of the afflicted woman. At length came on a frightful paroxysm. Miss George was present at the

* The case has already been referred to at page 171.

time, and thus describes it: "At about three o'clock,
or a little after, she commenced beating her head, and
tearing her hair. A good woman, the newly-converted
Mrs. N., cut off the hair, and bathed her head, and
begged her to be patient. Her eyes assumed a wild and
ghastly appearance. She said, 'she only wished to swear;
she had no hope of ever being saved, and no wish
to be saved; she was lost,—going to hell directly!'
She struck any one she could reach, and swore terribly.
She could not bear to be looked at. All thought her to
be dying; I thought so myself for a time. I went to
her, held both her hands firmly, that she might do me
no injury. She said, with a horribly fierce look, 'Miss
George, I'm going to the devil: I shall be lost; I shall
be in hell directly!' 'No, Mrs. H.,' said I; 'you need
not: even now, if you look to Jesus, He will save you.'
'But I don't want to look to Jesus: I only want to
swear and be wicked; and swear I will.' And then, as
I held her, and looked at her, she would gnash her
teeth, and mutter curses and blasphemies, and would
then say, 'It has struck me all the time that I should
be lost at last, and now I know I shall. L——,' (to a
brother,) 'you'll have a sister in hell!' 'No, Hannah,
I hope not.' 'You will, I tell you; you'll have a
sister in hell, and that for ever. I hope I shall be
there before morning; I want to go.' As she had
frequently refused my request to pray with her, here I
said, 'Mrs. H., would you like me to kneel down and
pray that the Lord will send you to hell at once?'
She appeared startled for a moment; then, with a look
of blackest despair, she said, 'If you like, Miss George:
it'll make no difference. I'm going there. I am sure
I shall never be saved: so you needn't talk to me, or
pray for me. Leave me.' I trembled from head to

foot, and then proposed to L—— that I should pray (without her consent) that the Lord would rebuke Satan, and again impart the Holy Spirit. He took my place, and Mrs. N. knelt by her as well; for we did not know what she might do. I prayed, but in such awful trembling as I never felt before. Faith and hope for her seemed to increase, as I pleaded God's promise to hear prayer, His power to cast out devils, &c. She remained pretty quiet; and I began to feel that, perhaps, in answer to *violent* prayer and faith, she might yet be saved. She lay still afterwards, but continued to say very bad things."

Miss George stayed with the miserable woman until peremptorily ordered to leave the house, and then retired to her own chamber. The scene she had witnessed sank deep into her heart. For two whole years she had prayed on behalf of that poor sufferer; and was this to be the end? The thought was intolerable. Far into the hours of that night she wrestled with God; and early the next morning she rose, and again besieged the throne of grace. "I still held the last night's promise with firmer grasp. My prayer now was not exactly for her salvation, but that the Lord would rebuke Satan. I opened to John xv., a chapter that has often helped me in pleading with God. 'If ye abide in Me, and My words abide in you, ye shall ask what ye will, and it shall be done unto you.' Also verse 16. Here I fully claimed the promise, and soon cried out, 'Praise the Lord, it shall be done! it must be done! God cannot deny Himself.' I felt my Jesus peculiarly near and precious: He seemed to say He could deny me nothing."

Now for the issue. That surely is a cold and stubborn scepticism, that will discern here nothing but the subsidence of delirium or the reaction of inevitable

exhaustion, and refuses to connect the altered scene of
the morning with the secret wrestling over night. "As
soon after breakfast as I could, I went down, and found
the devil cast out, and poor Mrs. H. lying perfectly calm.
I told her to praise God, and to believe that He was
willing to save her. I asked if she would now like to
go to heaven. 'O, yes! Miss George: I feel very different to what I did yesterday. It was Satan! O, it
was dreadful, dreadful suffering.' She soon fell asleep.
I sat still for a time, silently praising God, and then
attempted gently to leave. She roused, and said,
'Won't you pray? O, do pray with me! and may the
Lord hear prayer, and fasten it on me!'"

This was hopeful; but there was yet another obstacle
to be removed before the poor woman could die in
peace. The brutality of her drunken husband perpetu-
ally irritated and disturbed her. Even in the midst
of her terrible agony on the preceding day, he had
heightened the horror of the scene by the oaths and
curses of his own furious passion. But Miss George's
faith in the power of prayer had gathered strength
from what had transpired in the wife's case, and she
resolved to try whether even the hard insensate heart of
the husband could not be forced to yield to it. "I
prayed," she continues, "that the Lord would at least
restrain Satan's power in him till his wife was dead, that
so she might have one or two quiet days to die in. The
Lord answered. On Wednesday and Thursday he began
to feel, and even to express, concern about her. He
behaved properly, and appeared to feel much. On
Friday morning he met me in the street, and stopped to
speak about his wife,—a thing he had never done for two
years. The tears were in his eyes. He questioned
me as to her state of body and mind. I answered

as best I could, without reproaching him for his
brutal conduct. This was great encouragement. I
prayed on that the Lord would bring his unkindness to
his mind, and trouble his soul. That same day Mrs. H.
died; that is, she was dying from two till half-past
twelve P. M. The lion was tamed; he wept most
bitterly; sobbed as though he were in the extreme of
wretchedness. Those who witnessed it are perfectly
astounded. It was an open reward to secret prayer. I
do truly believe the woman is in heaven, and that in
answer to violent prayer and faith. The Lord has
blessed me abundantly every time I have prayed for
her. I have had strong faith imparted, the blessed
faith which

> 'Laughs at impossibilities,
> And cries, It shall be done!'

I have felt such great love for this poor creature; she
has been so ill-used. The Lord has known her complicated trials, and that she was but dust. I wept, and
was unspeakably happy on her funeral-day. I wished
myself in heaven; but was willing to stay on earth, if I
could do good to poor sinners."—Thus in charity and
faith did she leave in the hands of the All-merciful
this poor object of her pious care; trusting that after
long trials the weary desponding soul had found rest at
last.

Miss George's labours at this time were incessant.
Her zeal glowed daily with a purer flame; experience
gave her tact and courage; God's evident blessing
animated her faith. If she had felt a foreboding that
her day of work would prematurely close, she could
hardly have turned its hours to better account. Indeed,
it was her maxim, " to live each day as if the last."

R

Towards the close of this July, she paid a short visit to those old and valued friends from whose ripe experience, twelve months before, she had reaped so much profit. Even here, in a strange place, and during a stay of but few days, she could not be idle. " I have spent most of my time," she writes, "in visiting the sick, &c.; and not, I think, in vain. One soul, at least, the Lord has saved; a wicked old woman, aged seventy-one, who was taken ill with water at the heart. I saw her five times, and read and prayed each time. Many of the neighbours came in to listen: I spoke to each one. On Thursday the poor old woman's mourning was turned into rejoicing. The Lord pardoned her while she was praying, 'God be merciful to me a sinner,' as I had directed her. She was filled with joy, and commenced singing the only hymn she knew—one verse of a Christmas carol about Jesus, and sang till she was exhausted. She then exclaimed, 'Sweet Jesus! sweet Jesus! Precious Jesus!' &c. May I meet her in glory ! "

A few weeks later, having occasion to pass this way again, she called on this old woman, and her brief record is, "Found Mrs. O. happy in God."

She returned home, to hear immediately on her arrival of the mortal illness of a poor girl of her acquaintance, and to sally forth at once to the bedside of the sufferer. A day or two after she writes, "Yesterday morning, a woman, entirely careless about her own soul, came to me in great concern about a wicked old woman, begging me to go to see her, and to *try to change her a bit before she died.'*" This will show the kind of reputation Miss George had by this time acquired in the village.

Another incident, narrated under date Wednesday,

August 9th, is of deeper interest, and deserves a fuller record :—" I was requested to visit old Mr. H., who was thought to be at the point of death. He had been ill one month ; and having led a pretty moral life, and always attended church, &c., he had never seen any necessity for a change of heart; consequently had manifested no concern on the subject, but told every one that " he was not afraid to die; he should go to heaven.' I had visited him occasionally, but never felt any deep responsibility on his account, as he was residing with a pious daughter. I went tremblingly, praying the Lord to send by whom He pleased, to speak by me if He would. I found him extremely ill. It appeared cruel to speak to him, on account of the difficulty of his breathing. As there were a number of persons present older than myself, and as I could not get near him, I said but a few words. I simply related the conversion of Mrs. O., of Eatington, showing that a real change had taken place in her, &c. I then prayed, and left. Miss H. said, at the door, ' It 'll be of no use, Miss George: father never will be brought to see as we do. He has always been brought up in the Church, and thinks there is no need of any change. Indeed, I don't think he believes in the forgiveness of sins, though he says he does, in the Church Service.' I replied, ' Miss H., nothing is too hard for the Lord. He can spare your father's life a little longer, and enlighten his mind, if *we* only pray in faith.' I retired ; and, encouraged by the numerous answers to prayer I had lately received, resolved to ask in faith, nothing doubting, that the old man's life might be lengthened, and that he might be led to see that his heart had never been changed. I pleaded the promise, ' If ye shall ask anything in My Name, I will do it.' I also requested that I might

have an answer *that afternoon*. I called again about
seven o'clock, though I scarcely liked to do so. Miss
H. met me in the garden, and, before I could speak,
said, 'O, Miss George! I am so very thankful you came
to see my poor father. He has been talking so about
that old woman you told him of; and I really believe it
has led him to see that no change has ever taken place
in him.' Strange as this news was, it was exactly
what I expected. I praised God, indeed, and resolved
to pray on. I did not see him; but went home, and
prayed that he might be led to feel deep concern and
distress about his soul, and to pray for pardon. I was
quite sure the Lord would do it. I called next morning.
Miss H., with tears of joy, said, 'O, Miss George, you
told father to be in earnest; and I believe he has not
had a moment's sleep all night for praying. I never
believed that such a change could have been wrought
in him in so short a time. He has been entreating the
Lord to have mercy upon him, and to pardon his sins.
He knows himself to be a poor lost sinner now.' He
was too ill to be seen then; so I called again at night,
and found him in deep concern. He acknowledged that
he was a lost sinner, and said that he was praying for
pardon. He listened most eagerly while I read some
hymns to him, and talked of the brazen serpent, &c.
I believe I saw him on Friday in the same state. On
Monday, the 14th, I called again, and found the poor
old gentleman very, very ill. He knew me, and seemed
delighted to see me. He had the restlessness of death
upon him. I talked to him for some time, and asked
before leaving him, 'Do you think the Lord has pardoned your sins? or do you think that He will do so?'
He paused, and then said, with a very confident tone,
'He will do it, Miss George.' He said very little more,

and in the evening he died. I have a hope, a good hope, of him. If I see him saved when I enter heaven, I shall believe that I was permitted to reap in his case: his daughter had sown tears and prayers for many long years."

It was now two years since she first proved that the blood of Jesus Christ cleanseth from all sin. The anniversary of this memorable epoch in her religious life calls forth reflections at once thankful and sad. Signally as of late God has honoured her faith and blessed her labours, there is no self-complacency in the glance she throws back over the past. She discovers much to praise God for, much also to charge herself with. For a new life, animated by Divine love, filled with a pervasive peace, crowned by immortal hope, words are all too weak to express her gratitude. Yet the more vilely contrasts her own unfaithfulness. She has "never altogether lost her faith in the sanctifying blood;" but there have been times when the approval of God has not been so vividly "testified" to her own conscience as at others. There have been denials of self she has flinched from; occasions when she has picked her way with over-dainty care along the rough path, instead of enduring hardness, as a good soldier of the Cross. She has lacked somewhat of devotional fervour and faith: if she had prayed more, or if in prayer she had grasped the promises with a firmer hold, might she not have rejoiced over some for whom she must still weep and tremble? Such self-accusations humble her; but from the depth of her humiliation she rises to new resolve and hope. "Lord," she writes at the close of the retrospect, "I wish to be ever at Thy beck and call, ever employed in Thy service. I offer myself as a whole burnt-offering. Lord, I am entirely Thine, body and soul: do with me

R 3

as Thou wilt, put me where Thou wilt; only use me, my Father, as an instrument in saving souls. Now, Lord, I

> ' Give myself up, through Jesu's power,
>   Thy name to glorify;
> And promise, in this sacred hour,
>   For Thee to live and die.' "

CHAPTER VIII.

THE THIRD TWELVEMONTHS.—TROUBLE.

" When my father and my mother forsake me, then the Lord will take me up." (Psal. xxvii. 10.)
" We glory in tribulations also." (Rom. v. 3.)

THE time had now arrived which must dissolve Miss George's connexion with Welford, the scene of so much happy Christian fellowship and toil. For a long while, as we have seen, nothing had been certain beyond the fact, that she and her mother would have, in the autumn, to leave their present residence: where they were to settle next had lain in doubt. At length providential indications seemed to point to the neighbouring town of Kineton, in Warwickshire. Friends, who knew the place, urged that it presented a favourable opening for such a school as Miss George proposed still to conduct. Accordingly, in the course of the summer, she paid a visit to it; and, having obtained promises of support from several of the inhabitants, she at last definitely determined that the experiment should at all events be tried. In the midst of all the perplexities of this period, her simple faith in Providence preserved her from anxiety: she only sought to do the will of God; and was prepared to follow, with prompt unhesitating step, wherever He appeared to point the path. " O, Matty," she writes to a friend, " the ways of God are mysterious! I cannot think why I am going to Kineton; but I am going simply in

faith, believing it is the will of God. My soul finds
abundant sweetness in looking to Jesus, and resting in
His almighty arms. I am entirely His, and at His
bidding. May He place me where He will, and use me
for His glory ! "

There was great lamentation throughout the village,
amongst young and old, as the hour of separation drew
nigh. For more than two years Miss George had looked
upon the rich and poor of Welford as her Saviour's
representatives, and, by ministrations of love to them,
had sought to evidence her devotion to Him. Deeply
had all this kindness graven itself upon their hearts;
much had they loved and valued her while she was yet
among them; yet they felt as if they had never known
how estimable and dear she was, until now that she
was about to leave them. The young wept at losing
a faithful monitress, whose very rebukes had been so
lovingly spoken, that they only enhanced the worth of
her friendship by proving its truth; the aged sorrowed,
because they had hoped that her prayers and whispered
consolations would cheer their dying beds; the sick
mourned, as they thought how they should miss one
whose periodic visits had so often brought vigour and
refreshment to the soul amidst the body's decay. Some
covered her hands with kisses and tears, unable to
suppress their affection and grief. One poor, sick
woman, whose name had stood long on Miss George's
visiting-list, said, with emphasis, "she would rather
live on bread and water for a year, than have her go."
On the last occasion of her meeting with the class, one
woman present burst into tears, and exclaimed, passion-
ately, "It's of no use: I cannot give you up!" That
same evening, on leaving the chapel, she found some two
dozen children congregated at the door. She was

passing through them, wishing them good-night, as usual, when one girl took her hand, and gave the explanation of their assemblage, by saying, with tears, " We want to wish you good-bye, Miss George."

To herself, too, as may well be imagined, this was a time of solemn and painful feeling. The sundering of so many connexions—connexions, too, of the tenderest and strongest; such, namely, as had been cemented by Christian fellowship, and the conferment and reception of spiritual obligation—greatly afflicted her. It was with a torn and bleeding heart that she left her friends at Welford, to go and live amongst strangers. But, quite characteristically, her deepest sorrow flowed from the fact, that she left those behind her on whom her faithful warnings and entreaties had wrought no abiding effect. Over such she shed her bitterest tears; for she trembled lest they should now relapse into utter callousness. Thus she writes, shortly after her settlement at Kineton :
" I felt parting with some of my dear Welford friends extremely, and I am fully sure they felt it too. Many bitter tears did I shed over some backsliders,—some whom I felt almost positive I should see with my own eyes turned into hell with all who forget God. I warned, exhorted, and entreated them to repent and be in earnest. The love of souls and of Christ constrained me to use the plainest language possible. My feelings were unutterable when I had to bid Miss —— good-bye. I had said all that I could say, and apparently to no purpose. I took her hand, but could not speak. She held mine, and very solemnly said, (it was what I was thinking,) 'Miss George, you will be clear from my blood.' But is *that* consolation sufficient to allow me to stand by, and see her going down to perdition ? May the God of all mercy save her ! "

On Wednesday, the 6th of September, Mrs. and Miss
George arrived at Kineton. " I have not," writes the
latter, " chosen my own inheritance. I am entirely
the Lord's. He shall ever choose for me."

The Rev. H. Laugher had been appointed by the
Conference of 1854 to labour in the Kineton Circuit.
Both Mr. and Mrs. Laugher had long been numbered
among Miss George's most valued friends; a circumstance
which considerably mitigated the pain of removal. The
new Minister found Methodism in Kineton depressed
and languishing; the congregations small, the Society
obscure and inactive. There existed, also, in the place,
a zealous and influential High-Church party, which
evidently regarded Methodism altogether as an intrusion,
and was only restrained, by contempt, from active anta-
gonism. Mr. Laugher soon began to organize plans of
aggression on the surrounding ungodliness; and sought,
both by word and example, to stir up into new life the
drooping activities of the people whose oversight he
had taken. In Miss George he found a useful coadjutor.
She shared his cares and hopes, and threw herself,
with her wonted energy, into such departments of
church-work as were suitable to her sex and age. True,
it required a struggle at first to divert her sympathies
from the old, and turn them into the new, scene of
labour. She shrunk, too, from using amongst strangers,
who did not yet know her, and might, therefore, easily
misinterpret her conduct, the same bold directness in
urging on individuals the claims of religion, which had
become habitual to her at Welford, and which all there
had learned to respect on account of its thorough consistency with the rest of her character. And there were
distractions and absorbing demands upon time and
attention, incident to the commencing of life in new

scenes, of which she had known nothing in the quiet monotony of former days. For all this, it was impossible for a spirit like hers to be idle. It is not, therefore, surprising to find her writing thus to a friend, not long after her final settlement at Kineton: "I commence an adult class on Tuesday night, if anybody should come. The Tract-Distributers will mention it at every house to-morrow. I have been superintending the covering and marking of two hundred tracts, which will be taken to each house in Kineton to-morrow. We are commencing all sorts of new things. We had a Ladies' Committee Meeting a few days ago. I was scribe; had to write down all the resolutions, &c. A vast deal of work is *cut out ;* but we must *wait* to see it done. I shall love tract-distributing dearly. I hope to be made useful here: I want to know *why* I have come." Again, a few days after, to another friend: "We are really expecting a revival of God's work in this wicked and prejudiced town. Last Sunday I visited fifty houses, with tracts; and the Sunday before, eighty."

The first notice of her religious state, since removing from Welford, given in her diary, bears date Sunday night, October 22d. There is throughout it a tone of abasement and self-reproach. Perhaps she judges herself too harshly for those invasions upon old habits which could not be prevented during this time of change. It is plain, at least, that her heart has not at all moved from its fixed anchorage: the presence of God still makes her heaven on earth ; His service commands her entire devotion.

"The last fortnight," she writes, "I have not been able to secure time for writing here. It has been a fortnight of profit. I have been greatly humbled at my weaknesses and imperfections, and have thrown my

whole self at the Lord's footstool in deepest abasement,
resolved to pray and wait for grace and a fresh baptism of
the Holy Spirit. On our quarterly fast-day I renewed
my covenant with the Lord; and resolved to look into
myself, and wait in faith to be made more holy, more
like Christ. I have had many blessed seasons in prayer.
I feel very deeply lest I should dishonour Jesus, and
bring reproach upon His holy work and cause. I feel
that I have given way to my besetment, lack of earnest
seriousness in my deportment among Christians. I am
too apt, when amongst strangers, to forget the presence
of God, and suit myself to my company. This is a
great evil, and one that cannot be avoided without
constant prayer and recollectedness. It has grieved me
exceedingly, because the people here do not know me,
and have to judge by what they see. I have mourned,
and do mourn before the Lord, on account of this evil,
which I could bear if it only tended to *humble me;* but
it does harm to others in a thousand ways. I know
the Lord will help me. He has promised that His grace
shall be sufficient to enable me to conquer, if I be
watchful. I want 'holiness unto the Lord' to be seen
written on all my words and conduct. I want to order
all my words with a holy, reverent feeling of the
presence of God. I want to be unlike the world. . I
have an earnest longing to glorify my Saviour, to be a
faithful and true witness for Him, to have the abiding
testimony that I please Him. I know not why He has
brought me here; but I want to be made useful, to be
an instrument in the Lord's hands of saving souls. More
than ever I feel that the Lord will not use me, unless I
am wholly given up to Him, and that continually;
ever at His beck and call, as Kempis says.

, "The night before last, I had sweet communion with

God. I felt that He did indeed fully accept of me as a labourer; that the blood of His dear Son cleansed me from all sin, that I was holy and unblamable in His sight.

"I have not done much yet. This has been a sorrow of sorrows. I have written some letters for the Saviour, and am trying to lead my dear little pupils to Him. They seem much affected at the story of the Cross, which is quite new to them. May the impressions they receive never, never be effaced!

"Since I have been here, my cry has been, 'Lord, what wilt Thou have me to do?' The church and Pastor are replying by appointing me a district for the distribution of tracts. Thus I shall get an opportunity of speaking to sinners in many families, as well as visiting the sick. I humbly ask that the Lord may make me a blessing to the sick here, and that I may rejoice over more conversions than at Welford. O my Jesus, keep me ever near Thy side! Hold me ever in Thy arms! Make me a blessing to Kineton!"

Amongst the letters she had "written for the Saviour," during the first few weeks of her Kineton residence, must be reckoned one to her former Class-Leader at Welford, upon whom great perplexity and trouble had descended shortly after her removal. Her heart turns often at this time, with much solicitude and love, to her Welford friends; and her letters to that village are full of inquiries and messages, hopes and prayers. The sick, the aged, the newly-converted, and the unstable, lie especially near her sympathies. From the letter to her Leader the following is an extract. It is dated, "Sunday afternoon."

"I wish I were at school at home. I feel as if I had been here quite long enough, and wanted to get

s

back to old friends and old employments. I thought last
week I would have given anything to attend our prayer
and class meetings. My affections and interests are
divided. I think I want *two hearts,*—both good ones
though.

"I do not forget my Welford friends, but think of
them with much affection. I shall be happy to write
to any that would trouble to write to me. I shall feel
especially anxious about Mrs. ——, &c. [Here follows a string of names.] I hope ever to hear of their
steadfastness. I think I felt more at parting with ——
and —— than with any others. I hope and pray that I
may meet them in heaven; but I shall not, without a
change.

"I am convinced that the best and happiest way of
getting through this changing, troublesome world, is to
keep an eye on the glory that awaits us, on our future
inheritance. And not an eye only, but our whole heart
and affections: then trials and changes will appear
trifling in comparison. With this in view, time will
quickly pass away, and we shall be enabled to declare
plainly, that we are rather citizens of heaven than of
earth.

"During the last week I have had a delightful
realization of the happiness of sitting down on our
Father's throne above, when this world's pain and
parting, cares and tears, will be known no more; when
we shall be for ever out of Satan's reach, all saved
beyond the possibility of falling. I have conceived, as
I never did before, how the company of our friends will
augment our bliss. How shall we rejoice on behalf of
those for whom we have often wept and cared below!
This I *knew* before, but never *realized* it. It has taken
away the pain of parting. Let us henceforth live with

heaven much in view, realize a present heaven, walk with God, who is in heaven. If we do so, we shall know little of care or grief; we shall be happy, and enabled to 'rejoice evermore.' Although I feel a clinging to Welford, I am quite happy and contented here. I feel that I could be so anywhere. The matter is, what I am, and what I am doing, more than where I am. May I ever be just where the Lord would have me, and be doing His work. May His entire will be done in me, that I may be holy and unblamable in His sight. For this I have resolved to wait before Him.

"My great desire is to glorify the Saviour, to be a faithful witness for Him. I want to be made an instrument of saving souls in Kineton. For this end I have consecrated my whole self afresh to the Lord.—I must say to you what I have said before: Acknowledge the Lord, and I am sure He will direct your paths. You are not your own, but the Lord's. Will He not direct and provide for His own? If you are where God would have you be, it must be the best place in the universe; and if you are not, He will remove you. 'Casting all your care upon Him;' and why? 'For He careth for you.' With best wishes,

"I am

"Your sincere friend,

"E. A. GEORGE."

The following extracts from a letter to her valued friend, Mr. Reacher, written about this time, are also characteristic. They will show that she has not lost her simple, unsophisticated faith in the power of prayer.

"WE are getting many new tracts for Kineton. I shall write one or two of a simple narrative kind, as

s 2

soon as I get time; but I am much taken up with my
little ones and domestic matters. All are agreeable,
when Jesus is near.

> When I am happy in Him,
> December is pleasant as May.

Verily there is a God that heareth prayer! I have this
noon proved it: will the case interest? You love little
ones, so I will tell you. My ingenuity and grace have
been tried this morning by an obstinate little fellow,
the first case of the kind at Kineton. His little proud
heart, under the control of the 'naughty angel,' has
led him to stand on a locker the whole two and a half
hours, rather than say, 'Thank you!' After twelve
o'clock he remained still speechless, and firm as a rock:
what was to be done? I took him down, talked to
him, as you may guess, about his sin, and Jesus, and
Eli and his naughty sons, &c.; but nothing moved
him. So I said I would go and pray to Jesus to help
him to feel sorry. I did so, in faith; and got my own
soul blessed while pleading the promise, 'Ask, and it
shall be given you.' When I came down, I soon discovered that the little rock was broken by power
Divine. He was very sorry, acknowledged the sin,
and, with a clear voice, even said he should like to pray
himself. He knelt by my side, and I dictated a very
humble, penitential prayer to Jesus. His full heart
could scarcely permit him to utter the words, 'I feel I
have been very naughty this morning, and grieved
Thee.' It was a new thing: it was prayer, and not

'Matthew, Mark, Luke, and John,' &c.

May the impression never be effaced!
"You still 'walk in the light of the Lamb.' And

so do I, by grace Divine. May we ever stand by the Cross, and catch from the Saviour something of His dying love for sinners. The *word*, it appears, is still ' a hammer and a fire,' and that in Scotland.

"Your affectionate sister,

"E. A. GEORGE."

The wounds inflicted by her reluctant separation from her Welford friends were now fast healing; she was becoming reconciled to other faces and scenes; a new sphere of labour was supplying fresh interests and employments in the place of those she had been compelled to surrender; when, unlooked for, another sorrow came,—the darkest, heaviest of all. Her mother, the only relative that death and removal had spared to her, whose feeble health had long called forth those tender anxieties and attentions which more than anything else deepen the fondness of natural affection, was at length smitten with mortal disease. Of her last illness Miss George has given a detailed account in her diary, a few extracts from which will serve to show how the same sure faith and hope at once smoothed the final passage of the departing, and comforted the heart of the surviver.

" Sunday, Dec. 10th.—It is just six weeks since I penned a line here, not for want of inclination, but of time. What changes have since occurred! The first three or four of those weeks I think I lived nearer to God, and enjoyed more of His love. His precious promises were my stay and trust, the cleansing blood was my glory. I got out tract-distributing two or three Sundays, and was hoping to be made a blessing to many. But, about the beginning of November, my beloved mamma was taken with the appearances of

s 3

dropsy." She then details the progress of the disease
up to Sunday the 26th. "That day was mamma's last
down stairs. She sat sleeping most of the time. In
the evening I read the fifth chapter of the second of
Corinthians, and, as a correspondent hymn,—

'We know, by faith we know,' &c.

Mamma listened, and said it was very beautiful. I
requested her to pray, though she could scarcely kneel.
It was her custom at night, and my own in the
morning. She did so, most affectingly. She remembered very affectionately all her children, this town and
Circuit, Evesham and the friends there, and herself;
and prayed that she might be prepared for all God's
will, whether life or death. I was affected to tears;
but little did I think that would be her last audible
prayer. On Monday she was too unwell to get up, and
had no resolution. That night the doctor told me that
he considered the case hopeless; that he could not
depend on her life twenty-four hours together; and
that I was not to be surprised at any change that
might take place. Next day I wrote to a number of
friends to that effect. On Wednesday and Thursday
she did not appear much worse: she sat in an easy
chair for a few hours in the evenings. On Thursday
night I read to her, before retiring, the fifth of the
second of Corinthians again. I had been reading during
the evening some hymns, and selections from Baxter's
' Saints' Rest,' which seemed to send the thoughts more
glory-wards. That night I intimated that I thought
she would never recover: she did not reply. On
Friday the doctor said she had better not try to get
up. She did not; but I sent for Mr. Laugher to
converse with her. She talked of death with com-

posure; said she had no fear, and was quite ready and willing to depart. She had one strong tie, one trial; that was leaving me alone. I assured her I did not fear; I had a Friend who would take care of me and provide for me, a heavenly Father. She said also that the religion which had sustained and rendered her happy through life, afforded solid comfort in the prospect of death. Mr. L. prayed, after considerable conversation of the most satisfactory kind. The next morning I perceived a change had taken place: she looked thinner and more deathly. She lay with her mouth open, making much noise in breathing. I wrote a line to the doctor and to Mr. Laugher, who both came in a little time; but nothing could be done. I saw that death was approaching: still I was kept from all fear. Jesus said, sweetly, 'It is I; be not afraid.' Dear mamma never spoke again. Once she appeared to notice a little; but, as we were fully satisfied as to her state, we did not disturb her by talking to her. Just as the clock struck one on Saturday noon, Dec. 2d, she drew one long breath, and fell asleep in Jesus. Praise the Lord! She is now with Him in paradise!"

Thus closed the earthly career of one whose outward lot for many years had been pain and trouble; but to whom the grace of God had given in life, cheerfulness and patience,—in death, calm and hope. By this bereavement, Miss George was left alone. Three short years back there had been a large family of them under the parental roof-tree. Then came the marriage of her sisters, and the emigration of her brothers, and the number dwindled down to three. In the autumn of this year the one remaining brother had followed in the wake of the others to the land of the stranger. After that came the departure from "the old house at home," with its hallowed associations. Yet, while her mother survived, the first and dearest friend was spared; and there was still a gathering-point for the heart's affections, a spot on earth to answer to the name—*home*. But she was now gone, and Miss George was utterly bereaved. She was not, however, overwhelmed under this heavy sorrow. She felt it indeed acutely; for religion soothes, without deadening the sensibilities; but she felt also that her heavenly Father mingled and gave the bitter cup. Hence her trust was never shaken, her will never rebelled. Nay, so steadfastly were her thoughts fixed on that "rest" into which her mother had now entered; so near and sure appeared the reunion there; so brief the separating interval; so confident and blessed was her communion with the all-wise Friend who had appointed the affliction; and so mighty were the consolations He imparted with it, that she hardly knew whether to sorrow most or rejoice. To her, indeed, was given "beauty for ashes, the oil of joy for mourning, and the garment of praise for the spirit of heaviness." She thus closes the record of her mother's death, from which the preceding extracts were taken :—

"This trial would have been overwhelming, had it not been for the comforts of religion. Never, never did I know the value of an interest in Christ half as I did then. I could not grieve for a friend, even so beloved, taken to the skies; and I could not grieve on account of my own loss, because I had the fullest assurance possible that Jesus would be my Friend, that He would support and care for me as His own, and that, therefore, I need not fear. O the exceeding goodness of God! I do not know how to express it. During the days that the precious remains of my mamma lay uninterred, I spent most of my time in the room; many, many times

in the day and night gazing on the face, so placid, so
beautiful. I seemed to be so near heaven. I felt that
the happy spirit was with Jesus, and that Jesus knew
all about me, that He cared for me as a kind and
affectionate Friend. I used to weep much in private,
for hours; but they were tears of joy and gratitude,
not of sorrow. On Thursday, the 7th, the funeral took
place. In the chamber here was sung the hymn on
the death of a widow; mamma having expressed a wish,
months ago, to that effect.

"I soon began to feel my own condition, that of an
orphan, unprovided for, cast upon my own resources,
without a home; but all this never moved me. Satan
never tempted me to doubt God's faithfulness, and I
rested implicitly on it. 'Blessed is the man that
trusteth in the Lord!'"

There was some debate on the part of Miss George
and her friends, as to what course it was advisable for
her now to pursue. At length it was determined,
Providence seeming to point that way, that she should,
for another quarter at least, continue to make trial of
the school, though the scheme, owing to circumstances
which will have again to be adverted to, had not
proved so successful as she had hoped. Her friends
also feared for her, lest now, when the excitement and
distraction incident to the first shock of bereavement
had passed away, and quiet and solitude afforded
temptation to brooding reverie, the sense of her great
loss should overwhelm her. But their fears were
dissipated, as weeks rolled on, and they found her still
equable, cheerful, and abounding in Christian labours.
Her sorrow, for she felt sorrow, was not that "which
worketh death;" she did not blaspheme life, as robbed
of all worth and happiness, because to her its sun was

shaded for awhile; she had lost something, but retained more,—all, in fact, to which her heart had clung as essential to happiness, or in which she had sought her most powerful incentives to activity. The following extracts from a letter bearing date Dec. 27th, will show in what state the close of the first month of loneliness found her:—

To the Rev. J. Reacher.

"I HAVE so many letters now to write, that it is quite a formidable task. I take yours first, being the one that most pleased me in my sorrow. But what must I say? where must I begin? The goodness and faithfulness of God must be my theme. On these I have dwelt with great pleasure lately. *God is a faithful God.* I have indeed proved it: every promise made to me in days bygone has been fulfilled. Without these blessed promises, I should have been overwhelmed with sorrow during my past trial; but I have trusted implicitly in them, and in the faithfulness of Him who gave them, and I have not trusted in vain.

"The Lord has blessed and supported me, kept me free from all fear and anxiety, (when all my friends were fearing for me,) mapped out my way before me, removed every obstacle, and given me just what I desired. I can only praise Him, and wonder at His love. I praise Him, too, for the exceeding kindness of my friends, who have been anxious to meet every wish. I never had such an idea of the value of religion as now. I *cannot* fear: God is unchangeable; He will provide in the future as well as now. Why need dear mamma have feared leaving me in the hands of an almighty God? I do not feel that I am cast on the mercy of the wide, wide world; but that I am 'cast upon the Fatherhood of God.'

"For a long time, nobody could advise anything; all seemed mystery and darkness. I was passive. Many things were proposed, and many arrangements made: but, at last, the good lady of the house asked me if I would stay with her; she would comply with any conditions. Such a thing had not been spoken of before; but, as I was perfectly agreeable, all fell in with it immediately. So I am still at Kineton, in the same house, but have different rooms.

"But no more about myself at present. The good work of God is beginning to revive here. The ice is broken; five penitents have knelt at the communion-rail in prejudiced Kineton. I am hoping now to have time and opportunity for usefulness. May the Lord deign to use me for His own glory! But my position in this town is a most difficult one. I have to labour to please the Wesleyans, the Church people, my own conscience, and God. Who is sufficient for these things? We are making good use of sterling tracts. I have had six hundred of various kinds,—three hundred like the enclosed, to present one to every Wesleyan in this Circuit. 'A lost Opportunity,' I am ashamed to say, is mine."

On the last night of the year, Miss George, as usual, solemnly reviewed the past, committing to paper the thoughts which the retrospect awakened. She did not spare herself: it was not her habit to err on the side of self-flattery. True, the last few months had been months of change and unsettlement; but, with her, "circumstances" were never admitted to be a sufficient apology for spiritual short-coming,—at least, not in her judgment upon herself. She does not fail to specify one occasion, in particular, on which she had been "overtaken by a fault" altogether foreign to her general

character. She was usually remarkably guarded against
the practice of evil-speaking. Few Christians have
maintained such unimpeachable consistency in this
respect.* But in one instance about this time she
transgressed. It was not that she spoke falsely; but
she gave rash and impetuous utterance to what she
believed at the time to be true. Her words were at
once carried to the person whose conduct she had
stigmatized, and great umbrage was taken. Miss George,
feeling that, if she had spoken truly, she had not
spoken Christianly, that what she had said had not been
consistent with the charity which "thinketh no evil,"
wrote forthwith to the offended party in frank acknow-
ledgment of her error. Her apology was disregarded,
and for a long time she had to suffer acutely from a
resentment which, if justifiable in the outset, had now
certainly ceased to be so. Very deeply did she humble
herself before God, for what in His eyes, however, she
believed was infirmity and not sin; and very fervently
did she pray that His cause might not be injuriously

---

* On this feature of Miss George's character, an intimate friend of
hers, in a note transmitted to the compiler, thus remarks:—"In a
letter of Elizabeth's to a correspondent, bearing date Christmas, 1854,
occurs this sentence, ' I have solemnly resolved before God, in the
strength of His grace, to speak evil of no man.' To this resolution
those who were best acquainted with her can testify how scrupulously
she adhered. Such was her sensitiveness to this too common evil, that
she would never suffer any remark of the kind made in her presence
to pass unchecked. She has been known to silence religious people
indulging in this fault by the simple word ' Detraction!' kindly yet
decidedly spoken ; and, when not successful, has shown her disappro-
bation by shunning their society. She used to say that, in order to
' speak no evil,' you must be content to be considered defective in
observation, and ignorant of character,—indeed, willing to be a fool
for Christ's sake ; and that no one who did not vigorously watch
against it would have any idea of the self-denial necessary."

affected : for, quite characteristically, her most poignant distress arose not from any private annoyance, but from her sensitive jealousy for the glory of her Saviour. Before closing the entry, she passes from the past to the future, from regret to resolve.

" Lord, help me to write down some resolves for the coming year; not one of which, however, I can keep of myself.

"1. To be extremely watchful over my words; to speak no evil.

" 2. To speak much more for God ; to be determined to take up my cross, and feel that—

> ' 'Tis all my business here below
> To cry, Behold the Lamb ! '

O that I could spend the year without neglecting one opportunity !

" 3. To strive after habitual recollectedness of the presence of God.

" 4. To meditate more on death, and heaven, and the realities of eternity.

"5. To rise earlier, in order to secure more time for prayer and reading. To read the Scriptures less hurriedly.

" 6. To pray oftener every day.

" Lord, I do indeed feel, Thou knowest, that I cannot do one of these things without Thy special aid. I feel this, and rely alone on Thy strength. O, bless me, and make me a blessing to Kineton !

" In about half an hour the new year will be ushered in. Thousands are in the houses of worship in our land ; but no watch-night service is being held here to-night. Lord, help me to watch; and, O, bless me ! I throw myself into Thy arms : I trust entirely in Thee. O,

T

may the next year be a far better one to me! May I
be a bolder witness for Jesus! Lord, give me souls.
Prepare me for life or death; for all Thy will. Where
shall I be this time next year? Who can answer? May
I be in Christ."

These resolutions and prayers were not in vain.
New-Year's day was "a very blessed day;" and of the
next she writes: "I was filled with happiness. I was
in my little parlour,—not alone, for God was with me;
and my communion with Him was sweet, my bliss was
great." Then followed a rambling visit to Welford
and adjacent places. "During this time," the diary
proceeds, "the Lord was with me, continually filling
me with joy unspeakable, with confidence unbounded.
I felt the Lord loved me a thousand times more than
any creature did, and that He would delight to do me
good." There was one night of peculiar blessedness,
which her labouring words struggle vainly to describe.
"I could never give expression to the amount of my
enjoyment. I thought then, and I think now, it was as
great as any soul out of heaven could bear. It was
heaven below. It was 'fulness of joy in the presence
of God.' It was the perfect approbation of the Most
High. I appeared to enjoy a present exaltation with
the Saviour, and felt as though all heaven could see it:
I could only weep and wonder, and cry, 'Lord, why dost
Thou thus delight to bless me? How can it be?' O,
how humbling is this to a sinner!"

The same rapturous tone pervades the following
letter:—

To the Rev. J. Reacher.

KINETON, *Jan. 22d,* 1855.

"IN reply to your last, I pray that your New-
Year's motto may be mine: 'I have set the Lord always

at
to
per-
s to
butes
tion
y all

to the
Kineton.
ywhere.
me: they
alone in
happiness
nd things
is so happy

here; but I
acknowledge
with as much
d to me only:
not fe

mind it more than I do the blowing of the wind. If God be for me, who can be against me? With the full approbation of God, I can face men or devils.

"I think now I have said enough about myself; but I cannot say enough about the goodness of God. I believe that many blessings I have received during the last two months, have been in answer to the prayers of my friends. Now, I wish you to praise the Lord with me. I know you will do so.

"We have about a dozen new members here : some three or four have found peace. There is a revival at Thame. You must look up, and not despond. 'Ye have not yet resisted unto blood, striving against sin.' Remember, you told me one day, we should be rewarded according to our *labour*, not our *success*. Still you will see fruit, souls saved, I believe.

"Your affectionate sister,

"ELIZABETH."

For three or four months this state of elevated enjoyment continued. The loss of earthly friends seems to have led her to turn the full tide of her heart's love upon God. And most faithfully did He supply the places of those He had taken. Bereft though she was, she felt no "aching void;" for God was with her, and in His presence was "fulness of joy." Her mother's recent removal to heaven had made heaven nearer and dearer; it was more frequently in her thoughts; and so vivid were her realizations of its blessedness and glory, that there were times when she seemed almost to pass the veil, and mingle her rejoicing and praise with departed loved ones. Perplexities were again darkening round her earthly path, but they had no power to disturb her strong, calm faith in God. The entries in her diary during this period are few and far between; but, as they are generally retrospective, they give a sufficiently faithful account of the intervening spaces.

Thus on Monday, March 4th, she writes: "I feel quite surprised to find that so many weeks have passed since I wrote here. How much of the goodness and love of God have I experienced since Jan. 22d! Had I written daily, my theme must have been the goodness of God. Never has my bliss been more full: my cup of joy has been full to the brim. Often I know not what to do for the sense of God's love to me that I realize. Both when in the house of God, and when at home, I am abundantly blessed. *The Lord delights to bless.* O, what a God is mine! I feel that God perfectly satisfies all the wants of my soul. He seems to fill me, so that I want no other good. The attributes of God have afforded me much delightful meditation the last few weeks. God is love, and He is my all in all!

"I shall always look back with great delight to the days spent alone in these 'Ebenezer rooms' at Kineton, I cannot conceive that I can ever be happier anywhere. People wonder greatly that I can be happy alone: they do not know the secret of finding happiness alone in God; and the reason why so many miss of happiness is, because they seek it in the creature, and things terrestrial. I believe no person in Kineton is so happy as myself.

"My way seems very much obscured here; but I rely on the promise, 'In all thy ways acknowledge Him, and He shall direct thy steps,' with as much simplicity as if it were made to me, and to me only: and *I know I shall be directed.* I cannot fear or be

T 3

uneasy in the least. I seem so surrounded and filled with God, that I could not fear. I have such a sense not only of His presence, but of His unchangeableness, that He will always be the same God. Glory for ever be to the Father, glory to the Son, and glory to the Holy Spirit! Lord, keep me ever near Thy side, and fill me with Thy love.

"I have been led to pray much for my brothers lately. I feel such an ardent longing for their conversion, a longing that cannot be satisfied until the glorious event takes place. I believe God will soon grant me the desire of my heart.

"March 21st.—' Goodness and mercy' have followed me 'all the days of my life;' and 'goodness and mercy *shall* follow me all the' remaining 'days of my life; and I will dwell in the house of the Lord for ever.'

"I have been reading over all that I have written by way of journal since August last; and, O, the abundant love of God that I have seen and felt since then! I am ashamed that I have not made to the Lord better returns. It is a deep grief to me that I seem to be doing no good here. Can it be to humble me? The Lord has blessed my own soul so superabundantly, that perhaps, if He had given me souls, I might have been 'exalted above measure.' For a few weeks past I have felt more fearless about confessing the great salvation the Lord has wrought out for me. I wish the members here could be stirred up to seek it, and the Leaders. O that the Lord would use me for this end, if it may be without provoking pride! For the last few weeks I have had a great dread of pride, spiritual pride, because the Lord has so wonderfully blessed me; so beyond all my anticipation or conception.

"May 22d.—During the last two months I have
kept no diary; for which I am sorry. I always find it
profitable to keep in mind the dealings of the Lord, my
own resolutions, &c. Writing down my experience
leads me to self-examination; and that to praise, prayer,
and self-abasement, as the case may be. I am conscious
of having neglected these duties to some extent, and I
believe my soul has been in a less prosperous state in
consequence. The Lord has been good to me all the
time, astonishingly good. In private prayer He has
often blessed me much, undeservedly: O, how undeservedly! I have prayed much and earnestly for my
beloved brothers, and wait expectantly for their
conversion. For all God's ministering servants I have
been led to intercede, especially on Saturdays, and
have felt it a sweet privilege. I have had some
especial and encouraging answers to prayers for friends
at a distance, open rewards to secret prayer. I am
truly ashamed before God that I make so little use of
the omnipotent power laid within my reach, the power
of prayer."

It was nearly three years now since her brothers left
their native land; and during the whole of that time
they had ever been upon her heart, ever remembered
in her prayers. Circumstances had conspired of late to
quicken, if possible, her interest and affection. One
brother had been for two years utterly lost to all the
inquiries of his friends; but now, at length, when hope
was expiring, intelligence arrived of his whereabouts
and well-being. As a set-off against this good news,
all her anxieties were awakened by hearing that her
third brother, the last emigrant, had soon after his
landing been seized with the perilous colonial fever.
Would God permit him to die in his sins? It was a

torturing question; but her strong faith in the ultimate
efficacy of so many prayers would not suffer her to
answer it despondingly. These, and other reasons, gave
at this time especial frequency and fervour to her
intercessions for those far-off but beloved wanderers.
Thus she writes, in conclusion of the last-quoted
entry: "I cannot describe what I sometimes feel when
praying for my brothers. My one absorbing desire is,
that they may glorify Jesus, that they may be made
one in Him and with me; that Jesus may be our
Brother, and take delight in us all. O, when shall the
happy time arrive? The Lord will do it in His own
time. Lord, remember Thy promise."

The following letter will explain, in part at least,
the allusion made above, to the "open reward of secret
prayer." It is addressed to her old Class-Leader, at
Welford.

"April 17th, 1855.

"MY DEAR MR. H——,

"THE reception of your kind and welcome epistle
afforded me much pleasure and relief. I was induced
to praise God on your behalf, as sincerely as I had
before offered up prayer.

"Your case was quite a trial and grief to me a time
back, because I felt I could do nothing. It was suggested to my mind, 'You can pray; and prayer moves
the Hand that moves the universe.' I was then encouraged, and saw that I had at my command infinite
resources of good. I entreated the Lord to do with you as
would most promote His glory and your good;—either
to remove your difficulties, or to fill you with His
strength; to increase your faith abundantly; in a word,
to sustain and carry you above your trials, as He had
done with me in my late bereavement. I left the matter

in the Lord's hands, feeling that He could not refuse my request. Lately I have felt easy, occasionally reminding Him of my desires, and knowing that He would grant them.

"You may imagine your letter afforded me fresh cause for rejoicing. May it lead me more than ever to trust in God!

"During the last three months, I have been led to intercede much for my brothers' conversion; I think, in faith. I am very anxious for the end of May to come, that I may know how they received the intelligence of dear mamma's removal. I am almost more anxious about Eden Hughes than about them. I have heard nothing of him; but have resolved that, if prayer to God can keep him out of hell, he shall never enter.

"So it is probable that your aged father has reached the borders of the heavenly Canaan; the dangers, and sorrows, and trials of the wilderness nearly over; the glorious land in view, only the Jordan rolling between. I should think he looks with wishful eyes. And he need not fear the swelling stream, with his Joshua standing in the midst. How delightful is the thought of death!—our entrance into eternal life, into endless glory! May we ever keep it in view, that we may form correct ideas of things seen!"

The views expressed in the foregoing paragraph, on the subject of death, were not the ebullition of transient feeling, but the fixed habit of Miss George's mind. Of this the reader has already had many evidences in the course of this biography. The last grand event was with her the subject of glad and frequent anticipation. She loved to meditate upon it. The thought was her solace in times of grief, and shed an intenser brightness upon days of gladness. Her experience was remarkable

in this respect; for there are many Christians, fully
assured of their preparedness for the great hereafter,
and doubting nothing that when death comes the
sufficient grace will be given, upon whose hearts,
nevertheless, the thought of the parting struggle strikes
chill and sad. That it was otherwise with Miss George,
was not because she saw no beauty and happiness in
this earthly life; she spoke no evil of the lesser lights
because she looked forward to the eclipsing glory : still
less did it result from the apathy of a careless mind, to
which the thought of death is seldom present, and never
realized : but it sprang rather from the near and vivid
distinctness in which she viewed the heavenly state,
and the strength of her affection for Him whose
revealed presence is " the light thereof." Perhaps the
following short extract from a letter written about this
time may also help to account for this feature of her
character. The influence of some one strong book or
person, in the impressible days of childhood, will not
unfrequently give a shape and tone to the sentiments,
which they never after lose.

"Last Friday I was twenty-four years of age. I
sang in my bedroom, 'God of my life, to Thee,' &c.,
and the two next hymns. I do now, indeed, 'bless the
day that I was born.' I exceedingly rejoice that I have
commenced an existence never to terminate. How
delightful is the thought of man's immortality! I
remember Young says,—

'Henceforth 'tis blasphemous to call man mortal.'

Since I read the ' Night Thoughts,' I have ever regarded
this short life as but the preface to my existence. I
can quite realize this. I *feel* that I am immortal. I
suppose that is why I look upon death with such com-

posure, as being simply the entrance into glorious life.
That book had more to do in forming my character than
any I have ever read. It made an impression which
will be 'lasting as eternity.' Let us look forward more,
and contemplate our distant selves."

Close upon these few months of almost unclouded
happiness, there followed a period of conflict and
depression. The general complexion of Miss George's
piety was eminently cheerful. There was nothing morbid
about her mind. The views she took of her relations to
God, as a believer in Jesus, were thoroughly scriptural,
and therefore confident and joyous. Yet she had, as we
have already seen, her seasons of depression. She walked
at times in the Valley of Humiliation. Such was the
character of the period upon which she now entered.
The extracts which follow may give encouragement to
some of the young readers of this Memoir, as showing that
it is " no strange thing " which happens to them when
they are in heaviness through manifold temptations.
It would be presumptuous to profess to explain fully
the phase of experience which these extracts present.
Perhaps long enjoyment was beginning to produce false
security; perhaps, even as she accuses herself, she had
relaxed a little her jealous self-watchfulness and earnest
endeavours to do good; or, it may be that she wrote
bitter things against herself, condemning where God
had not condemned; or, yet again, all this may have
been but another phase of Divine discipline: God may
have been revealing to her her nature's deep corruption
and utter feebleness, in order that, with self-renunciation yet more entire, she might abandon herself to
the merit of the atonement, and the upholding of the
Spirit. That she had not faltered in her whole-hearted
devotion to God, the following passage from a letter

written in the midst of her trouble will sufficiently
prove. After complaining bitterly of her short-comings,
she adds, "I feel that I am in Christ a new creature.
For this I am very thankful. I never feel any rising
of anger, fretfulness, or self-will, that I am aware of.
The Lord's will in everything is mine: therefore I
receive everything as from Him, and can rejoice evermore, and in everything give thanks. I fear lest a
sense of my deficiencies should cause me to forget to
praise God for present attainments."

On June 5th she writes, she had been reading the
"Devotional Remains of Mrs. Cryer," records of the
holiest moments of one of the holiest of women :—" I
think I have never been so humbled in reading anything, never felt myself so far below any one. For
about a week, Satan tempted me powerfully to despair
of ever being as holy and as useful as she was, and to
sit down carelessly. When I attempted to pray, and
to rouse myself, I felt no power to do so. For one or
two days my prayer seemed not to ascend so high as
the ceiling. Often I ceased speaking in the middle of
a petition; it seemed useless. I felt that this must be
from Satan; because I had lately been blessed whenever I prayed, and especially in praying with the
children in opening school. Since I finished Mrs.
Cryer's ' Remains,' I have been reading over my own
diary; and I see and acknowledge, with shame and
tears, that I am *a dreadful backslider*. There was a
time when I lived each day as if my last; when I had
eternity full in view; when I warned sinners as from
the margin of the grave; when my Saviour held constant communion with me, and I felt an abiding witness
that I pleased Him, and was not ashamed to speak of
spiritual things to anybody. But it is not so now. I

am altered. My Saviour is unchangeable : He is just
as willing now as then to impart the same amount of
grace, the same constraining love of sinners. And my
one great desire is, that He will do so. I desire to be
wholly given up to Him, and not to strive to please the
creature; for I feel that no created thing can satisfy
the wants of my soul. I still come daily to the
precious, the all-precious, blood of the Lamb, for cleansing; and I feel that it does cleanse me, a sinner, from
all sin. Last night, at the prayer-meeting, when Mr.
L. was praying for our families, I thought, ' Ah! our
family is scattered and gone. I belong to no family. I
am all alone.' My heavenly Father appeared, and said
sweetly, ' You belong to My family ; you are one with
Us; you are My care and charge.' O! I felt unutterable
sweetness. I saw that my Father still owned me as
His child. And this morning I have felt peculiar
peace and satisfaction in reflecting that I am cast upon
the Fatherhood of God. What a Guardian have I! I
never need fear. O that my whole soul's affections may
be continually yielded up to Him! "

This was a gleam of sunshine; but the darkness soon
gathered again.

" June 22d.—During the last week or two I have
been almost overwhelmed with a sense of my failings
and weaknesses. I think I never lay so utterly in the
dust. I never felt myself to be such an impotent
worm, ' less than the least of all saints,' unworthy to be
called a saint; far below everybody. A week or ten days
ago, a friend, at my own request, very kindly told me
of some faults which she and others had observed, and
which some people fancied were sin, though she did
not. I felt exceedingly obliged to her, and looked upon
her as one of my best friends. But I think, perhaps,

U

Satan took advantage of it, to make me look too much
to myself. I was very, very sorrowful. I seemed to
be too vile to live, and wished I had never been known,
lest I should have dishonoured Christ. I would willingly have flown away. Next day, while reading
some psalms, I was much blessed and comforted. The
Lord assured me of His love. I rejoiced with tears.
But, during this week, I have had to *make myself* pray,
and have neglected many opportunities of speaking for
Christ. I am afraid to speak, lest the people should
think I am taking too much on myself.

"I think of going to Prestwich, to visit my sister,
on Tuesday next. I shrink from going, because I am
so unfaithful; but I renounce myself entirely, and look
to God. I take hold of His strength. He giveth more
grace. Again I come, just as I am, to the blood of
atonement. O my Saviour, sprinkle my soul, and
cleanse, and keep me clean!"

The visit to Prestwich did not, however, take place
till towards the middle of July, when she spent a fortnight with her sister. Of the whole period she writes,
on her return, in a tone of self-rebuke. "I have spent
a fortnight at Prestwich, but was ashamed of myself
all the time. I have lost every shade of confidence in
myself." The cloud has not yet broken: she is still
diffident, struggling, and sad.

From this state of morbid self-reproach and depression
she was only driven by a fresh access of trouble from
without. It had now become impossible that she
should continue longer in Kineton. From an influential
section of the inhabitants, she had from the first en-
countered much opposition in her endeavours to establish
a school, on account of her connexion with Methodism.
This opposition became, at length, so determined in its

spirit, and so dexterous in its methods of attack, that Miss George and her friends were obliged to give way before it. A rival school was opened, supported in part by voluntary subscription, and thus able to receive pupils at a much lower rate than Miss George could compete with. The result was, the gradual withdrawal of almost all her children. After this Midsummer, therefore, she resolved not to re-open school at Kineton. There was some discussion as to her future course; but she, at length, determined to accept the pressing invitation of her sister, at Prestwich, and go to reside with her, until Providence should open to her some other path.

These vexations and perplexities did her spiritual good. They drove her to her old resort in trouble, the Divine mercy-seat; and revived her old spirit of simple child-like trust in God. Again she drank comfort from the promises, and rested in the everlasting arms. Compelled to look less inwardly upon her own defects, and more outwardly on the provisions of Divine grace, she found that the former were best overcome by the maintenance of a steadfast, confiding grasp upon the latter. Her wonted peace returned, and with it occasional ecstasies, as of old, of a "joy unspeakable."

Under date July 26th, she writes: "The way for me to leave Kineton seems clearer than ever it did before. I can trust in God, and believe that all things are working together for my good, though it may be hard to see how. May the Lord's will be done!"

Again, Aug. 16th: "During the last three weeks, I have had little time for writing, or I should certainly have recorded the exceeding great goodness of God to me. I feel that God is a very present help in time of trouble, and that it is blessed to trust in Him.

"Good is the will of the Lord! I am going to Prestwich, from a sense of duty. For how long, or for what purpose, I know not. For a day or two I feared it much, on account of the dangers of a formal religion, together with the bustle and confusion of removal; and I prayed, in an agony, that the Lord would at once take me to Himself, rather than permit me to go to Prestwich, to dishonour Him, or to lose my religion. The Lord comforted me abundantly, by assuring me that He was my Leader, my Protector, and my everlasting, all-sufficient Friend. I was so filled with joy, that I could scarcely feel the trouble at all. All the time I have been packing, my head has been very bad from the confusion and perplexity; but my heart has been rejoicing in God, and glorying in tribulation. One night especially, I rolled about on my bed for hours, unable to sleep for praise. I feel very thankful for this time of trial, because it has been a time of great blessing, as my times of trial always are. I praise God for trials : they carry me nearer to Himself and heaven. O, to be for ever with the Lord! Haste, happy day!"

This entry was written on the day after she had bidden farewell to her friends at Kineton. She had resided there about twelve months, during which time the Lord had showed her many and great troubles, but more and greater mercies.

CHAPTER IX.

LAST DAYS.

" Therefore be ye also ready: for in such an hour as ye think not the Son of Man cometh." (Matt. xxiv. 44.)

Miss George did not proceed directly to Prestwich on leaving Kineton. An interval of some weeks occurred, which she spent in a tour of visits amongst her friends. Most of these were Christians, like-minded with herself; and in converse with them, on the theme of common interest, she found delight and profit. At the same time, she was ever on the alert for opportunities of doing good. She was not one of those who can only labour in a beaten routine. Amidst perpetual change and distraction, she kept her soul steadied to its one purpose; and many were the faithful words which, during these few interrupted weeks, she dropt in the ears of those whom the casualties of travel and social intercourse threw in her way.

Under date, Bidford, Sept. 5th, she thus writes, in hasty retrospect: "I find friends and homes everywhere. At Mr. and Mrs. G.'s, of L——, I greatly enjoyed myself. Mr. G.'s prayers, and deeply-spiritual conversation, were delightful. At R. H—— I found a converted dress-maker in one of the bedrooms, at work: we had some profitable conversation and prayer. In the house I found a volume of Edmondson's ' Sermons on the Holy Spirit.' I read four of them with ex-

ceeding delight and profit. I had clearer views than
ever of the presence, personality, and work of the Spirit.
I rejoiced with joy unspeakable in what He had done
for me. I was filled with joy, and love, and praise. I
seemed to be 'strong in the Lord, and the power of His
might;' yet, that very afternoon, I had such a proof of
my weakness and liability to err, as humbled me in the
dust, and filled me with penitential tears. O that, by
continual watchfulness and recollectedness, I may be
kept from sin! What should we do, if we might plunge
but once in the purple flood! What a mercy that the
fountain is ever open!

" Last night I met with a young lady, undecided. I
walked with her, and earnestly pressed her at once to
give up her idols, and yield herself to God. Lord,
enable her to do so!

" I find my own soul daily rejoicing in God. I am
yielding myself up to the Holy Spirit to be just as holy
as He can make me, just as holy as God would have me,
just as holy as Jesus designed I should be. O, may I
never faint, but be a co-worker with God; or the work
will never be accomplished.

" The Bidford people have not seen me since my
beloved mamma was taken to glory. They wonder at
my composure in my present singular circumstances,
and at my manner of bearing mamma's removal; but
they do not know the grace of God. The week she
was removed was one of the most glorious and triumphant I ever enjoyed. I was full of tears; but they
were all tears of love, and wonder, and joy. I have
never shed a tear from a sense of loneliness : I never am
alone. I am not removed from mamma, nor is she from
me; we are together with and in Christ. I now know
what Mrs. Fletcher means, when she writes of union

with her husband after his departure from earth, though it was a mystery to me when I read the book. When mamma was taken, the Lord Jesus seemed to be removing her from me with one hand, and drawing me to Himself with the other. O the goodness of God! I never can sufficiently praise Him!"

One of the places she visited during this period was Welford, and it was with mingled emotions that she found herself again in the midst of scenes which such various recollections hallowed and endeared. It was pleasant to renew intercourse with those who had once travelled side by side with her in the path to heaven, and who still maintained their steadfastness. It was pleasant to talk of those who had since finished their course, and to hear what last words of trust and hope they had left as their dying memorials. But the pleasure was chequered with sadness : for some there were who had "died, and made no sign;" and others, for whom she had often wept and prayed, were still loiterers in the perilous border-land, or, belying the promise they once gave, had settled down in apathy and sin. Of her interview with one inveterate backslider, to whom she has more than once before made reference in her diary, she thus writes in her deep sympathy and love : " I could do little more than weep. He was greatly affected, sobbed, and wept. O that he were safe in heaven! I cannot give him up. Lord, have mercy on him! I feel that I would willingly die to save him." Her old habits seemed to revive with fresh force on this return to old scenes, and much of the time of her stay in Welford was spent in such ministrations to the sick, poor, and dying, as she had formerly delighted in.

To her dear friend, Mrs. Laugher, she thus writes of this visit : "Sunday was a strange day. I was filled

with exceeding joy and deep grief alternately, as I
heard of some souls holding fast their religion, and of
others drawing back unto perdition. I cannot describe
my feelings : they reminded me of olden times. I saw
a young man very ill, but in a hopeful state. But there
is a stern infidel, almost at the point of death, and at
present unmoved; the same man I have named to you
as holding the same views of the Sabbath with M——.
There has been another of those singularly-awful cases
here, for which Welford seems remarkable. A very
wicked woman, whom I have often faithfully warned,
and of whose blood I am clear, died in terrible despair.
People say that she frightened everybody from the house.
For many days she lay declaring that her room was full
of devils, and not allowing any one to pray with her;
saying, that prayer would only increase her torment, as
she was past hope. The neighbours sent for the Minister,
who was seized with alarm, and told them not to send
for him again till she was changed and composed.
Her friends literally left her to die alone; and she would
have done so, had it not been for a good woman, who
dared to go and stay with her till her wretched spirit
plunged into deeper woe. Before she died, she told her
sons and friends that, if any of them followed her to the
grave, she would come and torment them to their lives'
end! They were so alarmed that nobody dared follow
her. People say it was a strange sight to see her body
carried to the grave without any mourners. This is
how Welford sinners die, unless saved by the prayer of
faith.

"I feel as if I should like to live here again, if it were
the Lord's will; and everybody invites me : but I do
not think there are sufficient children of the class I
want for a school. I am going to stay another week.

I want to visit the people, lest I should not see them again, until it would be too late to do them any good."

The case of the dying infidel, mentioned above, lay so heavily on her heart, that, on being refused admission to his bedside, she went home and wrote him forthwith a short, plain, earnest letter. The rough draft of a portion of this letter has been found among her papers. It is only remarkable for the characteristic earnestness with which, foregoing for the present all argument on merely speculative points, she wisely seeks to smite straight home upon his conscience and heart. It runs as follows: —

"I FEEL greatly concerned for the salvation of your soul, and cannot help writing you a line upon the subject.

"From your conversation with me in past times, and from the fact that you do not wish to see any Christian friend now, I am led to conclude that you are still a stranger to the great change every sinner must experience before he can enter heaven. 'Except a man be born again, he cannot see the kingdom of God.' This is God's word; and if you deny it now, the time is fast coming when it will judge you. I hope you will ponder it well; and may the Holy Spirit of God give you light! Also the solemn words, 'Except ye repent, ye shall all likewise perish.' It will be in vain for you to try to satisfy your conscience with the plea that you have never sinned, that you have wronged nobody, and therefore have no need to repent. 'All have sinned, and come short of the glory of God.' You once told me that your father, who had been a constant Sabbath-breaker, died as peacefully as a lamb. Many sinners do so, who die in the dark; but I do not think *you* will do so. Already I believe you feel some slight misgiving that all is not right,

that your heart has not been made holy, that you have
not obtained a preparation to stand boldly before that
God whose Bible and day you have habitually slighted.
Have you a sufficient excuse to make? or will you be
speechless? I hope you will pardon my earnestness:
I feel constrained to write as I do. I shall continue to
pray for you, that God may give you light to see
yourself a *lost, hell-deserving sinner*. Without this you
will not flee to Christ to save you.

"I am your sincere friend,

"E. A. GEORGE."

Miss George reached Prestwich on Monday, the 10th
of September. After noting the fact in her diary, she
adds, "I am happy, trusting in God. May He direct
all my steps! Lord, make me useful."

The first five weeks after her arrival she suffered
much from violent pains in the head, together with
general bodily debility. Change of scene and circumstances also broke up her former habits of Christian
labour, and she shrank diffidently from saying and doing
much that she had it in her heart to say and do, lest
her zeal should be mistaken for obtrusiveness. Even
at Kineton she had never felt so free to yield to the
impulses of her earnest, devoted spirit, as at Welford,
amongst its poor unsophisticated villagers, whose faces
had been familiar to her from childhood. But at Prestwich it was worse in this respect than at Kineton. The
place was populous and strange; and the people,
perhaps, little disposed to approve of any deviation
from the conventional proprieties of Christian activity.
So for awhile she retired within herself; and, observing
much, lamenting much, panting to break through her
diffidence, she still led a more inactive life than she had

done since her first consecration of herself to God. Such a state of things was not, as may be imagined, very conducive to her happiness; and the tone of self-dissatisfaction which pervades the few disclosures she has made of her inner life during this period may thus be readily accounted for.

In the midst of all, however, she can write thus to a friend: "Through grace, I have power *just now* to lay my all—body, soul, time, talents—upon the altar that sanctifieth the gift, a complete sacrifice. O that I may ever keep it there! and, while there, it must be holy. I feel that I have peculiar temptations; but I determine to rely on God for strength. I am His, entirely His." And in the short scattered diaries of this period are sentiments to the same effect.

The anniversary of her mother's death has now come round, and occasions retrospections sad yet grateful. Thus she writes:—

"Dec. 2d.—This is a day never, never to be forgotten by me, nor indeed this season of the year. It is exactly twelve months since my beloved mamma passed into the skies. Every day of the past week has seemed sacred, this day especially; and will not the next three? My eyes fill with tears as I look back on the past, recall each trifling event, and think of the hours spent in that sacred chamber, gazing on the remains of her whose love I had known so long. I cannot forget the solemn joy I then experienced; the infinite kindness of my Saviour. O, how I was enabled to glory in tribulations, to cast myself entirely on the Fatherhood of God, to feel that I was given into His hands, that I was doubly His! My Jesus never permitted me to feel for a moment that I was alone, or left to chance.

"The Lord has graciously cared for my wants one year;

and shall I not trust Him for the future? I am very,
very unworthy of His love and watchful care; but I
hope, through grace, to be more devoted. This seems
a very proper occasion to renew my entire surrender of
myself to God. On this sacred day, Dec. 2d, by God's
grace, I offer my whole self afresh to Him, resolve to be
more interested and earnest in His service, and to be
more *holy*. O my Jesus, I want to enjoy constant
communion with Thyself! O, be my support in every
trying hour! Direct all my steps; teach me Thy will.
Thou knowest I have no will of my own. O, lead me
and guide me continually. May Thy glory lie very
near my heart! Keep me from sin; help me to deny
myself daily, and follow Thee fully. Amen."

Not in word only did she thus consecrate herself
anew to God. From this date, the tone of self-reproach
disappears from her diary; and to the end, almost
without exception, she writes of close communion, calm
trust, settled peace.

Miss George had come to Prestwich in uncertainty as
to her future path. She never contemplated fixing her
residence there, but had sought a temporary shelter
under her sister's roof, until circumstances opened to
her an opportunity of providing a home and maintenance
for herself. Meanwhile, her present position sometimes
pressed heavily on her spirits. It was not that her
friends failed at all in kindness : the place of her sojourn
was made to her, in the fullest sense, a home; and
thus the dear relatives who had received her wished
that she should regard it; but her active spirit would,
for all that, now and then chafe at the comparative in-
dolence and dependence which circumstances had forced
upon her. Thus, one day she writes: "Yesterday I
felt sorrowful and heavy. I began to wonder whether

I was in my right place; whether I was wanted;
whether I was not in the way. I could not help having
a good cry about it, in private." These, however, were
morbid and exceptional moods : generally, she waited
calmly, reliant upon Providence for the moving of the
cloud.

At length, however, the much-desired opportunity of
changing her position presented itself, bearing upon it
many marks of providential appointment. A lady
resident in the town, being compelled by circumstances
to give up a school which she had for some time
successfully conducted, offered to make over her entire
connexion and influence to Miss George. The proposal,
after some hesitation, was accepted. Whilst these nego-
tiations were going on, and, subsequently, while can-
vassing for pupils, Miss George was able to maintain
her usual calm trustfulness in God. The time of trial,
indeed, she ever found a time of profit; for it was then
she clung most lovingly to the guiding Hand and
upholding promise. After noticing the matter in her
diary, she writes : " I never left anything more entirely
in the hands of the Lord, or felt more calmness and
easiness about anything. It seemed, and seems now, to
be the Lord's doing altogether. My mind has been kept
in perfect peace. I have had no will of my own. I only
wish to do God's will. I feel that my ways please Him.
I yield my whole self to Him without any reserve."

To a friend she writes : " This school has been
given to me quite as unexpectedly as the Kineton one
was taken from me; and I am no happier over this
matter than I was over that. Then I rejoiced in the
very difficulty, through the grace of God, and delighted
to be left with only the promise to depend upon. Now
I have the utmost satisfaction in every step that I have

x

taken. I feel, daily, that I should do just the same, if Jesus were here, as He used to be with Martha and Mary, and I could consult Him on every little particular. He knoweth the way that I take, and approves it. I shall do my best; and then, if the affair succeed, it will be for my good; and if it result in disappointment, that will be best for me."

The following extracts are from a letter to Mr. Reacher, touching upon these and other matters:—

"It has been a matter of great thankfulness to me to know that *God* does not lead us into temptation, and that, *in stations where He has placed us*, He will not permit any temptation to happen to us, but such as He will give us grace to overcome. When I came here, a new temptation assailed me. For some time I was daunted: then I thought, 'I have not come here of my own accord, but by the direction of the Lord; and He has promised that I shall not be tempted above that I am able, but that with the temptation He will make a way to escape. It is, therefore, my privilege to rise superior to everything, and to be *holy*.' While I thus reasoned, and claimed the promises, the snare was broken, and I was more than conqueror.

"I do delight in the promises, as I suppose every Christian does. I have taken them as my heritage for ever. They are a precious bunch of keys, by means of which I can gain every blessing on earth or in heaven. (Don't smile at my homely comparison.) The last fortnight I have been making use of two,—those which unlock the treasuries of wisdom and Divine direction. (Prov. iii. 6, and James i. 5.) They have not failed; for I have been accustomed to the turning of them in bygone days."

After informing her correspondent of her new undertaking, and the circumstances which had led to it, she proceeds :

"I had no will of my own ; and knew that, if it were really the thing that God had designed for me, I should be helped through every difficulty: and so I have been. How completely are we freed from anxiety, when seeking only to know and do the will of God !

"I have been endeavouring to know more of Jesus; to walk more closely with Him; to know that His smile of approbation rests on all I do. You ask what I am reading. Very little. I manage to look into my Bible three times a day : besides that, I have only M'Cheyne in hand."

As coinciding in sentiment with the above letter, and showing that, through many of these winter weeks, the same happy state lasted, the following passages are extracted from her diary :—

"Sunday night, Dec. 30th.—The few last weeks I feel that my soul has been cleaving more closely to Jesus. My peace and joy have indeed abounded. I have held sweeter communion with Jesus, have realized His smile and approbation. Words cannot express the adoration my soul often feels for Him. I do indeed feel that He is the Beloved of my soul. My earnest longing is to be conformed to His will in all things. My faith in the sanctifying blood is clear and strong. About a week ago, when holding sweet communion with the Saviour, and groaning for His likeness, I felt that I was covered with the spotless robe of His righteousness; that I was meet, through His blood, for eternal glory ; that I was as beloved on earth as I should be if in heaven. A repetition of this feeling I have had at times since. 'If God be for us, who can be against us?' I feel that with Jesus I could be happy any-

x 2

where, under any circumstances.   May the Lord make me faithful!

"Jan. 20th, 1856.—' Bless the Lord, O my soul; and all that is within me, bless His holy name!' 'Goodness and mercy have followed'—will follow—' me all the days of my life.'   I have been reading over what I wrote Dec. 30th, and find I have nothing more to say. Jesus is precious, the well-beloved of my soul, my All in all.   I feel that I want no other good.   I have, daily, great delight in private prayer, and in reading God's holy word.   O that I may daily become more like Christ!

"At the beginning of this year I gave myself up afresh to God, and I daily offer my whole self as a living sacrifice."

Miss George opened her new school on Wednesday, Jan. 23d.   The pupils were few in number at first, but there was the prospect of more as the year advanced. And, at all events, she was glad to be doing something for herself again.   With the resumption of school-duties, her activity in other wonted departments of labour seemed to be quickened.   The following Sunday saw her installed as Teacher of the senior female class in the Sabbath-school, a class consisting of between twenty and twenty-five grown girls.   The godless, uncared-for condition of the poor in this populous district also began to awaken her sympathies.   She sought out, according to her former wont, some of the most wretched cases, and looked forward to yet more extensive operations in this line.   It was now highly probable that Prestwich would be her future home, and this fact caused her to regard it with new eyes.   How she began to scheme, and resolve, and hope, the following extract from her diary will show :—

" Feb. 18th.—I have been much ashamed of the little that is being done here for perishing sinners. I have realized the fact, that hundreds of Prestwich people are living and dying in heathenish darkness, and we are sitting still and doing nothing. I have prayed for these people; and then the thought has followed me, 'God works by means; He allows His creatures to be co-workers with Himself: what can *you* do?' Then, with a sad and heavy heart, I fell on my knees, and entreated the Lord to show me what I could do; for I felt that I should lose my own religion if I did not put forth all the efforts I could to save some. The Lord graciously heard me, and showed me that I had influence here, and that I might do and get others to do a great deal. I saw that, by using my influence and aid, I might,

" 1. Get a system of general Tract-distribution set on foot.

" 2. That I might myself read the Scriptures in cottages, and explain them to the family, and perhaps get others to do the same.

" 3. That in the Sabbath-school, by conferring with the Superintendent and principal Teachers, I might, (1.) Get the ' Teachers' Magazine' circulated; (2.) Introduce the ' Sunday-School Union Lessons,' or those published by our Book-Committee in the ' Reporter;' (3.) Get the children throughout the school to learn texts of Scripture from the Lesson of the day; (4.) Introduce a system of rewards and punishments, the former chiefly in order to attract and encourage the children, and please the parents; (5.) Have the ' Child's own Hymn-Book' used in the school, and taught in the junior classes; (6.) Persuade the leader of the singing to introduce little pieces, as well as hymns, for

x 3

the children to sing; (7.) Have little books, and the
'Band of Hope,' given as rewards.

"All these things may, I think, be accomplished in
time, if I propose them to the necessary parties in an
unassuming way, so as that they shall forget or not
notice who made the first proposition. I thought also,
while on my knees, that I would present a copy of
'Rules for Holy Living' to each member, through the
Leaders, privately; and try to get the friends of my
day-pupils to take the 'British Messenger,' and to secure
subscribers for the 'British Workman' and the 'Band
of Hope.' O that these things may be done, and that
the blessing of the Most High may rest upon them!

"Feb. 19th.—I have only named two of the above
matters yet, and they are well received to some extent,
—the Tract movement and cottage-visiting. A Tract
Committee has been formed, and will meet here to-night
to make arrangements. I have visited, several times, a
blind, ignorant, old man, who has died; and an enlightened one, who still lives. O that I may live to purpose!
I want to do all I do with a single eye to God's glory."

Thus she proposed, but God disposed otherwise.
This is the last entry in her diary. With these hopes
and plans of future usefulness, abruptly yet fitly closes
this faithful record of her spiritual history. Her purposes were not permitted to ripen and bear fruit; but
did not He, who saw what was in her heart, accept the
will for the act; the desire, for the effort to realize it?
When we speak of premature death, we must remember
that God notes and approves what the heart purposes
to do, as well as what the hand has actually done.

A few days from the date of the above extract, Miss
George heard of the dangerous illness of her oldest
sister, the wife of the Rev. E. Thorley, then resident at

Thame, in Oxfordshire. With the tidings came an urgent request that she would, if possible, come in person to minister comfort and help. There were difficulties in the way; her new school might suffer by so early a suspension: but the claims of affection were paramount; and, calmly leaving consequences with Him whose faithfulness had never failed her, she went. The illness proved unto death. It was, indeed, a scene of surpassing sorrow to which she had been summoned. Three times, in the course of as many years, had death visited the domestic circle of her brother-in-law; and now the dart hung quivering over his wife and one remaining child, and threatened to leave him utterly desolate. The child recovered; but it was soon evident that the mother's days were numbered. It was, however, a Christian's deathbed; and trust, and peace, and holy triumph were there. To Miss George, with her habitual views of death and the great beyond, the scene was one of mingled sorrow and rejoicing. She sorrowed in sympathy with the bereaved husband, and in the natural pain of wounded sisterly affection; but her vivid realizations of the happiness of the dead in Christ, and the strong simplicity of her trust in God, inspired, as formerly, on the occasion of her mother's departure, such abounding consolations, as often to turn the voice of lamentation into the song of praise. The following extracts from letters which she wrote at this time are worthy of preservation, both as containing some record of this glorious exit, and as showing the emotions with which she regarded it :—

To Mrs. Laugher.

" AT about ten minutes to eleven on Saturday night she ceased to breathe; for it was nothing more,—

there was not the faintest struggle or groan: she sweetly
fell asleep. I shall ever be thankful that I was permitted to be present, to see another saint enter heaven.
Is not heaven becoming more and more *homely* ? Joseph
Benson said, he had 'more friends in heaven than on
earth.' I cannot, perhaps, say that; but I have a great
many there. O that I may some day join them, to be
with Jesus!

"We have eleven or twelve pages of precious sentiments, uttered by my departing sister. I cannot write
many now. One was, 'Happy? Of course I am
happy! I am always happy! For me to live is Christ,
and to die is gain!'

> 'The arms of love that compass me,
>   Would all mankind embrace.'

She very often said,

> 'My God, I am Thine, what a comfort divine,
>   What a blessing to know that my Jesus is mine!
>   In the heavenly Lamb thrice happy I am;'

and oftener still, 'Eye hath not seen, nor ear heard,
neither have entered into the heart of man, the things
which God hath prepared for them that love Him.'
This she said with much emphasis and heavenly smiles.
Once she said, 'Sanctified throughout body, soul, and
spirit! Glory! glory! glory! I know that I shall
soon rise to glorious immortality.' Again, 'I shall
soon drink of that wine, that blessed wine, in the kingdom of my Father.' One remarked, 'The Lord is very
good still.' 'O, yes! my name is graven on His hands.'
She said she was one of the happiest creatures living;
that she should soon be with mamma and her own
four children; and 'I shall see Jesus, and be with
Him.'"

To her Sister Louisa.

"DEAR sister's happy spirit is released. It is no longer an inhabitant of its clay tenement. 'Absent from the body, present with the Lord.' We all continued watching, and silently lifting up our hearts to God in praise and prayer, till the change occurred. She did not speak or stir; only breathed short, till she breathed no more. The unbounded goodness of God prevented a single groan, or gasp, or death-struggle. O, how could we praise Him enough! We all knelt down, and offered silent thanks. Then Mr. U. and Edwin, amidst sobs and tears, praised God aloud, and implored blessings on us and ours. We have left her. She looks sweetly calm and placid.

"We were seven; but now the number is broken into by death, and we are only six. Which of us shall go next? O that I may be ready,—as ready as my now-glorified sister! O that my end may be as calm and peaceful as hers! Her happy, loving spirit is now freed from all entanglement: she can love as she would, and adore as she would. She is with Jesus, made like Him, a partaker of His nature, of His holiness. She is singing the new song that she learned on earth, which the Lord's redeemed alone can sing. Christ's spotless righteousness is her white robe, and God Himself beholds her faultless."

The following rhymes have also been found, scribbled hastily, partly in ink and partly in pencil, on a fragment of paper, and evidently of this date. It was her last attempt at verse-making, a mode of giving utterance to her emotions which from a child she had been fond of. The lines claim little poetic merit; but are remark-

able as showing of what at this period her heart was
full, and as written so short a time before her own
translation into the presence of God.

> "Fulness of joy! what pen can describe it,
>   Of joy in the presence of God and the Lamb!
> Fulness of joy! what heart can conceive it,
>   Or put into numbers the glorious theme!

> "Fulness of joy! our thoughts still dwell on it,
>   Nor can we confine them to earth and its gloom;
> We'll let them ascend, and behold the departed
>   Triumphing over both death and the tomb.

> "The warfare is past; the struggle is o'er;
>   And sickness and sorrow shall trouble no more;
> The soul, disentangled from earth's weary clod,
>   Shall triumph for aye in the presence of God!"

CHAPTER X.

DEATH.

" Blessed are the dead which die in the Lord from henceforth : Yea, saith the Spirit, that they may rest from their labours; and their works do follow them." (Rev. xiv. 13.)

MISS GEORGE returned from Thame on Monday the 17th of March, and immediately resumed her school-duties. From the very commencement of the week she showed signs of indisposition, yet not so as to awaken alarm in herself or others. Rapidly, however, she grew worse; an internal fever was drying up the springs of life. On the Friday, Good Friday, she used her pen for the last time, before hand and brain both lost their cunning. It was to write a few lines in the album of a friend. They are quoted below, and will show with what thoughts of God she began to tread that dark valley, where failing heart and flesh most need to find their "portion" in Him.* On the Sunday the symptoms

---

* *" Thoughts on the Attributes of God.*—If God is a God of infinite *love,* then I, as His child, may rest assured that all His dealings with me are the result of that love. He is a Father, and cannot do harm to His child; He pities, He cares for, and He will surely provide for me in the best way. If He has occasion to correct, love holds the rod, and numbers the stripes. He afflicts not willingly. If the bitter draught be needed, His own loving hand prepares the cup.

" If God is infinite in *wisdom,* He knows precisely what is best for His child : He sees to the end, and knows why, and when, and how, to appoint whatever His love designs. I may safely trust Him.

" If God is infinite in *power,* I may rest assured that, if I trust in Him, I shall never want : all hands and hearts are under His control ; the earth is His,—the gold, the silver, the cattle on a

became so much worse that a medical man was called in, who at once pronounced the disease to be typhus fever. This alarming announcement was made audibly in Miss George's presence, but excited not the slightest perturbation. When some one present remarked that she would now "have to become worse before she became better," she replied with a smile, uplifting her hot unmoistened hands, "Then these hands and arms will have almost to dry up and burn away with fever!" During the next two or three days she maintained the same unruffled composure. On one occasion her bereaved brother-in-law, who had returned with her to Prestwich, said to her, "Well, my dear girl, it is easy in health to write respecting the attributes of God; but do you now in the furnace of affliction feel that they are all at work for you?" She smiled, and spoke in strong, unhesitating terms of her faith in God. He then asked her, how she felt with regard to the issue of the illness; whether she were willing that it should terminate in death, if her heavenly Father saw fit. She replied, "I do not think it will be unto death. I have no presentiment of the kind; I believe I shall recover: but if I do not, do you think *that* will trouble me? Only one thing would trouble me," she continued. Being asked what that might be, she said with strong emotion, "That I have done so little for Jesus, when I might have done so much." An expression of fear was dropped

---

thousand hills. He has only to will it, and I shall want no good thing. In the darkest day I need not fear.— *God is mine.*

"If God is infinite in *holiness*, not one of His promises shall ever fail. He will see that sin and injustice do not go unpunished; that all good is rewarded, and that with the utmost faithfulness. Am I oppressed and persecuted? I may commit myself to Him in all meekness; for whoso toucheth me, toucheth the apple of His eye."

lest her school-project in Prestwich should be seriously injured by her illness, even supposing she recovered. To this she promptly rejoined,

> " ' Make you His service your delight,
> Your wants shall be His care.'

I went to Thame delighting myself in the service of God, and I have no fear as to the result. Should the present door close, another will be opened."

It is not always that a holy and devoted life is "crowned" by an end of unmingled triumph. Without directly deserting His servants in the last struggle, God does sometimes withhold those special manifestations of His presence which give rejoicing in that hour of especial need; or He suffers unwonted license to the powers of darkness; or the soul itself will in some cases look so exclusively to the more awful attributes of Him into whose presence it is entering, as to shrink, and tremble, and cry, like the Prophet in the glory-filled temple, ' Woe is me!' Inscrutable are these withholdings and permitted conflicts, the last mysteries through which the Christian has to walk by faith, before he quits the dark path of trial to see light in the light of God. Some such discipline her heavenly Father saw fit in His wisdom to appoint to Miss George in the closing scene of her pilgrimage. On the Wednesday her mind dwelt much on the holiness of God; and at length so overpowering became her conceptions of it, that trouble and darkness fell upon her. In this strong and insufferable light she saw short-comings in her best works, the mingling of evil with her purest intentions. The standard of Divine requirement appeared to her loftier than ever, and her own defectiveness overwhelmed her. It was evident that these thoughts had become so

Y

absorbing for the moment as to distract her mind from
dying man's one hope,—the all-atoning, all-cleansing
blood. Her faith, usually so strong in its grasp upon the
Rock of Refuge, was beginning to waver in these great
floods. And then came terrible paroxysms of delirium,
lasting, with little intermission, until a day or two
before her death. During her delirium, the idea which
seized and kept possession of her mind was, the personal presence of the Spirit of Evil. She spoke of little
else. She would tell those around her, that he was in
the room, that he threatened her with fiendish threats,
that she was grappling with him in dreadful conflict.
Even in her rational intervals, still the same consciousness of powerful and incessant temptation distressed her
beyond measure. So morbidly was she now driven to
view all her conduct, that one day, questioning her
motives, she took from her finger the signet-ring which
she wore in memory of her brother; and the next
morning, still sorely harassed, she laid aside her dead
mamma's "keeper," saying, as she did so, " I never
thought there was any harm in wearing that." At
another time, after talking deliriously for a long while
under the influence of the one tyrannizing idea, she
called a relation to her bedside, and said, with unspeakable solemnity,—" I have one thing to tell you. During
this conflict I have been in the eternal world. I have
seen the abode of lost spirits; and the metaphors used
by the Saviour in describing the torments of that place
are not merely metaphors: each one represents a dreadful reality; there is the worm conscience that dieth not,
the smoke of the torment that ascendeth for ever and
ever, the lake that burneth with fire and brimstone, the
weeping and wailing and gnashing of teeth, and the
calling for water to cool the parched tongue."

At length, on Friday, April 4th, the day but one before her death, the delirium subsided somewhat, and her soul recovered its composure. She could look now over the swelling flood to the brighter shore beyond. Other and happier thoughts occupied her mind in its occasional wanderings. She sang of heaven frequently, and with fervour. The child's hymn,

> " There is a better world, they say,
> O, so bright! "

was often on her lips. Then, with eye dreamily fixed, as if the soul looked through it to visions which others saw not, she would repeat, again and again, " O, so bright! So bright! Beautifully bright!" The next day the same mood continued. After all, the end was " peace." There were occasional attacks from the evil one; but they were few and far between, and strength was given her to withstand and triumph. Her mind was at rest; so much so, that she was able to converse thoughtfully about certain domestic matters which interested her. During the day, she called for the servant, who had been with the family at Welford, and requested her to read a psalm, selecting the 103d. Afterwards, it being necessary to disturb her a good deal, she sang, with clear voice, the verse,—

> " Once they were mourners here below,
> And pour'd out cries and tears :
> They wrestled hard, as we do now,
> With sins, and doubts, and fears."

In the evening she spoke of the severe struggles she had passed through; and referred to a remarkable scene which occurred during the last hours of the Rev. John Smith, and is recorded in his biography, as a parallel case to her own. She would fain have had the passage forthwith read aloud; but, the medical man objecting on the ground of her weakness, she contented herself with securing a promise from her friends who were present, that they would read it for themselves. During the night she talked much with the nurse who sat up with her; gave her the history of her mother's death; spoke, as dying saints often do, of glimpses vouchsafed her into glories beyond the veil, and of anticipatory greetings from departed loved ones; and with strong, calm assurance, looked forward to her own speedy reunion with them. About two in the morning, all enfeebled as she was, she turned round in the bed, and, fixing her eyes upon one corner of the room, exclaimed many times, "Yes, mamma, I am coming! Yes, mamma, I am coming!" She then slept till six in the morning, was at that hour aroused of necessity, for a moment, and then slept again until about five minutes before twelve, when, without sigh or struggle, the spirit took its flight.

She was within three weeks of completing her twenty-fifth year. Her remains lie in the Wesleyan Cemetery, Cheetham-Hill. On her tombstone is inscribed, "The memory of the just is blessed."

She wished to die young, for heaven had long been to her more "homely" than earth; and God gave her her wish. Her life was short, if we reckon it by days or months; long, if degrees of progress and deeds of service be our measure.

CONCLUSION.

THE REV. JOHN REACHER, who knew Miss George well for some years, has kindly furnished the following remarks upon her character:—

"My acquaintance with the late Miss George dates from September, 1852, soon after my appointment to the Evesham Circuit; and during the remainder of her life I enjoyed her friendship and regular correspondence. As requested, I will here set down a few things relative to her religious character, as they occur to myself.

"Her piety was *distinct and elevated.* She was able to speak in the language of the primitive Christians: 'I know that I am of God.' No ambiguity pertained to her experience: all was clear. At the outset, she obtained the witness of the Spirit to her adoption, and then she continued to 'walk in the light of the Lord.' For some time, however, her views of Christian privilege were contracted, and she did not see that her 'calling's glorious hope' was 'inward holiness.' But when she was more perfectly instructed in the way of the Lord, and when she had ascertained from the written word that the Holy Ghost was willing to cleanse her from all iniquity, with her characteristic ardour and constancy she pursued the blessing. And what she sought, she found; what she found, she kept. She not only *sighted* the good land, 'the land of uprightness,' but she followed the leadership of the good Spirit until He brought her into it, and caused her to dwell there. Faithful to His promise, the Lord sprinkled His believing one with clean water, and she

Y 3

was clean; from all her filthiness, and from all her idols
He cleansed her. Nor that only: when the eternal
God had thrust out the enemy from before her, He also
filled her with holy, happy love. Henceforward her
progress was clearly and strongly marked. Her experience deepened, her communion with the blessed Spirit
grew more intimate; and they who saw her took
knowledge of her that she had been with Jesus.

"In Miss George, religion appeared in its *loveliness*.
She exhibited 'the beauties of holiness.' Though raised
by natural endowments and culture above most of those
with whom she came in contact, she assumed no superiority. The villagers were attracted by her kindness.
Aged people reckoned on her visits with joy; for the
winsome graces of humility and love adorned her. Her
determination to be a thorough Christian laid her open
to unkind remarks: but some of her friends she won by
her loveableness and calm decision; while others could
not but feel that *she*, at any rate, was happy without
worldly pleasures, and amiable, notwithstanding her
'pious strictness.' Elizabeth was no borderer. She
could not bring down piety to the standard of the
world. Against all worldly conformities she held
strong and scriptural opinions, and was free to express
them; but even the half-hearted confessed that her
happiness and her consistency commended religious
thoroughness. In an eminent degree she adorned the
doctrine.

"All who knew Miss George remember *her Christian
activity*. As a visiter of the sick, she was unwearied.
All the sick of the village, to whom she could gain
access, found in her a patient and faithful friend.
Entertaining large views of the length and breadth of
the love of Christ, she had hope for the worst, for aged

sinners, for all ; and this feeling was of eminent use to
her when she had to deal with the ungodly. Even
when persons had repented and sinned, then repented
and sinned again, and had worn out the patience of
others, Miss George still plied them with the warnings
of the word, and with the overtures of free grace, and
still pleaded for them in her closet. And frequently
were her visits owned of God, and blessed to the conversion of souls. It is believed that numbers are in
heaven who from her faithful, hopeful lips first heard
the saving truth with power.

"As a *Sabbath-school Teacher* she was truly exemplary, as well for the care which she bestowed on her
preparations, as for the Christian anxiety with which
she watched over the souls of her scholars. And then
her pen also was devoted to the cause of her Saviour ;
and by her tracts and pithy papers she endeavoured to
awaken neglecters, or stimulate believers. Indeed, in
one form or other, she was a constant labourer. Of set
purpose, and from Christian motives, her piety was
diffusive. She *meant* to glorify God. She *resolved* to
win souls : and, having yielded up her heart to this
design, the means for prosecuting it were readily found.
Now she would post tracts; at another time would write
an earnest letter; and again would seek an opportunity
for conversation. With less piety, her outward exertions
might have been a snare to herself; but, as she walked
with God, they were natural, healthy, and abundantly
useful, both to herself and others.

"Miss George's *trust in God* was singularly strong,
and it exercised upon her mind and movements a
benign control. The circumstances which occasioned the
family's removal from Welford cost her much mental
pain; but she committed all to God, and waited for

the guidance of the cloud. On the death of her
excellent mother, sympathizing friends were astonished
at her freedom from anxiety, her entire and grateful
submission, and, indeed, her holy joy. She was fully
persuaded that He who was the God of her good
mother, and who had afforded her 'solid comfort' in
the death-hour, would guide *her* also with His eye.
And events showed that her faith was honoured. Tried,
indeed, she was, and even painfully; but the Lord
wonderfully upheld, directed, and comforted her. In
recognition of these mercies, she named her home at
Kineton, 'Ebenezer.' And, obtaining help of God, she
trusted on, and still was blessed; until, in a little while,
she exchanged the militant life for the life triumphant.

"One of the latest letters, if not the last, which the
writer received from the departed, was written from her
elder sister's home. Death had been there. It had cut
down tender children, and now the mother; but, while
Elizabeth sorrowed, it was not for her glorified sister,
but for the mourning husband, and for herself,—that
she was a while detained behind. Yet it was not long.
A few weeks more, and she rejoined her kindred. She
had been in the habit of singing, 'Ah! lovely appearance of death!' for she *did* think death lovely; and
soon she passed through death, to live with Him who is
'the Life,' and 'who is alive for evermore.'"

To this excellent delineation of Miss George's character, all that need be added is a word or two, for the
sake of pointing out some of the principal truths and
lessons which her life exemplifies.

First, and most obviously, then, we learn from it the
importance of obtaining, at the very outset of a religious
course, *a certainty of the Divine forgiveness and favour.*
"Being justified by faith, we have peace with God."

Such confident language, with regard to her own spiritual state, Miss George could use at any time during the last three years and a half of her life. She had so trusted in the great atonement for sin, as to leave no doubt on her mind concerning her relations to God. And this faith, once reposed on Christ, became thenceforward a habit; her life was one of "faith on the Son of God, who loved" her, "and gave Himself for" her. She received the child's heart of affection and trust, and, taught by the Spirit of adoption, could ever look up, and cry, "Abba, Father!" It was this which made her piety so singularly happy. It was this which inspired her with that tranquil trust in God, the outward manifestations of which, in the midst of much perplexity and sorrow, were sometimes absolutely startling to those who did not understand the secret. It was this which gave her, in her addresses to God, a confidence so simple as to deem everything to belong to the province of prayer, and so strong as to believe everything to be within the power of prayer. All these happy traits of her piety had a close and obvious connexion with the clear assurance she possessed of the forgiving love of God. In all this she did but stand on her child's privilege. God was her Father; she knew it; and, as a child, she rejoiced in His love, she trusted in His care, she took all her wants and troubles to His ear.

Now, there are persons who, possessed of much religiousness, yet halt short of this state of happy assurance. They have penitent feelings, good desires and aspirations; they wish to serve God and get to heaven; they devote much time and thought to the concerns of their souls; they pray, and read the Scriptures; are exemplary in their attendance on the ordinances of religion; and perhaps diligent and self-denying

in works of charity : and yet they feel no certainty on
so vital a point as their souls' relations to God. The
result is, their piety is not confident and cheerful.
Their addresses to God are pervaded by a tone of confession and deprecation. When trouble comes, they are
doubtful whether they may venture to regard it as the
kind chastening of a heavenly Father. And their want
of confidence is also want of strength : they lay no
vigorous hold on the provided aid of the Spirit; they
are weak in the presence of temptation; they fail in
carrying out their own resolves; they bewail perpetual
defects; they are conscious of living below the standard
of their own aspirations. Their religion has been as yet
a thing of desire, not enjoyment; of hope, not possession.
Now, let such individuals be assured that there is a state
attainable far superior to that in which they have been
living. Let them read the Epistles of the New Testament with care, and they will find throughout them
the assumption, that the Christian believer enjoys a
state of conscious reconcilement with God. Let them
take this life of Miss George as a testimony of fact to
the possibility not only of entering into such a state, but
of maintaining it uninterruptedly. Let them rely upon
it, that they never will live as they aspire to live, never
so as to satisfy their own convictions and desires, until
they have themselves attained to satisfaction on this
all-important point. And, instead of going about to
establish their own righteousness, let them simply trust
in that Saviour, by whom, *while yet sinners*, we are
reconciled to God; and they, too, shall *know that they
have passed from death unto life.*

Again : Miss George's life teaches how *promotive of
Christian enjoyment and stability is a state of entire
devotion to God.* Very early in her religious career, as

we have seen, she enjoyed a consciousness of her
"entire sanctification." That is, she gave herself
wholly up to God, that she might, with every power of
her nature, and through every hour of her life, do His
will and promote His glory; and she was persuaded
that God had thus accepted of her. And this covenant,
once made, she was continually renewing; this sacrifice,
once presented, she was careful never to withdraw.
She believed, therefore, that God regarded her as one
wholly and constantly dedicated to Himself. And,
without doubt, this belief, and the actual consecration
on which it was founded, contributed greatly to her
happiness. She knew nothing of the misery of a heart
at variance with itself. She had *one* purpose, and that
purpose fixed as the magnet to the pole. She had
drawn away her heart from this world, from its interests
and pleasures; and said, with the consent of her whole
being, "Whom have I in heaven but Thee? and
there is none upon earth that I desire beside Thee."
Thus, in her nature there was harmony and peace. In
response to her devotedness, God gave Himself to her, to
be to her an infinitely more secure and satisfying Fount
of happiness than all the fickle bitter-sweet springs of
earthly good from which she had turned away. And
thus elevated piety is ever elevated enjoyment. *They*
have never yet tested the full power of religion to
confer happiness, who have never tested the Spirit's
power fully to sanctify; nay, they know nothing yet
of their own nature's capacity of *receiving* happiness.
When the Christian gives himself wholly up to God,
then God reciprocates; and He, in whose "presence is
fulness of joy," makes His abode in that dedicated
heart. And then is heaven begun below; for the
essential element of heaven's happiness is then enjoyed.

"There be many that say, Who will show us any good?" It is the great outcry of humanity, ringing through all centuries; but when any soul, centering its all of desire and affection upon God, exclaims, "Lord, lift Thou the light of Thy countenance upon us," then, at once responding in fuller revealings of His glorious presence, God "puts gladness" therein, "more than in the time that their corn and their wine increased."

Further: Miss George derived increased *stability*, as well as increased happiness, from the entireness of her devotion to God. From the day on which she dated her sanctification she suffered *no relapse*. There came, subsequently, times of diminished enjoyment, times even of diminished earnestness; but no time when she "looked back," or faltered in her purpose to be the Lord's. Nay, the general character of her spiritual life was progressive. She obviously gained month by month, and year by year, in closeness of communion with God, in depth of spiritual affection, in maturity of Christian graces. For this absence of all vacillation, this steadiness of religious growth, she was without doubt indebted in great measure to that whole-hearted consecration of herself which marked the outset of her career. None are so little in danger of deserting a cause as those who have espoused it with the full consent of their judgment, and the full devotion of their affections; who from the very beginning have made up their minds, at the risk of any danger, at the cost of any sacrifice, to abide by it. None, on the other hand, are so likely to play the traitor as those who cherish secret reservations, or suffer their hearts to harbour competing interests and affections. These propositions sound, in fact, like truisms. But they have their application in the spiritual life. The best security against back-sliding from God lies in a state of entire devotion to God. When temptation comes to such a one, and it will come to him as to others, it finds in him no waver-ing thoughts, no rival affections, on which it may fasten. Such a Christian comes nearest to the character of Him who, speaking of His own spotless humanity, could say, "The prince of this world cometh, *and hath nothing in Me.*"

Again : we learn from Miss George's life how much of Christian labour and achievement *one faithful servant* may accomplish. The sphere in which Miss George moved was neither large nor inviting. She resided the greater part of her life in a small country village; and many would have pleaded, that in such a neighbour-hood there were really no materials for Christian acti-vity to work upon. She was very superior, in position, taste, and culture, to the class to which most of the villagers belonged; and many would have thought that utter want of congeniality was excuse sufficient for leading an isolated life. She was occupied with the duties of her school the greater part of the day; and, after the fatigue and worry of such an employment, many would have felt comfortably exonerated from all further labour. She confesses, more than once, in her diary, that when she first began to visit her poor neigh-bours she was shy and embarrassed; it was "a cross" to go; and when she went, she knew not what to say : many would have seen in this a sign that they were "not cut out for that kind of work," and would have delegated it to those who were better qualified. But Miss George, instead of contenting herself with excuses which might have sounded well enough in theory, wisely put them to the test of actual experiment; and

z

she soon discovered that, thus tested, they were nothing worth. Contracted as the sphere around her was, she found in it more work than with all her diligence she could overtake. The superiority of her position, instead of opening a gulf between her and those she sought to benefit, only caused her visits to be better received, and her opinion more respectfully listened to. Her diffidence gradually vanished; and her aptitude for the work increased as she persevered in it, both by the natural law, that faculty improves by exercise, and by the direct blessing of Him who giveth wisdom "liberally and without upbraiding" to those who ask it of Him. What amount of good she actually effected, what comfort and strength she imparted to Christ's poor and afflicted ones, what saving light to those who were dying in darkness, only "the day" will declare: but the foregoing Memoir will at any rate serve to show, not only how faithfully she laboured, but that her labours were crowned with a very fair proportion of visible success.

Would to God that such instances of Christian activity and devotedness were more numerous than they are! This Memoir will probably be read by some of Miss George's own age and sex: let them especially consider well this aspect of her character. There are departments of Christian labour for which none are so well qualified as they. How many young females, much of whose time is now spent in profitless gaieties, or employments which are little better than a busy idleness, have it in their power to move as beneficent spirits through the neighbourhoods in which they dwell! They might teach the dark, and comfort the sorrowful, smooth the beds of suffering, and whisper words of faith and hope in dying ears. In such work their own souls would be often refreshed, and " the blessing of him that was ready to perish" would come upon them. Let none say, " I am but one, and what can one do?" The example which these memorials exhibit shows that one may do much. Let them not plead inaptness for the work; for experience will bring skill, and the blessing of God will rest upon the honest though imperfect endeavour. And, as the crowning thought,—that which should sweeten all sacrifice, and kindle sloth and coldness into ardour,— let them remember that the day is coming " when the Son of Man shall come in His glory, and all the holy angels with Him;" and "then shall the King say unto them on His right hand, Come, ye blessed of My Father, inherit the kingdom prepared for you from the foundation of the world: for I was an hungred, and ye gave Me meat : I was thirsty, and ye gave Me drink: I was a stranger, and ye took Me in: naked, and ye clothed Me: I was sick, and ye visited Me: I was in prison, and ye came unto Me. Then shall the righteous answer Him, saying, Lord, when saw we Thee an hungred, and fed Thee? or thirsty, and gave Thee drink? When saw we Thee a stranger, and took Thee in? or naked, and clothed Thee? Or when saw we Thee sick, or in prison, and came unto Thee? And the King shall answer and say unto them, Verily I say unto you, INASMUCH AS YE HAVE DONE IT UNTO ONE OF THE LEAST OF THESE MY BRETHREN, YE HAVE DONE IT UNTO ME."

LONDON:

PRINTED BY H. T. & J. ROCHE,

25, HOXTON SQUARE.

WORKS PUBLISHED

MEMORABLE MEN AND MEMORABLE EVENTS.

Each Volume, Price 1s., 18mo.

I.

COLUMBUS;

OR, THE DISCOVERY OF AMERICA.

By the REV. GEORGE CUBITT.

II.

CORTES;

OR, THE DISCOVERY AND CONQUEST OF MEXICO.

III.

PIZARRO;

OR, THE DISCOVERY AND CONQUEST OF PERU.

IV.

GRANADA;

OR, THE EXPULSION OF THE MOORS FROM SPAIN.

Others are in preparation.

THE IRISH CONVERT;

Or, Popish Intolerance illustrated.

By the REV. WILLIAM LUPTON.

18mo. Price 1s. 6d., cambric, gilt-lettered.

HELEN LESLIE; OR, TRUTH AND ERROR.

By ADELINE. 18mo., cambric. Price 1s. 6d.

MEMORIALS OF MISS MARY FISHWICK,

Of Springfield, near Garstang: containing Selections from her Correspondence.
With an Introduction, by the REV. PETER M'OWAN.
Third Edition. 18mo. Price 1s. 6d., cambric; or, gilt edges, with a Portrait, 2s.

ATTRACTIVE PIETY:

Or, Memorials of William B. Carvosso, Grandson of the late Mr. W. Carvosso.
By his FATHER. Second Edition. 18mo. Price 1s. 4d.

WORKS PUBLISHED

THE INFIDEL'S OWN BOOK.
A Statement of some of the Absurdities resulting from the
Rejection of Christianity.
By the Rev. Richard Treffry, jun.
18mo. cambric. Price 2s. 6d.

THE SAINTS' EVERLASTING REST.
Extracted from the Works of the Rev. Richard Baxter,
by the Rev. John Wesley, A.M.
Royal 18mo., cambric. Price 3s.

THE IMPORTANCE OF PRAYER-MEETINGS IN PROMOTING THE REVIVAL OF RELIGION.
By the Rev. Robert Young. 18mo. Price 1s.

HYMNS FOR CHILDREN, AND FOR PERSONS OF RIPER YEARS.
By the Rev. Charles Wesley, A.M. 24mo. Price 3d.

THE WORK OF THE HOLY SPIRIT IN THE HUMAN HEART.
By the Rev. Jonathan Edwards, M.A.
Abridged by the Rev. John Wesley, A.M. 18mo., cambric. Price 1s. 6d.

REVIVALS OF RELIGION:
Their Nature, Defence, and Management.
By the Rev. J. Edwards, M.A. Abridged by the Rev. J. Wesley, A.M.
18mo., cambric. Price 2s. 6d.

A SHORT EXPOSITION OF THE TEN COMMANDMENTS.
Extracted from Bishop Hopkins, by the Rev. John Wesley, A.M.
18mo., cambric. Price 1s. 6d.

THE PROPER NAMES OF THE BIBLE;
Their Orthography, Pronunciation, and Signification. With a brief Account of
the principal Persons and Places. By the Rev. John Farrar.
Sixth Edition. 18mo., cambric, gilt-lettered. Price 2s.

PRAYERS FOR THE USE OF CHRISTIAN FAMILIES:
Containing a Morning and Evening Prayer for each Day in the Month, &c.
By several Wesleyan Ministers.
8vo., cambric,.Price 7s.; also in 12mo., Price 4s.

WORKS PUBLISHED

BY THE REV. JONATHAN EDMONDSON, A.M.

SHORT SERMONS ON IMPORTANT SUBJECTS.
2 Vols., 8vo., cambric. Price 10s.

A CONCISE SYSTEM OF SELF-GOVERNMENT
In the great Affairs of Life and Godliness. 18mo., cambric. Price 2s. 6d.

SERMONS ON THE NATURE AND OFFICES OF THE HOLY GHOST.
By the Rev. J. Edmondson, and the Rev. R. Treffry.
12mo., cambric. Price 3s. 6d.

SCRIPTURE VIEWS OF THE HEAVENLY WORLD.
18mo., cambric. Price 2s.

ELEMENTS OF REVEALED RELIGION.
12mo., cambric. Price 5s.

AN ESSAY ON THE CHRISTIAN MINISTRY:
Including a General Outline of Ministerial and Pastoral Duties; for the Use of Young Preachers. 12mo., cambric. Price 5s. 6d.

BY THE REV. RICHARD TREFFRY.

MEMOIRS OF THE REV. RICHARD TREFFRY, JUN.;
WITH SELECT REMAINS,
Consisting of Sketches of Sermons, Essays, and Poetry.
Including Extracts from his Correspondence. With a Portrait.
12mo., cambric. Price 5s.

A TREATISE ON SECRET AND SOCIAL PRAYER.
12mo., cambric. Price 3s.

A TREATISE ON THE CHRISTIAN SABBATH.
12mo., cambric. Price 3s.

A TREATISE ON CHRISTIAN PERFECTION.
18mo., cambric. Price 2s. 6d.

A PARENTAL PORTRAITURE OF THOMAS H. TREFFRY.
18mo., cambric. Price 1s. 6d.

MEMOIRS OF MR. RICHARD TREWAVAS, SEN.,
Of Mousehole, Cornwall.
To which is prefixed, An Account of Methodism in Mousehole.
18mo., cambric. Price 1s. 6d.

WORKS PUBLISHED

MISCELLANEOUS.

DELINEATION OF ROMAN CATHOLICISM,
Drawn from the authentic and acknowledged Standards of the Church of Rome :
in which her peculiar Doctrines, Morals, Government, and
Usages are stated, treated at large, and confuted.
By the Rev. CHARLES ELLIOTT, D.D.
A new Edition, corrected and revised throughout, with numerous
important Additions.
Imperial 8vo., cambric. Price 10s.

SHORT DISCOURSES, PRACTICAL AND EXPERIMENTAL.
By the late Rev. RICHARD TREFFRY.
With Biographical Reminiscences of the Author.
12mo., cambric. Price 4s.

A HELP TO EXTEMPORE PRAYER.
And an Aid to Private, Domestic, and Public Devotion.
By the Rev. JOSEPH WOOD. 18mo. Price 9d.

PRACTICAL CONSIDERATIONS ON THE CHRISTIAN SABBATH.
By the Rev. PETER M'OWAN.
Third Edition. 18mo., gilt-lettered. Price 1s.

A TREATISE ON JUSTIFICATION.
By JOHN GOODWIN. 12mo., cambric. Price 2s.

EMINENT CHRISTIAN PHILANTHROPISTS.
Brief Biographical Sketches, designed especially as Studies for the Young.
By the Rev. GEORGE MAUNDER.
Royal 18mo. Price 2s. 6d.

THE DOCTRINE OF UNIVERSAL RESTORATION EXAMINED AND REFUTED.
By the Rev. DANIEL ISAAC. 12mo., cambric. Price 2s.

DIALOGUES ON SANCTIFICATION.
By the Rev. J. S. PIPE. 18mo., cambric. Price 1s. 4d.

THE CHRISTIAN MIRACLES:
Or, Conversations on the Miracles of Christ, &c.
By the Rev. GEORGE CUBITT.
18mo., cambric, gilt-lettered. Price 2s. 6d.